SHARE THE LIGHT

WITH THE GIFT OF A

B ♥ Ø ♥ Ø ♥ K

This material has been generously provided by the Kwantlen University College Buy-a-Book Campaign.

RENAISSANCE BEASTS

RENAISSANCE BEASTS

Of Animals, Humans, and Other
Wonderful Creatures

Edited by Erica Fudge

University of Illinois Press
Urbana and Chicago

Library of Congress Cataloging-in-Publication Data
Renaissance beasts : of animals, humans, and other wonderful
creatures / edited by Erica Fudge.
    p.   cm.
Includes bibliographical references and index.
ISBN 0-252-02880-5 (cloth : alk. paper)
1. Animals and civilization—Europe—History—16th century.
2. Animals and civilization—Europe—History—17th century.
3. Animals (Philosophy)—Europe—History—16th century.
4. Animals (Philosophy)—Europe—History—17th century.
I. Fudge, Erica.
QL85.R455   2004
590'.9031—dc21   2003007986

❦ CONTENTS

✖ ACKNOWLEDGMENTS

Any collection of essays is, by necessity, a collaborative enterprise, and I would like first of all to thank the contributors for their work. It has been a real pleasure bringing these essays together. Help has also come from Lawrence Normand, Patricia Parker, Jonathan Burt, and David Kastan, for which I am extremely grateful. Tracey Hill and I co-organized a conference, "Animals in History and Culture," at Bath Spa University College in 1999 at which a number of the contributors here first came together, and I am immensely grateful to Tracey for all her work on the conference. Carol Anne Peschke copyedited the collection with precision, and the collection has also benefited greatly from the work of Elizabeth Dulany at the University of Illinois Press. Her interest in and support of all things animal is a gift to those of us in the field, and this collection is a tribute to her.

Throughout, early modern *u, v, i,* and *j* have been silently modernized. In some essays gendered terms such as *man, mankind,* and *horsemanship* are used. Although these terms may cause discomfort to modern readers, they reflect early modern usage, which prioritized the male over the female and often (in relation to horsemanship, for instance) assumed a male subject.

❧ INTRODUCTION

Erica Fudge

In 1634 William Prynne was called before the Star Chamber for "writing
and publishinge a scandalous and a libellous Booke againste the State, the
Kinge, and all his people." The book, *Histrio-Mastix,* was "condempneth . . .
to bee in a most ignominyous manner burnte by the hande of the hangman," and Prynne himself was condemned, among other things, "to loose
an eare at eyther place."[1] Three years later, after an apparent plot "to set up
the puritan or separatist faction,"[2] Prynne, with John Bastwick and Henry
Burton, was once again sentenced to have his ears clipped and to have his
cheek marked with the letters *S* and *L,* for "a seditious libellour." Because
of the previous punishment "the court examined whether Prin had any eares
left; they found they were cropt, soe they went to sentence."[3] This time Prynne
lost his ears completely.

Nine years after the punishment of Prynne, Bastwick, and Burton, protest
against which Christopher Hill has seen as one of the key starting points of
the English Revolution,[4] the birth of a child with its *"face upon the breast, and
without a head"* in Lancashire put a new spin on the story. The mother of the
child, a Catholic, had been heard to declare, *"I pray God, that rather than I
shall be a Roundhead, or bear a Roundhead, I may bring forth a Childe without
a head."* Her neighbors agreed that her words "might be a great meanes to
provoke God to shew such testimony of his displeasure against her, by causing her to bring forth this Monster." But it was not only the woman's words
that were at issue, according to the pamphlet that recorded the appearance of
this wonderful child. The actions of the woman's mother were also presented
as part of the context for understanding the advent of the aberrant infant. The
pamphlet records, "amongst other scornes which her mother cast upon religious people she too her Cat; and said that it must be made a Roundhead like
Burton, Prinne and *Bastwicke,* and causing the eares to be cut off; called her
cat Prynn (instead of Puffe)."[5]

This story, involving politics, religion, punishment, and justice, offers a
picture of human-animal relations that is extreme, but that simultaneously

calls up an attitude that is typical of the period under discussion in this collection. What is brought to the fore is the dual nature of animals that pervades much of the thinking on the subject in northern Europe in the sixteenth and seventeenth centuries.

At first glance, the story of the crop-eared cat called Prynne testifies to a completely instrumental use of animals. The cat becomes the means for this Catholic woman to mark her protest and to mock the beliefs of her neighbors. The cat as cat disappears; it is a blank page onto which she writes her message. But persisting throughout the period, and in this sad story, is the danger represented by the animal. The pamphlet's linking of the mutilation of the cat to the birth of the monstrous child offers in microcosm the connection that was often traced in this period between animals and the fragility of the status of the human. Animals may be mere instruments for human use, but that use can bring with it a reminder not only of human dominance but also of human vulnerability. Even as it sets the cat up as the opposite of the human, the story reveals that God's punishment here, as in the case of so many other monstrous births, is to destroy human status or to reveal the stability of that status to be brittle.[6]

But there is more. The story also implies a link between the "Roundhead" human, Prynne, and the "Roundhead" cat, Prynne. On one level, of course, this animalizes the Protestant protestor, but on the other it bespeaks a belief, present in popular if not comfortably in literate culture, in the similarity of human and animal abilities to suffer.[7] Ear-clipping moves from being the sign of possession by a shepherd on his sheep, to a sign of punishment by the state on its prisoner, to a sign by a Catholic of her power over her cat. Human and animal are marked by the same means, are linked in their capacity to be interpellated into a community: of ownership, state justice, or dominion.

Thus an instrumental attitude, by which animals are objectified, coexists with concepts of the frailty of humanity as a species and the shared sentience of human and animal. The boundary between the two groups, apparently so clear and unbreachable, is revealed to be, to use Margaret Healy's description of the human body in this period, "porous [and] vulnerable."[8] But the boundary between human and animal is also, and inevitably, firmly reiterated throughout the period. Where there is a fear of the collapse of difference, there is also an urgent need to reiterate human superiority. This reiteration can be found in the ways in which people use animals (hunting, riding, eating, vivisecting, staging, and caging them), and it can also be traced in the ways in which people thought with them in different discourses: religious, demonological, satirical, linguistic. The chapters in this book, in a variety of ways, address these different dominions and dangers.

But the chapters also address another issue: that of the place of animals in historical work. In their history of the English pig, Robert Malcolmson and Stephanos Mastoris note that "history being written by humans, is mostly about humans."[9] They go on to argue that ignoring the presence of animals in the past is ignoring a significant feature of human life. Such a recognition, obvious as it may seem, is reflected in the emergence of new ways of thinking about the place, role, and understanding of animals. Historians such as Harriet Ritvo, Kathleen Kete, and Joyce E. Salisbury have offered new and important evaluations of the past through an attention to attitudes toward and uses of nonhumans.[10] This collection is an attempt to take that work into the sixteenth and seventeenth centuries.

That is not to say that animals have until now been wholly absent from the study of this period. What I think is important is that these chapters read the animal as a significant figure in early modern cultural and intellectual history. This has not always been the case: often animals, even when present, are not assessed as animals. Keith Thomas's magisterial study, *Man and the Natural World* (1983), showed that animals (and nature more generally) were an important aspect of intellectual, cultural, and social debate in the early modern period.[11] However, in his book animals, like plants, were objects of analysis, not, as Jonathan Burt has recently argued in his study of the development of film technology in the nineteenth century, "an important motive force."[12] Setting aside the very different subjects being analyzed in their work, the difference between Thomas's and Burt's ideas about animals is crucial: the latter's proposal allows us to think about animals as creatures who are objects of human analysis (such has ever been the case) but also as beings in the world who may themselves create change. These change-provoking animals might be real. Joan Thirsk and Peter Edwards both have shown how significant the horse was to the development of the economy of Tudor and Stuart England, and Lisa Jardine and Jerry Brotton have shown the horse's importance in East-West relations and trade in the fifteenth and sixteenth centuries, for example.[13] But change-provoking animals might also be housed in the realm of ideas: concepts of human status in religious, humanist, legal, and political writings were in part motivated by an understanding of the nature of animals, as I have argued in *Perceiving Animals*.

Chris Philo and Chris Wilbert, writing from a geographic perspective, likewise propose that we need to rethink how we conceptualize animals, but they go further than Burt. They argue that the proliferation of nonhumans in "human society" makes it "impossible to recognize a pure 'human' society." Using actor network theory, they propose that "resources, technologies, animals, and so on, all actively participate in, refine and frame . . . processes of interaction."[14] Their focus is on modern culture, but the same would, I think, hold true of early modern culture. Animals can be agents within culture; they are never always only objects. Furthermore, humans cannot think about themselves—their cultures, societies, and political structures—without recognizing the importance of nonhumans to themselves, their cultures, societies, and political structures. To assert such a possibility is to propose a reevaluation not only of the period of study—in the case of this collection, from 1550 to 1700—but also of how we conceptualize the nature of that study itself. New questions must be asked if we begin to think about animals in different ways, and this is where these chapters represent a shift in our conceptualization of both subject matter and period. An example of how this shift might work can be traced in a brief look at one recent text.

In his fascinating study *Travesties and Transgressions in Tudor and Stuart England,* the eminent historian David Cressy unearths what he calls "some of the strangest and most troubling incidents from the byways of Tudor and Stuart England."[15] His work is particularly useful here not only because it contains two stories of human-animal interactions but also because Cressy is very self-reflexive about his role as historian. The eccentricity of the stories he is dealing with leads him to wonder about his own place in relation to the material, to contemplate the nature of the questions he should ask of it. What this allows for is twofold: we get to hear of extraordinary events, and we are asked to think about how we analyze those events. It is the bringing together of these two issues in the stories about animals that is particularly useful for me here.

In the first animal story Cressy tells the tale of Agnes Bowker's cat.[16] It begins with "the unwanted pregnancy of an unmarried domestic servant," Agnes Bowker, who, "in 1569, at Market Harborough, gave birth to a cat." Cressy's essay about what he calls "a unique and unsettling incident" traces the context, testimony, and evidence in the subsequent case that came before the church courts and is an attempt, he writes, "to capture some lost voices and anxieties from early modern England." In one piece of evidence, given by a midwife, Bowker was reported to have said that she had been approached by "a thing in the likeness of a bear, sometimes like a dog, sometimes like a man and [that this thing] had the knowledge carnal of her body in every such shape." Bowker later claimed that this thing also came to her "in the likeness of a black cat" and again had "knowledge of her body." The suggestions here of bestiality fit, as Cressy notes, with contemporary belief in the possibility of cross-breeding.

However, the commissary of the enquiry into the case of the cat, Anthony Anderson, was unsatisfied with this explanation and decided to investigate the matter further. In an undertaking that displays the emergence

4

of empirical science in the mid-sixteenth century, he writes, "I caused another cat to be killed and flayed, and betwixt the one [Bowker's] and the other in the whole this was the difference and only the difference, the eyes of my cat were as cats' eyes that be alive, and the monster cat's eyes were darker than blue. I cast my flayn cat into boiling water, and pulling the same out again, both in eye and else they were altogether one." Cressy notes that despite clear evidence to suggest the fraudulent nature of the cat's birth, no confession from Bowker was forthcoming, and the truth of the matter was never fully established. Bowker "soon returned to oblivion, her subsequent history unknown."

Having offered such a detailed description of the case and of some of its possible meanings, Cressy then turns from the evidence to think about his role in this narrative: "how does the historian," he asks, "decide what questions to ask, what lines of inquiry to pursue?" He offers a number of suggestions: "a deeper political and religious contextualization . . . [a] detailed local and cultural account . . . [c]omparative reading of the history of bastardy . . . [m]ore work on sorcery and diabolism." Never does he mention a more profound understanding of human-animal relations, which is interesting because he has offered a fascinating insight into those relations in his essay. It is as if that aspect of the context is not perceived to be worth further development or understanding but that more established modes of scholarship—political, social, and demonological history—must take over.[17] Or, and I think this might actually be the case, Cressy has not recognized that human-animal relationships might have a role to play in understanding the past.

This marginalization of the animal is also the case in the second animal story in Cressy's collection; this time it is the tale of the baptism of a horse. In 1644, as Thomas Edwards recorded in *Gangraena*, a horse was baptized with urine by parliamentary soldiers in a church in Yaxley in Huntingdonshire. Cressy notes other similar "mock religious" ceremonies involving animals in the period: in the same year another horse was baptized, this time with holy water, at Lostwithiel in Cornwall; earlier "travesties" (to use Cressy's term) included the baptism of a cat, the marriage of a goose and a gander, and the mock churching of a cow. Cressy looks to the religious context of some of the actions—citing the possibility that the baptisers of the horse had taken the concept of "the priesthood of all believers" to its extreme—but he also recognizes briefly the role of the animal in these tales, proposing that the baptisms "profaned sacred ceremony and blurred the boundary between humans and beasts." However, this question of the boundary is taken no further, and Cressy proposes that the actions of these men were "not just a profanation of the church but a dishonour to God."

The alternative possibility he cites comes from "a tradition of folk magic" in which it might be believed that "the baptism of beasts was intended to secure them benefits." He sees this suggestion as "more ingenious than persuasive," however.[18]

What follows should not be interpreted as a wholesale criticism of Cressy's work. Indeed, the two essays offer fascinating and disturbing glimpses of the early modern period that might be lost, ignored, and remain unknown without his important archival work, and his questions about the incidents are significant in that they recognize the difficulty of understanding them. What is worth highlighting is that in both essays the animal is a persistent problem for the historian. I am (perhaps unfairly) using Cressy's work as a way of thinking through broader problems of historical analysis that seem to be concentrated in his two chapters.

In the first chapter the cat and the meanings associated with it are simultaneously central to Cressy's discussions and sidelined in his list of potential further areas of research. This sidelining is reiterated in his summing up. He writes, "the testimony in this case touches a range of issues: normal and abnormal childbirth, gender relations and sexuality, monsters and the imagination, the proceedings of ecclesiastical justice, community discourse and authority, storytelling and the standards for establishing truth."[19] Here animals are missing, perhaps replaced by monsters, but these are two very different things. It is as if the cat cannot be regarded as a significant aspect of history, as if boiling a moggy is an event unworthy of comment or understanding.

The essay on horse baptism poses a different problem, one that Cressy himself is aware of. "Baptisms of beasts," he writes, "are puzzling phenomena, and it is by no means clear how they fit into our larger understanding of history."[20] The problem, I argue, is not Cressy's but history's. The categories that we use to think about the past do not comfortably offer explanations for such enigmatic events, not because there are no explanations but because those explanations may come from categories within which we might find it difficult to think. This is a part of Cressy's implicit, if not explicit, focus in his book, and his self-reflexive understanding of the puzzling nature of the baptism of the horse reflects his recognition that the event is worth understanding even if, as it stands, we can only offer very partial explanations. One thing that comes from Cressy's work is a recognition that we constantly need to develop our ways of reading the past. Including animals would be a sensible and productive development.

If we agree that there is no such thing as a pure human society (and I think the number of day-to-day interactions between humans and animals in all areas of life make this a fair possibility) and if we don't expand our horizons to include animals, ultimately we will be ignoring an important aspect of the cultures we interpret. Furthermore, we should remind ourselves that the conceptualization of animals in historical work will replicate in some ways (although somewhat less physically) the conceptualization that is present in the ear-clipping incident recorded in 1646. Where in that incident the cat was merely a blank onto which the Catholic mother could write her own meaning, we would be taking animals to speak about issues already in place in social and cultural history, and this would ignore the animality of the animal and overlook its presence as meaningful in itself. In doing this we might not only be underestimating the importance of animals but also denying ourselves access to an enhanced understanding of the past.

But this is beginning to change. Scholars of the sixteenth and seventeenth centuries, as Cressy's two essays show, are starting to recognize the importance of animals. This in itself is not a new development, but the motivation for the recognition of the importance of animals does seem to have shifted. In older scholarship much work on animals was a part of antiquarian research and represented animals often in order to depict folk rituals and the pleasures of "the lowest of people."[21] Alternatively, it was presented as an attempt to contextualize a canonical author such as Shakespeare, to understand the references to different creatures in his work.[22] Early theater history of the period also provided a context in which to study entertainments such as bear-baiting, but again, the focus was on the differences and similarities between the two sorts of entertainment, not on the animals in anything beyond a very general sense.[23]

Although current Shakespeare studies have thrown up some interesting analyses of animals in early modern culture, the study of animals here is still, inevitably, merely a means of further understanding the plays rather than further understanding the animals (although this is often a welcome byproduct).[24] However, contemporary theater history is somewhat coyly shifting its focus. In a fascinating article on dogs on the early modern stage, Michael Dobson rather self-consciously begins by saying, "my field of inquiry may seem a twee one." What follows in his article makes a strong case for overturning such a suggestion.[25]

Social and cultural history, perhaps recognizing a progression from the study of the working class, women, ethnic minorities, and homosexuals to the study of animals,[26] has begun to pay attention to the nonhuman in new and productive ways. Recent work by Dan Beaver, Mary Fissell, and Mark Jenner has begun to correct this gap in our historical record by looking at, respectively, the social networks of honor involved in the hunting and possession of animals, the confusingly humanizing discourses in writings on the eradication of vermin, and the "cultural logic" of the dog massacres that were so central to attempts to wipe out plague.[27] All of these essays ask us to reevaluate not only the particular aspects of the period—social relations, concepts of cleanliness and fear—but also to think again about the role and function of animals.

Intellectual history is likewise revealing the importance and value of turning to animals. Just as medical history has noted the important differences between the Galenic, Paracelsian, and Vesalian conceptualizations of the human body and its treatment in the sixteenth and seventeenth centuries, so animals were represented via competing worldviews, and historians are beginning to recognize this. In an essay on "the virtues of animals," for example, Peter Harrison sees "three distinct positions" being taken up in philosophical debate: theriophilic, Aristotelian, and Cartesian.[28] In another article looking at the concept of the animal soul he highlights panpsychism as an argument offered against Cartesianism during the period.[29] Other competing cosmologies that have been posited to offer an understanding of early modern attitudes toward animals include William B. Ashworth Jr.'s "emblematic worldview," characterized by adage, allegory, and analogy, and its replacement, the empiricism that emerged during the Scientific Revolution.[30] The study of animals in the early modern period is no longer a simple one.

Other work on sixteenth- and seventeenth-century ideas is also showing the important role that animals can play in our understanding of the period. In the work of Thomas Tryon, a late seventeenth-century vegetarian, Nigel Smith has traced a link between the religious enthusiasm of the Civil War and Enlightenment ideas, modes of thinking routinely regarded as antithetical in scholarly work.[31] Susan Wiseman has shown how ideas in the political sphere can be traced alongside empiricism in comparative anatomy and has argued that it is only by paying heed to both that we can achieve a full comprehension of the meaning and status of animals and of politics.[32] Karen L. Raber has read William Cavendish's horse training manuals as a way of rethinking current scholarly assumptions about the emergence of "notions of identity and self-possession" in Locke's work.[33]

Certain fixed hypotheses about the period seem to be dismantled when animals enter the equation, and there is no intellectual sphere that did not take up and develop (to greater or lesser extents) the animal question in the early modern period. Even in areas that might be regarded—especially in the so-called age of Descartes—as the realm of the human, animals raise their heads, and this is something that is now being taking note of. Discussions of concepts of language and reason in the period have turned to think about concepts of *animal* language and *animal* reason to extend our understanding of those "human" debates but also to extend our understanding of animals.[34] For example, when Laurence Babb, in his study of Renaissance physiology and psychology of 1951, argued that "in human nature . . . there is a continual warfare between the rational and the sensitive, the human and the bestial, the intellectual and the physical," what he was proposing was a simple—and classical—opposition between humans and animals in the discourse of reason in which animals are mere emblems of what humans can become.[35] In 1998 Peter Harrison proposed something rather different. Like Babb before him, Harrison traced the fear of the postlapsarian bestiality of human nature in sixteenth- and seventeenth-century ideas but took it further, arguing that the animal is by no means to be read in this debate as a mere metaphorical presence. By understanding the passions, Harrison argued, humans "established three levels of control: of self, of others, and of nature."[36] The decline in human control of the self—the fall into passion—caused a loss of command over the natural world itself; metaphorical animals are simultaneously real. What appears to be a debate about human nature is shown also to be about human relationships with nature. It seems that such a possibility was not within Babb's "field of vision," a vision that, in 1951, was wholly focused on humanity.[37] By shifting our gaze we can learn something new.

So far I have attempted to show how animals might be important in this period; that is, I have thought about Renaissance *beasts*. It is worth now shifting the focus of the question to ask, Why *Renaissance* beasts? Why might this period be important in the history of animals?

For Harrison, the seventeenth century is linked to the twentieth by the sheer volume of discussion in both about the place of animals.[38] The early modern and the modern share a fixation on them that marks both periods as crucial to developments in the understanding of human relationships with animals and also marks animals as vital figures that historians of all kinds must take notice of if we are to offer a full assessment of that past and if we are to fully understand our own interests in the present.

The history of animals, a new and evolving subdiscipline, might be figured as requiring two things, which are focused in my differentiation of Renaissance *beasts* from *Renaissance* beasts. First and foremost it must be "good" history; that is, it must fulfill the standards of research and analysis set in all other areas of history. In the case of the early modern period, it must offer us a new way of thinking about a well-established area of study. Without both of these things—standards of research and a new approach to the period—it can never expect to be taken seriously. Second, it should evaluate its relationship to the modern world in which it is created. For example, it might be empowered by recognizing the fact that, like history from below, women's history, the history of ethnicity, and so on, it has a role to play in current ethical, environmental, social, and political debates. I am not prescribing that one position be taken up in the history of animals but that a link might be made between scholarship and society, between the academy and the abattoir.[39]

By understanding the past we can begin to reassess the present in ways that might upset some of the apparent stability in our current modes of living. As the editorial collective of the first issue of *History Workshop Journal* wrote in 1976, "History is a source of inspiration and understanding, furnishing not only the means of interpreting the past but also the best critical vantage point from which to view the present."[40] Their focus is on the history of the working class, labor history, and women's history, but as the inclusion of Mary Fissell's article on vermin in early modern England in the journal in 1999 shows, the history of our relationships with animals can respond to these same ideas; our current relationships with animals can be better interpreted and criticized from a historical perspective. The study of the early modern period has much to offer to the understanding of human-animal relations in the present because it unsettles the naturalness of those contemporary relations.

But this collection is not called *Early Modern Beasts;* it is called *Renaissance Beasts.* The distinction between the two can be made not in terms of the representations of particular formations of culture, particular conceptions of a period in the past; rather, the title *Renaissance Beasts* refers to an idea as much as (if not more than) a period.

The title is in direct opposition to its more famous forebear, "Renaissance Man." Jacob Burckhardt's great individual was a creation, as Tony Davies reminds us, of the nineteenth century, to be found not only in Machiavelli and Vasari but also in Samuel Smiles and "the ethos of manly independence forged by the public school."[41] "Renaissance Beast" may well be an equivalent creation of the early twenty-first century, reflecting the unease with which much contemporary philosophy has come to view humanity, but like Burckhardt's creation, it might offer a way of thinking about the earlier period. Where the animal, for Renaissance Man, was a mere instrument for use and, as scholars such as Lawrence Babb have shown, was the aspect of Man that needed to be tamed, kept under, the Renaissance beasts of this collection have a more active role in their historical moment: they have the power to create new ideas.[42]

❦

The chapters in the collection are arranged in broadly chronological order. The collection begins with the use of speaking animals in satire and ends with the liberation of the animals from Louis XIV's Ménagerie in 1792. Between these starting and ending points the chapters introduce some of the many ways in which animals were used and thought with and about in early modern culture. In many ways, the uses of animals represented in these chapters are unsurprising: in science (Cummings, Harrison), religion (Fudge, Wiseman), literature (Perry, Sheen, Knowles), and sport and pastime (Schiesari, Stewart, Graham, Senior). However, each of the chapters offers a new way of thinking about these uses, and each proposes that we revise our assumptions about the place, role, and function of animals in early modern thought.

In her chapter Kathryn Perry proposes that the use of talking animals in satire has a role beyond mere convention—that it impacts on the boundary between human and animal, a boundary often established through the possession or lack of speech. Reader pleasure comes through the overwhelming animality of the animals and the brutal reduction of the status of some humans, she argues.

This notion of the brutality of humanity emerges once again in Juliana Schiesari's study of Henri III's desire for "little dogs." Schiesari argues that the pet is a figure of desire that uproots social, sexual, and gender identities and that brutalizes the desirer. Criticisms of the rule of Henri III, concentrating as they did on his love of dogs, bring this bestialization of humanity to the fore.

Species identity is once again scrutinized in S. J. Wiseman's study of werewolf texts from the late sixteenth and early seventeenth centuries. Discussions of the human and the werewolf, Wiseman argues, are an exploration not only of religious issues (does a werewolf have a human soul?) but of social and civil debates in the period. Ultimately, the early modern werewolf is interpreted as being generated by the very civility it seems to challenge.

The dead animal, in the form of meat, is the focus of my chapter, in which I trace the role of animal flesh in Reformed theology and read the act of eating meat as an expression simultaneously of human dominion and of human vulnerability. Consuming an animal enacts human superiority, but it may actually also undo it: human status is a fragile thing in the face of even the dead animal.

Erica Sheen's chapter turns to Shakespeare and links the use of animal imagery in play texts to legal debates about property rights over animals. Discussions about originality and textual transmission are read through the literary use of animals, and as we recognize this, animals become not mere imagery but producers of meaning, Sheen argues.

Alan Stewart's chapter likewise takes up what has been assumed to be a purely conventional use of animal imagery: James VI and I's naming of his chancellor, Cecil, his "Little Beagle." Stewart traces a direct link between

James's predilection for hunting and his method of rule in which Cecil's role as "beagle" is revealed as more than mere frippery. The animal here is revealed as simultaneously real, emblematic, and politically powerful, and it reveals much about the operation of power in early seventeenth-century England.

This multifaceted role of animals is also recognized in Elspeth Graham's chapter on the horse. Graham argues that in two different seventeenth-century texts in which horses play central roles, one can trace not only details of human-animal relations but also some of the key cultural shifts of the period. The horse is never a mere object of discourse, she argues; it is a producer of meaning.

James Knowles returns us to a royal court, this time that of Charles I and Henrietta Maria. Taking as his focus the status of the ape in early modern thought and the problematic place of the actor as the "ape" of humanity, Knowles reads Aurelian Townshend's masque, *Tempe Restored,* as a response to the attacks on the queen's masquing by William Prynne. In the neoplatonism of the masque, the status of the monarch is defended against the accusations of descent to the beast that can be traced in Prynne's antitheatrical diatribe, and the possibility of human agency and reason is used as a way of countering his fear of becoming animal.

Brian Cummings takes Pliny's oft-repeated work on elephant language as his focus and traces the ways in which Renaissance thinkers abandoned a conception of animal language and reason that can be traced in this classical source. Looking at discussions of animal language in Montaigne and Descartes, Cummings traces early modern concerns about human language and human reason that distinguish that work from its classical forebears.

Peter Harrison also looks at the significance of mechanical philosophy in ideas of the period and reads works by a range of experimental philosophers arguing that, rather than regarding vivisection as evidence of a disregard of animals, we should pay attention to early modern scientists' perception of their work as actually raising the status of animals by revealing them as the sources for an increased understanding of God. The new science spelled the end of the medieval worldview but actually produced a new sense of the powerful emblematic qualities of animals.

Finally, Matthew Senior turns to Louis XIV's Ménagerie, which he reads as containing a range of different and competing discourses: of science, display, fable, and politics. Caught up in this royal spectacle, Senior argues, is the issue of consciousness and the differences and similarities of human and animal vision. His chapter ends in 1792, when the animals were released from Louis's Ménagerie by a committee of Jacobins. What is traced in this "liberation" is a shift in understanding, he argues, from animals as signifiers of royal power to animals as symbols of virtue. However, the Revolution does not undo all existing relations: even in the new zoo of the republic, human difference from animals is reasserted.

This collection is about animals, but among those animals it is perhaps the human itself that comes under the greatest scrutiny. In the early modern period, as now, animals were not easy beings to contemplate. They raised the specter of human limitation; they provoked unease about the distinct nature of humanity; they undid the boundaries between human and beast even as they appeared to cement them, and in so doing they offer us another way of thinking about Renaissance Man and a way of configuring our new entity, Renaissance beast.

NOTES

1. S. R. Gardiner, ed., *Documents Relating to the Proceedings against William Prynne in 1634 and 1637* (London: Camden Society, 1877), 1, 17.

2. P. S. Seaver, *Wallington's World*, cited in John Spurr, *English Puritanism, 1603–1689* (Basingstoke: Macmillan, 1988), 94.

3. Gardiner, *Documents*, 76, 75.

4. Hill argues that the Revolution was "started by a wave of popular protest at the cruel sentences passed on the Rev. Henry Burton, lawyer Prynne and Dr Bastwick." *The World Turned Upside Down: Radical Ideas during the English Revolution* (London: Temple Smith, 1972), 241.

5. *A Declaration of a Strange and Wonderfull Monster: Born in Kirkham Parish in Lancashire* (London, 1646), title page, 6, 5.

6. See *A discription of a monstrous Chylde, borne at Chychester in Sussex* (London, 1562); *A Most certaine report of a monster borne at Oteringham in Holdernesse* (London, 1595); and *Signes and wonders from Heaven* (London, 1645). The theme of Edward Fenton's statement that "It is most certaine that these monstrous creatures, for the most part, do proceede of the judgement, justice and chastisement of God, which suffreth that the fathers and mothers bring forth these abhominations, as a horrour of their sinne" is repeated in all of these pamphlets and broadsheets. *Certaine Secrete wonders of Nature* (London, 1569), 12v.

7. This, I have argued elsewhere, is part of the power of bear-baiting in the period. See Erica Fudge, *Perceiving Animals: Humans and Beasts in Early Modern English Culture* (2000. Reprint. Urbana: University of Illinois Press, 2002), 17.

8. Margaret Healy, "Bodily Regimen and Fear of the Beast: 'Plausibility' in Renaissance Domestic Tragedy," in *At the Borders of the Human: Beasts, Bodies, and Natural Philosophy in the Early Modern Period,* ed. Erica Fudge, Ruth Gilbert, and Susan Wiseman (Basingstoke: Macmillan, 1999), 53.

9. Robert Malcolmson and Stephanos Mastoris, *The English Pig: A History* (London: Hambledon Press, 1998), 29.

10. See Harriet Ritvo, *The Animal Estate: The English and Other Creatures in the*

Victorian Age (1987. Reprint. London: Penguin, 1990) and *The Platypus and the Mermaid and Other Figments of the Classifying Imagination* (Cambridge, Mass.: Harvard University Press, 1997); Kathleen Kete, *The Beast in the Boudoir: Petkeeping in Nineteenth-Century Paris* (Berkeley: University of California Press, 1994); and Joyce E. Salisbury, *The Beast Within: Animals in the Middle Ages* (London: Routledge, 1994).

11. Keith Thomas, *Man and the Natural World: Changing Attitudes in England 1500–1800* (1983. Reprint. London: Penguin, 1984).

12. Jonathan Burt, "The Illumination of the Animal Kingdom: The Role of Light and Electricity in Animal Representation," *Society and Animals* 9:3 (2001): 210.

13. Joan Thirsk, *Horses in Early Modern England: For Service, for Pleasure, for Power* (Reading: University of Reading, 1978); Peter Edwards, *The Horse Trade of Tudor and Stuart England* (Cambridge: Cambridge University Press, 1988); Lisa Jardine and Jerry Brotton, *Global Interests: Renaissance Art between East and West* (London: Reaktion, 2000), especially 145–51.

14. Chris Philo and Chris Wilbert, "Animal Spaces, Beastly Places: An Introduction," in *Animal Spaces, Beastly Places: New Geographies of Human-Animal Relations*, ed. Chris Philo and Chris Wilbert (London: Routledge, 2000), 17.

15. David Cressy, *Travesties and Transgressions in Tudor and Stuart England: Tales of Discord and Dissension* (Oxford: Oxford University Press, 2000), 1.

16. In the recent paperback edition of Cressy's book it has been retitled *Agnes Bowker's Cat . . .*, showing, surely, the publisher's belief in the popular interest in animals.

17. David Cressy, "Agnes Bowker's Cat: Childbirth, Seduction, Bestiality and Lies," in Cressy, ibid., 9–28, passim.

18. Cressy, "Baptized Beasts and Other Travesties: Affronts to Rites of Passage," in Cressy, ibid., 171–85, passim.

19. Ibid., 27.

20. Ibid., 174.

21. Samuel Pegge, "A Memoir on Cock-fighting," *Archaeologia* III (1774): 132–50, quote on 139. See also Pegge, "The Bull-Running at Tutbury, in Staffordshire, Considered," *Archaeologia* II (1773): 86–91.

22. See Sir Sidney Lee, "Bear-baiting, Bullbaiting and Cock-fighting," in *Shakespeare's England: An Account of the Life and Manners of His Age* (Oxford: Clarendon, 1916), II, 428–36; Herbert W. Seager, *Natural History in Shakespeare's Time* (London: E. Stock, 1896); A. E. Shipley, "Zoology in the Time of Shakespeare," *Edinburgh Review* 216 (1912): 120–33. As recently as 1972 a collection of Renaissance animal lore was compiled by Alan Dent under the title *The World of Shakespeare: Animals and Monsters* (Reading: Osprey, 1972).

23. For example, C. L. Kingsford, "Paris Garden and the Bear-baiting," *Archaeologia* second series 20 (1920): 155–78; and sections on the Hope Theatre, home of baiting in the early seventeenth century, in the classic studies of the theater: E. K. Chambers, *The Elizabethan Stage* (Oxford: Clarendon, 1923), II, 448–71; Gerald Eades Bentley, *The Jacobean and Caroline Stage* (Oxford: Clarendon, 1968), VI, 200–214; and Leslie Hotson's study of "Bear Gardens and Bear-Baiting," in Hotson, *The Com-*

monwealth and Restoration Stage (Cambridge, Mass.: Harvard University Press, 1928), 59–70.

24. See Jeanne Addison Roberts, *The Shakespearean Wild: Geography, Genus, and Gender* (1991. Reprint. London: Bison Books, 1994); A. Stuart Daley, "The Idea of Hunting in *As You Like It*," *Shakespeare Studies* 21 (1993): 72–95; Stephen Dickey, "Shakespeare's Mastiff Comedy," *Shakespeare Quarterly* 42:3 (1991): 255–75; Frederick B. Jonassen, "The Stag Hunt in *The Merry Wives of Windsor*," *Bestia: A Yearbook of the Beast Fable Society* (1991): 87–101; Jeffrey Theis, "The 'Ill kill'd' Deer: Poaching and Social Order in *The Merry Wives of Windsor*," *Texas Studies in Literature and Language* 43:1 (2001): 46–73. Bruce Boehrer's *Shakespeare among the Animals: Nature and Society in the Drama of Early Modern England* (New York: Palgrave, 2002) also falls into this category despite its attempts to enter into animal studies rather than only Shakespeare studies. Karen L. Edwards's *Milton and the Natural World: Science and Poetry in Paradise Lost* (Cambridge: Cambridge University Press, 1999) is another example of this type of work in Milton studies.

25. Michael Dobson, "A Dog at All Things: The Transformation of the Onstage Canine, 1550–1850," *Performance Research* 5:2 (2000): 116. An alternative argument to Dobson's can be found in Matthew Bliss, "Property or Performer? Animals on the Elizabethan Stage," *Theatre Studies* 34 (1994): 45–59.

26. This is always an unfortunate formulation that seems to reiterate some particularly unpleasant concepts of a chain of being that placed white, Western man at the top and animals at the bottom, with various human and "subhuman" groups in between. I have attempted to list the growing range of interests in historical study in a chronological order of their emergence. The placement of animals last merely represents them as the most recent addition to historical analysis. A parodic article signaling a fear about the possibility of a history of animals as a logical progression from the then-emergent social history is Charles Phineas, "Household Pets and Urban Alienation," *Journal of Social History* 7:2 (1974): 338–43.

27. Dan Beaver, "The Great Deer Massacre: Animals, Honor, and Communication in Early Modern England," *Journal of British Studies* 38 (1999): 187–216; Mary Fissell, "Imagining Vermin in Early Modern England," *History Workshop Journal* 47 (1999): 1–30; Mark S. R. Jenner, "The Great Dog Massacre," in *Fear in Early Modern Society*, ed. William G. Naphy and Penny Roberts (Manchester: Manchester University Press, 1997), 44–61. The repeated trope of "The Great . . . Massacre" here is evidence of the significance of Robert Darnton's seminal article on the emergence of the animal in social history. See "Workers Revolt: The Great Cat Massacre of the Rue Saint-Séverin," in Darnton, *The Great Cat Massacre and Other Episodes in French Cultural History* (1984. Reprint. London: Penguin, 1991), 79–104.

28. Peter Harrison, "The Virtues of Animals in Seventeenth-Century Thought," *Journal of the History of Ideas* 59:3 (1998): 469–71.

29. Peter Harrison, "Animal Souls, Metempsychosis and Theodicy in Seventeenth-Century English Thought," *Journal of the History of Philosophy* 31:4 (1993): 519–44.

30. William B. Ashworth Jr., "Natural History and the Emblematic World View," in *Reappraisals of the Scientific Revolution*, ed. David C. Lindberg and Robert S. West-

man (Cambridge: Cambridge University Press, 1990), 303–32. Other works on animals and early modern science include J. J. Macintosh, "Animals, Morality and Robert Boyle," *Dialogue—Canadian Philosophical Review* 35:3 (1996): 435–72; and Nathaniel Wolloch, "Christiaan Huygen's Attitude toward Animals," *Journal of the History of Ideas* (2000): 415–32.

31. Nigel Smith, "Enthusiasm and Enlightenment: Of Food, Filth and Slavery," in *The Country and the City Revisited: England and the Politics of Culture, 1550–1850*, ed. Gerald Maclean, Donna Landry, and Joseph P. Ward (Cambridge: Cambridge University Press, 1999), 106–18.

32. Susan Wiseman, "Monstrous Perfectibility: Ape-Human Transformations in Hobbes, Bulwer, Tyson," in *At the Borders of the Human: Beasts, Bodies, and Natural Philosophy in the Early Modern Period*, ed. Erica Fudge, Ruth Gilbert, and Susan Wiseman (Basingstoke: Macmillan, 1999), 215–38.

33. Karen L. Raber, "'Reasonable Creatures': William Cavendish and the Art of Dressage," in *Renaissance Culture and the Everyday*, ed. Patricia Fumerton and Simon Grant (Philadelphia: University of Pennsylvania Press, 1999), 61.

34. On language see Bruce Boehrer, "'Men, Monkeys, Lap-dogs, Parrots, Perish All!' Psittacine Articulacy in Early Modern Writing," *Modern Language Quarterly* 59:2 (1998): 171–93 (a version of this article is also included in Boehrer's *Shakespeare among the Animals*, 99–132); R. W. Serjeantson, "The Passions and Animal Language," *Journal of the History of Ideas* 62:3 (2001): 425–44; and Matthew Senior, "'When the Beasts Spoke': Animal Speech and Classical Reason in Descartes and La Fontaine," in *Animal Acts: Configuring the Human in Western History*, ed. Jennifer Ham and Matthew Senior (London: Routledge, 1997), 61–84. On reason see Raber, "'Reasonable Creatures,'" 43–66.

35. Laurence Babb, *The Elizabethan Malady: A Study of Melancholia in English Literature from 1580 to 1642* (East Lansing: Michigan State College Press, 1951), 18. A similar opposition between human and beast—and the fear of the possibility that humans might slide into the bestial—is also voiced in George Coffin Taylor, "Shakespeare's Use of the Idea of the Beast in Man," *Studies in Philology* 42 (1945): 530–43.

36. Peter Harrison, "Reading the Passions: The Fall, the Passions, and Dominion over Nature," in *The Soft Underbelly of Reason: The Passions in the Seventeenth Century*, ed. Stephen Gaukroger (London and New York: Routledge, 1998), 61.

37. The phrase "field of vision" was brought to my attention as an apt way of thinking about relationships with animals in Jonathan Burt's work. He, in turn, adapted it from Jacqueline Rose. Burt, "Illumination," 208.

38. Harrison, "Virtues of Animals," 463.

39. I have looked in more detail at the ethics of writing the history of animals in "A Left-Handed Blow: Writing the History of Animals," in *Representing Animals*, ed. Nigel Rothfels (Bloomington: University of Indiana Press, 2002), 3–18.

40. Editorial Collective, "History Workshop Journal," *History Workshop: A Journal of Socialist Historians* 1 (1976): 2.

41. Tony Davies, *Humanism* (London: Routledge, 1997), 15, 17. Burckhardt's influential study is *The Civilisation of the Renaissance in Italy* (1860).

42. It is worth noting that the term *beast* often is applied to many of the humans who inhabit the following pages; it is also notable how frequently certain groups—Turks, Jews—are associated with animals. The terms *"beast, beastly, beastliness, brute beast, brute, brutish* and *brutishness"* are, William Meredith Carroll argues, "favourite words" in the Elizabethan period. Carroll, *Animal Conventions in English Renaissance Non-Religious Prose, 1550–1600* (New York: Bookman Associates, 1954), 46.

1

Unpicking the Seam: Talking Animals and Reader Pleasure in Early Modern Satire

Kathryn Perry

Whether they are apocalyptically angry or merely scornful, satires can be recognized by the nature of their engagement with readers. They work toward constructing an alliance between the satirist and the like-minded reader, distancing the reader from the target under scrutiny. Regardless of the seriousness of the subject matter, this alliance typically depends on the satirist's ability to give the reader pleasure as well as to generate feelings of disgust, bitterness, or alienation. The pleasure taken in satire is not simply the pleasure of laughter; it is more fundamentally the pleasure of unruly fantasy, which might incorporate the manipulation of representations that point to the world outside the text or the dream of triumphing over an opponent through the power of rhetoric.

The satirist's interests, defined in this way, can be powerfully served by zoomorphism, by configuring satire as what Jennifer Ham and Matthew Senior call an animal act, in which the human shares space and consciousness with the beast.[1] Early modern English culture was saturated with animal metaphors and personae, and early modern English satire was compulsively zoomorphic. This could take a variety of forms. In the exchange of invective or abuse, the most direct form of satire, the target might be called an animal; the satirist might set out to expose the beasts within apparently civilized human society; or the satirical text, in the form of a fable or a longer, episodic narrative, might use talking animals as characters. In this chapter I discuss the first two categories, but my main interest is in talking animals and the nature of the pleasures early modern readers may have taken in them. Investigating talking animals as a source of pleasure is one way to find out how these chimerical literary and cultural constructions, surprisingly common in early modern satire, work.

The fundamental assumption on which this chapter is based is that the principal pleasure to be had from any talking animal text is the game of playing with recognized animal attributes, making apt, unlikely, or outrageous correspondences with human types or behaviors. The pleasure for authors is in reimagining the correspondences between the human and the animal; the pleasure for readers is in detecting them. The game may be ahistorical, but the cluster of attributes, often incompatible, associated with each species is historically inflected. Moreover, the attributes of a "rhetorical" animal, to borrow Harriet Ritvo's term, have very little in common with its "material" counterpart.[2] Early modern representations of the sparrow as lecherous or the pelican as self-sacrificing are no more unreasonable than the way the hippopotamus (responsible for more human deaths every year than any other African animal) is represented in contemporary children's culture as comic and benign.

From the beginning of the twentieth century, talking animals have been absorbed into the world of children's literature, film, and television, where they reign supreme. Talking animal texts occupied a different, though possibly analogous position in the hierarchy of early modern literature: rather than being set apart in a separate literary sphere, they were ranked at the bottom of the literary ladder and labeled "low." In both the early modern and modern periods, there is an insistence on the simplicity, triviality, and transparency of talking animals and their suitability for innocent readers. The most common form taken by early modern talking animal texts was animal fables, which could be used to instruct the young and socially subordinate, doctrinally (via homilies) or grammatically (via Latin primers).[3] Talking animals in these texts sugar the instructive pill; they exist to entertain. However, talking animals are unruly constructions, and "low" can easily become riotous or scatological, in the tradition of carnival formulated by Mikhail Bakhtin. As we shall see, Bakhtin's idea of carnival makes sense of many of the attributes of talking animals: his concept of the grotesque body, for example, is recognizable as the animal body or the human body in its animal aspect.[4]

The simplicity or "lowness" attributed to talking animal texts can become a specialized kind of pleasure when readers assume talking animal texts to contain encoded representations of recognizable and powerful individuals.[5] In these cases, the supposed simplicity or "lowness" of the animal vehicle is often remarked upon; it simultaneously attracts and deflects penetrating readings. In his *Dialogue of Comfort against Tribulation* (1534), written in the Tower, Sir Thomas More puts the tale of the Ass and his overscrupulous conscience into the mouth of Mother Mawd. The doubly humble form of the tale—an animal fable told by a woman servant—is protective coloring, discouraging unfriendly readers from taking it seriously. At the same time, More draws attention to the hidden gravity of the tale, which is clearly a commentary on his own predicament: "she was wont . . . to tell us that were children many childish tales / but as *plinius* sayth that there is no boke lightely so bad, but that some good thyng a man may pyk out therof / so thinke I that there is al most no tale so folysh, but that yet in one mater or other, to some purpose it may hap to serve."[6]

In *Mother Hubberds Tale* (1591) Edmund Spenser adopts the same device as More, putting a talking animal story into the mouth of an old woman. Spenser insists on the "base" style and "meane" matter of the tale,[7] but his protestations of innocence and triviality were not believed by officialdom or by the majority of readers at the time, who assumed *Mother Hubberds Tale* to be an encoded attack on Lord Burghley, Elizabeth I's chief minister. A letter written by Sir Thomas Tresham soon after the publication of *Mother Hubberds Tale* confirms that it was suppressed by the authorities and suggests the frisson of pleasure to be had from a dangerous jest. Tresham writes that "Tales, I meane no Tayles, are nowe on the soden in greate request; especiallie mother Hubburds tale. . . . The whole discourse of that ould weoman ys (as I heare reported) to showe by what channce the apes did loose their tayles. Thowghe this be a jest, yett is itt taken in suche earnest, that the booke is by Superior awthoritie called in."[8] The condemnation of writers of beast satire by moralists such as T.B. for "girding" or gibing at "the greatest personages of all estates and callings under the fables of savage beasts" tends to suggest that many contemporary readers may have taken pleasure in the subversive possibilities of the form.[9]

The body of this chapter amplifies the issues raised in the introduction, beginning with a discussion of how the boundaries between the human and the animal—the boundaries that talking animals breach—were prescribed in the early modern period. In practice, the boundaries often collapsed in the exchange of invective or the creation of monsters. The chapter continues with a closer look at carnival and the business of "girding" at authority, and at the ways in which the body of a thinking animal can become the satirist's subject. It concludes with speculations on how the pleasures of talking animals can be understood at the moment of reading and on how the seam between the human and the animal is unpicked.

BOUNDARIES

The ways in which relationships between the human and the animal could be known and represented are illuminated by Michel Foucault's definition, in *The Order of Things,* of a Renaissance episteme grounded in the assumption that the world is governed by laws of adjacency, emulation, analogy, and sympathy. The human being is the point where all things meet: "There does exist, however, in this space . . . one particularly privileged point: it is saturated with analogies. . . . This point is man: he stands in proportion to the heavens, just as he does to animals and plants, and as he does also to the earth, to metals, to stalactites or storms."[10]

The natural world, including animals, was held to correspond with the human world through the inexhaustible and orderly play of signs, demonstrating similitude and dissimilitude with bewildering variety. The history of human and animal relationships constructed by Keith Thomas offers evidence for the orthodoxy of this model. He describes theologians preaching a doctrine of human ascendancy and uniqueness. Animals were believed to serve humans discursively, as well as physically, providing a vocabulary and set of categories with which human qualities could be described and classified. Rather than being detached from the human world, the natural world was understood to be "redolent with human analogy and symbolic meaning."[11] The encyclopedic folios on the animal world produced by Edward Topsell at the beginning of the seventeenth century, in which he synthesizes contemporary knowledge about animals from the works of authorities on natural history, philosophy, and religion, are a monument to this orthodoxy.[12] Topsell's aim, in each case, is to uncover the true nature of the animal by discussing its name, habitat, and anthropomorphized characteristics, revealed through anecdotal evidence. The practical uses to which humans can put the animal, along with its symbolic significance, are an integral part of that knowledge.

The language in which these orthodox assumptions were expressed was surprisingly flexible. A favorite example demonstrating the relationship between the human and animal worlds, and one with political applications, was the beehive. In *The Boke Named the Governour* (1531), Sir Thomas Elyot lauds monarchy as the perfect system of government, ordained by nature: "For who can denie but that all thynge in heven and erthe is governed by one god, by one perpetuall ordre, by one providence? One Sonne ruleth over the day, and one Moone over the nyghte; and to descende downe to the erthe, in a litell beest, which of all other is moste to be marvayled at, I meane the Bee, is lefte to man by nature, as it semeth, a perpetuall figure of juste governance or rule: who hath amonge them one principall Bee for theyr governour, who excelleth all other in greatnes."[13] Elyot not only observes the principle of emulation in nature, with the heavens, small insects, and, centrally, humans, ruled by one monarch, but also interprets the naturally occurring hierarchy of the beehive as a lesson for occasionally wayward human societies. He goes on to discuss the expulsion of stranger bees and the formation of new swarms, concluding, "I suppose who seriously beholdeth this example, and hath any commendable witte, shall therof gather moche matter to the fourmynge of a publicke weale."[14]

In this case meaning flows in one direction: from the animal to the human. Sometimes meaning flows in both directions, and the animal and human worlds reflect one another. Charles Butler's treatise on bees, *The Feminine Monarchie* (1609), interprets natural order in this way. A comprehensive natural history and guide to beekeeping, it is unusual in that it recognizes that the monarch of the hive is a queen, not a king. Its subtitle announces Butler's aims and methods: *wherein the truth, found out by experience and diligent observation, discovereth the idle and fond conceipts, which many have written anent this subject.* However fresh his observations, the only way Butler can know and represent the workings of the hive is by comparison with human society: "Besides their soveraigne the Bees have also subordinate governors and leaders, not unfitly resembling Captaines and coronels of soldiers."[15] By understanding the bee world in terms of the human world, Butler's language is not so distant from that with which post-Darwinian biologists address lay audiences when they attribute human motivations and planning to the processes by which plants, insects, and animals ensure species survival, "enticing" or "employing" other organisms to spread pollen or remove pests. However, like Elyot and unlike modern biologists, Butler also sees the perfect, sustainable order of the bee commonwealth as a model for human societies.[16] According to this orderly vision, "the world remains identical; resemblances continue to be what they are, and to resemble one another."[17]

In this context, in which the pattern of correspondences between the human and the animal is prescribed and controlled, human superiority and uniqueness are asserted through the agency of speech. According to Ben Jonson, "speech is the only benefit man hath to express his excellency of mind above other creatures. It is the instrument of society."[18] Speech is the means by which other distinguishing features of humanity—reason and religion—can be asserted and the means by which human societies are created and maintained. Speech is liminal; it marks the threshold to humanity.

BEASTS WITHOUT AND WITHIN

In practice, there was much anxiety about maintaining the privileged position of human being separately from animal being.[19] It is all too easy to envisage, in a world of resemblances and analogies, the collapse of distinctions between the human and the animal. Humans stripped of reason and the consciousness of being created in God's image might sink into the bestial life of the body. Sometimes, this degradation was deliberately invoked: the ubiquitous human practice of labeling enemies, inferiors, and outsiders as animals was frequently and enthusiastically adopted in the early modern period. It is a tribal practice, observed by anthropologists such as Mary Douglas, readily translated into the multiple tribalisms of larger societies: "In each constructed world of nature, the contrast between man and not-man provides an analogy for the contrast between the member of the human society and the outsider."[20]

The power and rich allusiveness of abusive animal epithets were so great in the early seventeenth century that they could be used to structure formal invective, to the extent of shaping a long-running controversy. In 1615, Joseph Swetnam published *The Araignment of Lewde, Idle, Froward, and Unconstant Women,* in which, following the model of Diogenes, he represents himself as Cerberus. Swetnam's attack on women provoked several responses, some of which turned his self-representation as a snarling dog back on himself. Rachel Speght addressed Swetnam as black-mouthed Melastomus in *A Mouzell for Melastomus, The Cynicall Bayter of, and Foule Mouthed Barker against Evahs Sex* (1617); in *The Worming of a Mad Dogge; or, A Soppe for Cerberus the Jaylor of Hell* (1617), Constantia Munda pictures Swetnam as a mad dog returning to his vomit.[21] We can presume that the reading public enjoyed this language: it is no accident that in these and similar cases, abuse cast in animal terms is foregrounded on the title pages, and it was title pages that were used to market books.

The human can be defined in opposition not only to the animal but also to that which merely resembles the human. As Steve Baker points out, a common strategy in the definition of a privileged human community is to define the unprivileged, the outsiders, as half-human, or simian—a category more unsettling, in many ways, than the wholly animal.[22] In fiction, the half-human or imperfectly human and the metamorphosis between the animal and the human can be a focus for testing ideas about how human civilization originates and how it can be maintained. In *The Tempest,* Prospero's experiment to civilize Caliban, the imperfectly animal-like human, collapses. As a monstrous birth, a "puppy-headed monster" "not honoured with / A human shape," Caliban is often confused with the animal, particularly in the persistent joke that he is a fish. More fundamentally, his animal instincts, especially his susceptibility to lust and drunkenness, cannot be suppressed or reformed. Prospero shares Jonson's belief in the civic virtues of language. The key to his attempt to civilize the motherless Caliban, brought up in isolation with the motherless Miranda, is to teach him how to speak. In Caliban's case, speech allows him to attack his benefactor: "You taught me language, and my profit on't / Is I know how to curse." Prospero represents the failure of his project as the impossibility of inculcating superior human values in the imperfect human corrupted by animality. The experiment produced an angel in Miranda and, in Caliban, "A devil, a born devil, on whose nature / Nurture can never stick; on whom my pains, / Humanely taken, all, all lost, quite lost."[23]

Satire that questions the humanity, rationality, or civilization of human society sometimes embraces the animal; on occasion, the English Renaissance satirist casts himself as a kind of Caliban in the form of the rough, railing, half-animal satyr. The satyr's animality places him outside civilized society and sanctions his attacks on it.[24] George Wither, who enjoyed representing himself as an outsider, stresses this aspect of his chosen persona:

> Though in shape I seeme a Man,
> Yet a Satyr wilde I am;
> Bred in Woods and Desert places,
> Where men seldome shew their faces;
> Rough and hayrie like a Goate,
> Clothed with Dame Natures coate.[25]

In *The Muses Elizium* (1630), at the end of his career, Michael Drayton turns the role inside out, representing himself as an aged, harmless, melancholy satyr, driven away from human society by its cruelty and viciousness.[26]

In these examples the boundaries between the human and not-human are congruent with the boundaries between those inside and those outside society, illustrating Douglas's point about tribal practices. In other texts, appearances are less reliable, and categories of the human and the animal come under pressure. Turning to Drayton again, this time to *The Moone-Calfe* (1627), a monstrous birth is used to demonstrate the absence of fully human, civilized behavior in a degraded society. The androgynous Moone-Calfe is not shunned but sought out because of his wealth. Men are prepared to abandon their "perfect humane shape," imitating "this Beasts deformitie," in order to seek his favor.[27] The story of the Moone-Calfe is fairly extreme but follows a predictable path, demonstrating the bestiality of corrupt humankind. However, it is accompanied by tales told by the midwives who attended the creature's birth, which are more complex. They stress the confusion between the animal and the human and related problems of perception, contrasting consensus opinion, usually deluded, with the true perception of the clear-sighted individual. This opposition is explored in Mother Owle's tale, in which a werewolf preys on children. The only character to recognize the disguised werewolf in his human shape, to pick him out from a crowd of deceived villagers, is a man who has been metamorphosed into an ass but who cannot speak until he is magically restored to his human body.[28] The tale reverses assumptions: he who has the form of an animal is the only one to exercise the power of reason.

CARNIVAL AND "GIRDING" AT AUTHORITY

The ass and the werewolf, in Drayton's tale, are magically disguised, whereas the satyr persona is assumed self-consciously as a mask. Masks and disguises, actual or fictional, are one obvious way in which the boundary between the human and the animal can be breached. This was a practice condemned by the moralist William Prynne: "For doe not all Actors, Mummers, Masquers [put on] *the portraitures and formes of Lyons, Beares, Apes, Asses, Horses, Fishes, Foules, which in outward appearance metamorphose them into Idols, Devils, Monsters, Beasts,* whose parts they represent? and can these disguises bee lawfull, be tolerable among Christians? No verily."[29]

Animal masks are obnoxious, according to Prynne, because they obliterate the image of God in man. During carnival, which celebrates those aspects of human behavior condemned by moralists such as Prynne, masks and disguises are central to the abandonment of constraints: "The mask is related to transition, metamorphoses, the violation of natural boundaries, to mockery and familiar nicknames. It contains the playful element of life."[30] Bakhtin's formulation of carnival, although it refers to animals as such only rarely, illuminates ways in which the concept of the human—rational, controlled, transcendent—collides with the concept of the animal—instinctual, wild, and playful. Carnival is a release from officially sanctioned culture, an alternative world in which the community can revel at specified times of the year, with laughter (mocking and deriding as well as festive) and play as its key features. The language of carnival is often abusive; the practices of carnival are riotous, flouting established authority, reversing hierarchies, and rewarding rogues.[31] This is not to say that there is a simple opposition between authority and carnival: the liberty of carnival exists only because authority permits its own temporary suspension. However, the experience of that liberty might seem untrammeled; it is arguable that carnival is both contained by and a challenge to authorized power structures, that carnival "can both undermine and reinforce—it can constitute a process of adjustment within a perpetuation of order."[32]

The body, especially the lower body and its functions of defecation and reproduction, is celebrated in carnival; Bakhtin identifies this body as the grotesque body, but it is also recognizable as the human body in its animal aspect.[33] Keith Thomas records attempts by early modern commentators to resist or transcend the animal body and its functions: Cotton Mather, humiliated by the experience of urinating against a wall at the same time as a dog, resolved to fix his mind on specially pious thoughts on similar future occasions to distinguish himself from his companion.[34] Others revel in the pleasure of carnival, in the life of the body, in laughter, and the abandonment of the constraints of reason and hierarchy. This sense of bodily or anarchical pleasure is crucial to some kinds of satire, particularly texts with talking animals. The carnivalesque element in the texts in this study may be subordinated to an earnest desire to expose folly, but it remains a source of reader pleasure.

For example, in *Maroccus Extaticus; or, Bankes Bay Horse in a Trance* (1595), a dialogue based on the historical figures of the showman Banks and his performing horse, Morocco, the knowledgeable horse is overheard lecturing his ignorant master on sources of social evils. The joke is not only in the reversal of a hierarchical relationship and the overbearing way in which the horse addresses his master but also in the fact that the pair conceals the horse's ability: Morocco learned Latin at Oxford, for example, while he seemed merely to gambol in the college fields.[35] Talking horses tend to be superior creatures. At a much later date, the partnership between a man and his horse represented in *Maroccus Extaticus*—the arrogant horse, the secrecy about his ability to speak, the discussions in the stable—was recast, on precisely the same terms, in a popular American TV sitcom from the 1960s, *Mr. Ed, The Talking Horse,* suggesting that representations of talking animals that reverse the roles of master and servant are a reliable and repeatable source of consumer pleasure.

The archetypally carnivalesque animal character, who was of great significance to early modern satires, is Reynard the Fox. Cycles of stories starring the cunning Reynard appeared in Europe from the early medieval period; it was Caxton who introduced the Reynard epic to England in *The History of Reynard the Fox* (1481).[36] The controlling environment in Caxton's *Reynard* is a feudal court, ruled by the Lion, whose chief aim is to control his unruly barons, the most intransigent of whom is Reynard. The main impulse behind the many episodes in this narrative, and behind the Reynard cycle in general, is the Fox's duplicity. All the characters in the Reynard cycle are greedy and self-interested; only Reynard invariably satisfies his desires and escapes final punishment. He is indestructible because readers continued to demand and relish "the scandalous triumphs of a brazen reprobate"[37] and irredeemable because of his unchangeable animal nature.

A recurrent theme in the Reynard cycle is the enmity between the Fox and the Wolf and the Fox's repeated triumphs over his stronger rival through trickery. In Caxton's version, the feud culminates in single combat between Reynard and Isegrym the Wolf. Rukenaw the Ape, advising that "connyng goth to fore strengthe," recommends that Reynard be shorn and oiled so that the Wolf cannot get hold of him, that he stir up dust in his eyes, and that he urinate on his tail and beat the Wolf on the face to blind him.[38] Isegrym, who is characterized as a feudal knight, brutal but honorable, is exasperated by these tricks; declaring in chivalric language "I wyl sette it in aventure and seen what shal come thereof," he presses Reynard to the ground.[39] Under pressure, the Fox speaks sweetly and makes false promises; while the Wolf is distracted by this further proof of Reynard's falsehood, the Fox wrings the Wolf's testicles. Leaving the Wolf spitting blood and defecating in pain, the Fox is surrounded by friends and former enemies. Fortune has rewarded the rogue: "Thus fareth the world now. who that is riche and hye on the wheel. he hath many kynnesmen and frendes. that shal helpe to bere out his welthe. But who that is nedy and in payne or in poverte. fyndeth but fewe frendes and kynnesmen."[40]

Mocking laughter, the humiliating overturn of the stronger by the weaker, the ascendancy of the trickster, and the focus on bodily functions identify Caxton's *Reynard* as a carnivalesque and obviously "low" text. It remained popular, appearing in various editions, revised versions, and adaptations until the end of the seventeenth century, although its "lowness" became a source of embarrassment rather than a strength. Elizabeth Allde's version, for example, first published in 1620, promised to be *Newly Corrected and Purged from All Grossenesse.*[41] Caxton's *Reynard* is not a political satire, but it is politically configured: events and relationships are governed by the apparatus of a royal court. Therefore, it could be used as a basis for more explicitly political texts, such as *The Most Pleasant and Delightful History of Reynard the Fox: The Second Part* (1681), which focuses on factional maneuverings, conspiracies, rebellion, and executions, appropriate in the aftermath of Titus Oates, the Popish Plot, and the Exclusion Crisis.

At the end of the sixteenth century, Spenser incorporated elements of the Reynard cycle, including its episodic structure and the nature of the Fox, into *Mother Hubberds Tale.* In this satire, a criminally cunning Fox and an artful Ape perpetrate a series of frauds, disguised as shepherds, clerics, and courtiers, culminating in the Ape masquerading as the king, with the Fox as his evil counselor. In each episode, the Fox and the Ape exhaust the possibilities of the roles they assume and are either briefly punished or escape, but each failure positions them further up the social ladder rather than down. Their irresistible upward momentum is part of the satire—an outrage to morality and natural justice. The careers of the two animals could be, and were, read as a disillusioned commentary on contemporary politics and the inevitable ascent of rogues.[42] The indestructibility of the Fox and the Ape, and the concomitant lack of faith in those in high office, is attested by their reappearance in a new reign in a sequel to *Mother Hubberds Tale,* Richard Niccols's *The Beggers Ape* (1627). Mother Hubberd herself could be represented as a carnivalesque figure, as in Thomas Middleton's description of her as an alewife, "she that was called in for selling her working bottle-ale to bookbinders, and spurting froth upon courtiers' noses."[43] The rude and defiant Mother Hubberd, in this representation, stands in for the text that bears her name, with its irrepressible "girding" at the powerful.

TALKING ANIMALS ARE "GOOD TO THINK"

Despite the likenesses between the two texts, early modern readers evidently read Caxton's *Reynard* and Spenser's *Mother Hubberds Tale* in different ways: many of them assumed that the animals in the latter text were encoded representations of real and powerful individuals. For these readers, the interest and the pleasure in *Mother Hubberds Tale* lay not just in its carnivalesque attributes but also in decoding its hidden meanings. Claude Lévi-Strauss, commenting on totemic animals, suggested that they are chosen as totems not for naturalistic or empirical reasons but because they are a way of grappling with and expressing ideas about the world and the relationships within it, that they are "good to think" rather than "good to eat."[44] Talking animals can also be "good to think"; the thinking may be caught up in the game of decoding, or it may engage with the business of human-animal correspondences in other ways, including a device peculiar to talking animal texts in which the special attributes of an animal's body are given human functions. This device is used in similar ways and for similar purposes, in two texts, modern and early modern, in which part of an insect's body is recast as a human tool. The reader is given an imaginative jolt and forced to consider the human subject under totalitarianism deflated to the status of an ant or human governance as laughably weak.

The modern example is *The Sword in the Stone,* T. H. White's novel about King Arthur's boyhood, in which Merlyn transforms Arthur into a series of different animals in order to teach him, ostensibly, about animal life and, actually, about different forms of human social organization. In an episode in the revised version of the text, Merlyn changes Arthur into an ant; he learns that anthills are totalitarian dictatorships, where individual thought and action are suppressed. A physiological feature of ants is exploited to bring this about: the ants' antennae are permanent radio antennae, picking up commands, the Leader's propaganda, or relentless popular music and abolishing any ant's capacity to think private thoughts in silence. Arthur finds that the songs cannot be turned off: "He liked them at first, especially the ones about Love-dove-above, until he found that they did not vary. As soon as they had been finished once, they were begun again. After an hour or two, they began to make him feel sick inside."[45] Representing the ants' antennae as a fusion of technology and biology, and as the means by which a malign state could invade and eradicate individuality, embodied popular fears in the 1950s, when the revised version of *The Sword in the Stone* was published.

In *The Parliament of Bees* (1641), John Day also represents an element of an insect as both a tool and a body part. A soldier bee uses his sting in battle to protect his ruler, Prorex, who had been "beaten into a tuft of Rosemary."[46] This comic account draws on a tradition of mock heroic or mock epic writing about the doings of insects, which includes Spenser's *Muiopotmos* (1590) and Richard Carew's *A Herrings Tayle* (1598). The satiric bite in *The Parliament of Bees* comes from the fact that Prorex, ignominiously rescued by his pikeman, attempts unsuccessfully to govern an unruly parliament, which is very far from the orderly bee commonwealths represented by Elyot and Butler, discussed earlier in this chapter. *The Parliament of Bees* was published at a time when the real Parliament was in uproar and leaders on both sides would soon need to be defended by their pikemen.

These pleasures of these texts, and those cited earlier, are slippery; categories such as the carnivalesque and being "good to think" tend to slide into one another. This is particularly true of *The Flea* by Peter Woodhouse (1605).[47] Like Donne's flea, this Flea is aggrandized beyond reason; unlike Donne's flea, Woodhouse's Flea speaks for himself.[48] This is a satire that asserts the power of rhetoric: the Elephant, proudly claiming to be the greatest of beasts because of his strength, size, courage, and service to kings, is challenged by the Flea to test these claims in debate. The Elephant loses; the Flea, more dexterous rhetorically, confounds each claim with a greater one of his own. The Flea is a figure for the successful satirist, triumphing over his infinitely more powerful opponent because of his ability to manipulate words. The story satirizes both court parasites (the Flea represents himself as the perfect courtier) and arrogant notables. It is framed by two dreams: the unnamed narrator dreams of a meeting between Democritus, the laughing philosopher, and Heraclitus, the weeping philosopher; the debate between the Flea and the Elephant is a dream told by Democritus as evidence that laughter is the best response to the world. As a tribute to laughter, *The Flea* is positioned explicitly in the world of carnival described by Bakhtin; in carnivalesque mode, the Flea, the tiniest of creatures, is the only one to confront the Elephant's claims to supremacy and issues a bold and insulting challenge from the shelter of a Dog's ear. In his claims to greater courage than the Elephant, the Flea flaunts his intractable animal nature, making a virtue of his maddening persistence and indestructibility:

> When man with pressing nayle seekes me to kill,
> My guts about my heeles, I march on still.
> And though in this great broyle I was neere slaine,
> The daunger past, I boldely bite againe.[49]

Like Reynard the Fox, the Flea is an irredeemable rogue because of his unchangeable animal nature. His reply to the Elephant, in which he claims, among other things, that by dining on the blood of carnivorous man he revenges the rest of the animal world, is a triumph of perverse logic, demonstrating the power of the insignificant over the great.

UNPICKING THE SEAM

The previous sections of this chapter have largely been attempts to build on the texts under discussion, to construct boundaries, half-human monsters, carnival, and contexts in which talking animals could be applied to political realities. This last section seeks instead to undo the texts, to take them apart in order to understand something of the pleasure of the reading moment. This is Barthes's focus in *The Pleasure of the Text:* among his criteria for reader pleasure, Barthes includes the erotically charged notion of the collision, or seam, between conflicting textual elements. The example he uses is Sade, writing pornography in canonical, grammatically pure language: "Neither culture nor its destruction is erotic; it is the seam between them, the fault, the flaw which becomes so . . . what pleasure wants is the site of a loss, the seam, the cut, the deflation, the *dissolve* which seizes the subject in the midst of bliss."[50]

What Barthes seems to be describing is a process whereby opposing entities are sewn together and then ripped apart. Reader pleasure lies both in the unpredictable and playful collision between those entities and in their separation. When it comes to talking animals, this process can be seen in the construction of the fiction of the talking animal, as a creature with some human attributes, and in the moments when the fiction is undone, when the animality of the persona dominates. A particular version of this pleasure comes as a result of the collision, the seam, between elevated language and representations, and grossly animal bodily functions. Chauntecleer, in "The Nun's Priest's Tale," is a case in point: he is represented as a beast with heraldic beauty and as an exponent of *fine amour,* expert in learned debate. It is in the language belonging to that code that he expresses his explicitly animal desire for Pertelote as they perch on their roosts:

> For whan I feele a-nyght your softe side—
> Al be it that I may nat on yow ryde,
> For that oure perche is maad so narwe, allas—
> I am so ful of joye and of solas,
> That I diffye bothe sweven and dreem.[51]

Isegrym the Wolf speaks the same chivalric language when confronted with Reynard the Fox urinating in his face: "I wyl sette it in aventure and seen what shal come thereof." *The History of Reynard the Fox* stages continual oscillations between the human and the animal. Reynard's body is clearly an animal's body, although his voice is that of a courtier; his castle is a den as well as a baronial stronghold; he steals chickens as well as defying the king. In the comprehensively enjoyable text, *The Flea*, there is also a moment when the reader's attention is drawn to the seam between socially elevated and grossly animal behaviors and to the way that seam gapes. When the Flea issues his challenge to the Elephant, he throws down his glove in true chivalric style; however, he does it from the protection of the Dog's ear. The wretched and unwilling mediator, the Dog, offers to punish him in genuinely doggy style, "betwixt my teeth I soone would crush this patch," if only he could find him.[52] In these texts, in "The Nun's Priest's Tale," and in most texts with talking animals, the seam between the animal and the human is visible only intermittently; Barthes regards such intermittence, "the staging of an appearance-as-disappearance," as more desirable than open display.[53]

The seam is not always sewn between speech and action. In *The Calidonian Forrest* by John Hepwith (probably written in 1628 but first published in 1641), the relationship between a Lion and a Hart is represented at a critical moment through symbolic play; the meanings and consequences of that play, and the species of the talking animals chosen, flow from a collision enacted rather than spoken. The Lion encounters the Hart in the forest; becoming besotted with the stranger, he establishes him as royal favorite:

> Who in a jesting manner oft would throw
> His Royall Crowne upon his branched brow,
> And with some favour oft would grace his horne,
> Or with some goodly Gemme his eare adorn.[54]

The intimacy between the two animals, crossing the species barrier, is not just a fantastic impossibility but indicates the collapse of distinctions between royalty and commoners. The Hart's horns make him physiologically unequipped to wear a crown, suggesting that he is intrinsically unfit to be the Lion's deputy; the odd image makes the crown into a quoit, a plaything. It draws attention to the inescapable animality of the Hart and the gaping seam between that animality and the crown as a precious symbol of rule. The phallic overtones in the line "and with some favour oft would grace his horne" hints at the nature of the relationship between the Lion and the Hart. The established connections between lions and royalty are preserved in *The*

Calidonian Forrest, but the dignity of the analogy is undone. Furthermore, a knowing reader in 1628 might detect the great favorite the Duke of Buckingham under the mask of the Hart, given word play on the Duke's title and the representation of him as a buck in libels of the period, and might even ponder the significance of the Actaeon myth and the usual fate of metamorphosed deer.

In this chapter, I have constructed distinct categories—carnivalesque, being "good to think," the collision between elevated language and bodily functions—as a way of analyzing the mechanisms of early modern talking animal satires, but it is clear that these categories mingle and overlap. What is also clear is that all of these texts, from *Maroccus Extaticus* to *Mother Hubberds Tale* and *The Flea,* are preoccupied with the same issues of hierarchy, order, decorum, and the status of outsiders and that talking animals consistently flout hierarchy and shatter decorum. Contemporary reactions to these texts confirm that unruly talking animals were regarded by some as a threat and by others as an indulgent or possibly risky pleasure.

Why do talking animal satires work like this and provoke these responses? Because of speech. Animal invective and animal masks may breach the boundaries between the human and the animal, but something different happens when that chimera, the animal with the power of speech, is created. If Jonson is right, and speech is "the only benefit man hath" to assert his superiority, the existence of talking animals questions that superiority. In the fantasy world of the talking animal text, humans are not automatically the most excellent of creatures, nor are they the only ones capable of organizing civil societies. Within these social structures, the representation of figures of authority as talking animals often is undignified or derisory or, at best, encourages a sense of intimacy that is inimical to authority. Spenser's critic T.B. was right to fear the "girding" at authority that might be concealed in fables of savage beasts. By appropriating the power of speech, talking animals undermine convictions of human superiority and uniqueness and, by extension, hierarchical structures and discourses in general, such as the language of chivalry. Not all talking animal texts challenge notions of human superiority: many, like the fables used to enforce orthodoxy, are buttressed by authoritarian pronouncements by the narrator or by the moral that polices the fable. In Lyly's *Euphues and His England* (1580), old Fidus tells Euphues a tale in which the Fox and the Wolf try to exploit the Lion's sleep, only to find that he is perpetually vigilant. The moral of the fable is that subjects should not even ask whether the Lion is asleep or awake, "for this is sufficient for you to know, that there is a Lyon, not where he is, or what he doth."[55] The moral enforces the sovereignty of the Lion by taking away his speech, by transforming him into a symbolic lion: power lies in silence and mystery. Dissent, on the other hand, requires speech and, in the form of satire, thrives on fantasy and pleasure. Artful, rude, and unpredictable as they are, talking animals are the satirist's natural allies.

NOTES

1. *Animal Acts: Configuring the Human in Western History,* ed. Jennifer Ham and Matthew Senior (London: Routledge, 1997), 2.

2. Harriet Ritvo, *The Animal Estate: The English and Other Creatures in the Victorian Age* (1987. Reprint. Harmondsworth, U.K.: Penguin, 1987), 5.

3. See Thomas Blage, *A Schole of Wise Conceytes* (London, 1572), and John Brinsley, *Ludus Literarius; or, The Grammar Schoole* (1612. Reprint. Menston, U.K.: Scholar Press, 1968).

4. Mikhail Bakhtin, *Rabelais and His World,* trans. Helene Iswolsky (Cambridge, Mass.: MIT Press, 1968), 17–29.

5. Annabel Patterson discusses the ways in which animal fables can be read politically in *Fables of Power: Aesopian Writing and Political History* (Durham, N.C.: Duke University Press, 1991).

6. Sir Thomas More, *A Dialogue of Comfort against Tribulation,* in *The Complete Works of St Thomas More,* ed. Louis L. Martz and Frank Manley, 13 vols. (New Haven, Conn.: Yale University Press, 1976), XII, 114.

7. Edmund Spenser, *Mother Hubberds Tale,* line 44, in *The Yale Edition of the Shorter Poems of Edmund Spenser* (New Haven, Conn.: Yale University Press, 1989).

8. Richard S. Peterson, "Laurel Crown and Ape's Tail: New Light on Spenser's Career from Sir Thomas Tresham," *Spenser Studies* 12 (1998): 1–35; quote on p. 22.

9. Peter de la Primaudaye, *The Second Part of the French Academie,* trans. T.B. (London, 1594), Ff2v.

10. Michel Foucault, *The Order of Things: An Archaeology of the Human Sciences* (London: Tavistock, 1970), 22.

11. Keith Thomas, *Man and the Natural World: Changing Attitudes in England, 1500–1800* (1983. Reprint. Harmondsworth, U.K.: Penguin, 1984), 30–41, 61–64, 89.

12. Edward Topsell, *The Historie of Foure-footed Beasts* (London, 1607); Edward Topsell, *The Historie of Serpents* (London, 1608).

13. Sir Thomas Elyot, *The Boke Named the Governour,* ed. Henry Herbert Stephen Croft, 2 vols. (London, 1838), I, 11–12.

14. Ibid., I, 12.

15. Charles Butler, *The Feminine Monarchie; or, A Treatise Concerning Bees, and the Due Ordering of Them* (Oxford, 1609), A3v.

16. Ibid., A2r.

17. Foucault, *Order of Things,* 25.

18. Ben Jonson, *Timber; or, Discoveries,* in *Ben Jonson,* ed. Ian Donaldson (Oxford: Oxford University Press, 1985), 570.

19. Thomas, *Man and the Natural World,* 36–41.

20. Mary Douglas, *Implicit Meanings: Essays in Anthropology* (London: Routledge and Kegan Paul, 1975), 289.

21. Constantia Munda, *The Worming of a Mad Dogge; or, A Soppe for Cerberus the Jaylor of Hell* (London, 1617), 15–16; Linda Woodbridge, *Women and the English Renaissance: Literature and the Nature of Womankind, 1540–1620* (Urbana: University of Illinois Press, 1984), 77–101.

22. Steve Baker, *Picturing the Beast: Animals, Identity, and Representation* (Manchester: Manchester University Press, 1993), 108–14. Erica Fudge sets the human and half-human in opposition: the ape is disturbing because it is anthropoid, and "to be anthropoid is *emphatically* not to be human." Erica Fudge, *Perceiving Animals: Humans and Beasts in Early Modern Culture* (2000. Reprint. Urbana: University of Illinois Press, 2002), 11.

23. William Shakespeare, *The Tempest,* II.2.153–54; I.2.284–85; II.2.24–31; I.2.365–66; IV.1.188–90, in *William Shakespeare: The Complete Works,* ed. Stanley Wells and Gary Taylor (Oxford: Clarendon Press, 1988).

24. Alvin Kernan, *The Cankered Muse: Satire of the English Renaissance* (New Haven, Conn.: Yale University Press, 1959), 54–92.

25. George Wither, *The Workes of Master George Wither* (London, 1617), 307.

26. Michael Drayton, *The Muses Elizium* (1630); "The Tenth Nimphall," in *The Works of Michael Drayton,* ed. William Hebel, Kathleen Tillotson, and Bernard Newdigate, 5 vols. (Oxford: Shakespeare Head Press, 1931–41; corrected edition Oxford: Basil Blackwell, 1961), III.

27. Michael Drayton, *The Moone-Calfe* (1627), lines 229–30, in Drayton, *Works,* III.

28. Ibid., lines 1043–1212.

29. William Prynne, *Histrio-Mastix. The Players Scourge; or, Actors Tragedie* (London, 1633), 890.

30. Bakhtin, *Rabelais and His World,* 39.

31. Ibid., 5–26; Michael D. Bristol, *Carnival and Theater: Plebian Culture and the Structure of Authority in Renaissance England* (New York: Methuen, 1985), 19–25.

32. Leah S. Marcus, *The Politics of Mirth: Jonson, Herrick, Milton, Marvell, and the Defense of the Old Holiday Pastimes* (Chicago: University of Chicago Press, 1986), 7.

33. Bakhtin, *Rabelais and His World,* 17–29.

34. Thomas, *Man and the Natural World,* 38.

35. John Dando and Harrie Runt, *Maroccus Extaticus; or, Bankes Bay Horse in a Trance,* ed. E. F. Rimbault (London, 1843), 14, 9.

36. *The History of Reynard the Fox: Translated from the Dutch Original by William Caxton,* ed. N. F. Blake, Early English Text Society Old Series 263 (London: Oxford University Press, 1970).

37. *Early Middle English Verse and Prose,* ed. J. A. W. Bennett and G. V. Smithers, 2d ed. (Oxford: Clarendon Press, 1968), 67.

38. Caxton, *Reynard,* 97.

39. Ibid., 101.

40. Ibid., 105.

41. *The Most Delectable History of Reynard the Fox. Newly Corrected and Purged from All Grossenesse, in Phrase and Matter.* (London, 1620).

42. Many contemporary readers of *Mother Hubberds Tale* commented on its application to court politics. Gabriel Harvey, friend of Spenser, reproved him in print for being a malcontent (Gabriel Harvey, *Foure Letters and Certeine Sonnets, Especially Touching Robert Greene and Other Parties by Him Abused,* ed. G. B. Harrison, Bodley Head Quartos, 2 [London: Bodley Head, 1922], 15). An early and outspoken identification between the Fox and Lord Burghley was made by the Catholic exile and polemicist Richard Verstegan (also known as Richard Rowlands) in *A Declaration of the True Causes of the Great Troubles, Presupposed to Be Intended against the Realme of England* (Cologne, 1592), E2v.

43. Thomas Middleton, *The Black Book* (1604), in *The Works of Thomas Middleton,* ed. A. H. Bullen, 8 vols. (London, 1885), VIII, 31.

44. Claude Lévi-Strauss, *Totemism,* trans. Rodney Needham (Harmondsworth, U.K.: Penguin, 1969), 161.

45. T. H. White, *The Sword in the Stone,* in *The Once and Future King* (London: Collins, 1958), 120.

46. John Day, *The Parliament of Bees, with their Proper Characters; or, A Bee-Hive Furnisht with Twelve Hony-Combes, as Pleasant as Profitable* (London, 1641), D3r.

47. Peter Woodhouse, *Democritus his Dreame; or, The Contentions betweene the Elephant and the Flea (1605),* ed. A. B. Grosart, Occasional Issues of Unique and Very Rare Books, 4 (Manchester, 1881).

48. John Donne, "The Flea," in *The Complete English Poems of John Donne,* ed. C. A. Patrides (London: Dent, 1985), 47–48.

49. Woodhouse, *The Flea,* 25.

50. Roland Barthes, *The Pleasure of the Text,* trans. Richard Miller (London: Jonathan Cape, 1976), 7.

51. Geoffrey Chaucer, "The Nun's Priest's Tale," lines 3167–71, in *The Riverside Chaucer,* general editor, Larry D. Benson, 3d ed., based on *The Works of Geoffrey Chaucer,* ed. F. N. Robinson (Oxford: Oxford University Press, 1988), 257.

52. Woodhouse, *The Flea,* 15.

53. Barthes, *Pleasure,* 9.

54. John Hepwith, *The Calidonian Forrest* (London, 1641), 4.

55. *The Complete Works of John Lyly,* ed. Warwick R. Bond, 3 vols. (Oxford: Clarendon Press, 1902), II, 43.

2

"Bitches and Queens": Pets and Perversion at the Court of France's Henri III

Juliana Schiesari

Desire and the beast intersect in myriad and suggestive ways, to the point of becoming figures for each other: not only is desire metaphorized as beastly, but the beast is also represented as an emblem of desire, especially forbidden or perverse desire. The beastliness of desire is a common staple, since at least Plato, of moralizing discourses that prescribe moderation and restraint of bodily pleasures. However, what one could call (with a certain Lacanian irony), the desire *of* the beast retains its fascinating currency across a number of literary texts, going back at least as far as the ancient poems and epigrams featured in Maximus Planudes's *Greek Anthology* (first published in Florence in 1494). "Beauty and the Beast" is one of the most overt of countless narratives that phrase both the fear and attraction of desire as a confrontation with the nonhuman, which in a most magical way converts the beast into the human at the right moment. This conversion from beast to human also both represents and eschews the eroticism of the encounter and thus dispels its terror while underscoring pleasure. One might also interpret the narrative as a fantasy of a nonpatriarchal symbolic order whose expression is allowed ideologically to unfold to the extent that the conclusion of the narrative recodes the relationship between Beast and Beauty into the familiar patriarchal bond of husband and wife.

But often what one could call the desire of the beast raises hackles for a symbolic order predicated on a heteronormative ideal. In the Renaissance, what was commonly perceived by humanists from Ariosto to Conrad Gesner as the excessive attention of ladies to their lapdogs found its literarily respectable correlate in the *Greek Anthology*, where the loved object may be not only a male or female human but also a horse, a dolphin, a bird, or even a cicada.[1] Thanks to the editorial efforts of Maximus Planudes, the *Greek Anthology* had an enormous effect on Renaissance poetry, first in Quattrocento Italy, then in sixteenth-century France and England. In this regard, the court of King Henri III of France offers one of the best contexts within which to observe the slippery relations between petkeeping and divergent sexualities. Henri III was known for collecting both young boys (his infamous "mignons") and lapdogs (especially the papillon or *chien-lion*). It is not certain which of these two loves proved most shocking to a France wreaked by religious, civil, and dynastic conflict. Henri III's keeping of lapdogs—as was in vogue by contemporary, mostly aristocratic women—and his cross-dressing at elaborate costume balls with his mignons, blurred gender categories and sexual identities. Understood to be the ultimate drag queen in Agrippa D'Aubigné's satiric remark that "chacun estoit en peine / S'il voyoit un Roy femme ou bien un homme Reyne"[2] ("all had trouble knowing whether what they saw was a woman king or a man queen"), Henri III comes in the writings of his contemporaries to emblematize within the royal body the dissension and corruption of the body politic.

Brantôme, for example, describes with obvious disgust how the king's affection for lapdogs is manipulated by a gentleman seeking admission to a royal order of knighthood:

> [Un gentilhomme] arriva au bout de ces années, sur le poinct que le roi projectoit son Ordre et qu'il s'estoit mis en verrue d'aymer de beaux petitz chiens de lions et turquetz et autres. L'on dist au roy, et luy en fit-on grand cas, que ce gentilhomme avoit deux turquetz, les plus beaux qu'on sçavoit voir au monde. Le roy les vouloit voir, et les trouva encore plus beaux qu'on ne les luy avoit faictz, et pour ce les luy demanda, qui en récompense le fit chevalier de ce bel Ordre. Voylà un Ordre bien donné et posé, pour deux petitz chiens! Tant d'autres pareilz fatz contes apporterois-je, pour monstrer es abuz de ces chevalliers en leurs eslections, que je n'aurois faict.[3]

> [(A nobleman) came to court at the end of this time, when the king was making projects for his Order and had gotten all worked up with his love for beautiful little Lion dogs and Turqués and others. It was told to the king, and much was made of it, that this nobleman had two Turqués, the most beautiful that could be seen in the world. The king wanted to see them, and found them even more lovely than they had been made out to be, and on account of this, asked to have them, making the owner a Knight in this beautiful Order by way of recompense. There indeed is an Order easily granted and posited, for two little dogs! I could bring up many other such stories than I could have to show the abuse made by these knights in their appointments.]

In his *Histoire Universelle,* Agrippa d'Aubigné devotes a passage to Henri's "excessive" interest in dogs in order to develop a critique that moves from a simple moral indictment to a charge of *lèse-majesté* because the expense involved in Henri's habit travels the path from moral bankruptcy to the state's financial destitution and "sterility":

> Le roi . . . s'avance à Lion, où il donna plusieurs subjets de penser, dire, prescher et escrire contre les moeurs. Il lui prit un goust excessif d'amasser et de nourrir une telle quantité de petis chiens de Lyon qu'en une grande stérilité et destruction de finances, il en fit en estat, qui montoit plus de cent mille escus par an. Ceux qui en ont escrit, et mesmes aux histoires universelles, doublent ma dose, et, certes, il est constant qu'on lui en a veu plus d'un millier, desquels il en faisoit porter plus de deux cents avec lui. Chaque huictaine, ayant une gouvernante et une femme pour la servir et un cheval de bagage, si bien que ces deux cents chiens faisoyent six cents chevaux, et aussi la despence ordinaire estoit de huit cent francs par jours, sur quoi il faut déduire que le nombre n'estoit pas toujours complet.[4]

> [The king . . . advanced to Lyon, where he gave several occasions for thinking, speaking, preaching and writing against customs. He developed an excessive taste for collecting and nurturing so great a quantity of Little Lion Dogs that he brought about a state of great sterility and financial destruction, amounting to more than one hundred thousand écus per annum. Those who have written about this, even in universal histories, double the dose I list, and certainly, it is a constant that he was seen to have more than a thousand, of which he had over two hundred borne along with him. Each eight dogs had a governess and a servant woman and a pack horse, such that these two hundred dogs required six hundred horses, and so the normal expense was about eight hundred francs per day, from which it can be deduced that the number was not always complete.]

Not just an eccentric habit that makes for a colorful court history, Henri's petkeeping propensities emblematize the vice of his reign. The uncontrolled population of tiny dogs serves as a powerful synecdoche of the excess, sterility, and general ruin of the kingdom under his rule. Or, to be more accurate, the excess that is metonymized by Henri's immoderate taste in dogs (not just too many in number, but too little in size; earlier French kings had kept large hunting dogs, such as "les grands chiens blancs du roi," by the hundreds, but these were obviously of "practical" value, nor would their upkeep have been as expensive as what D'Aubigné describes, with a governess, servant, and pack horse for every eight dogs) is the sign of a "sterility" that is as sexual as it is financial and moral. In turn, all such excesses become seen as the cause of much ruin and destruction, if not the very disintegration of the nation. And although the category of deviance may prove anachronistic when applied to the Renaissance, the concept of luxury certainly is readily available to a contemporary Huguenot reader and thus able to be subsumed into a broad spectrum of vices. Indeed, in the Calvinist imaginary, luxury is the antithesis of the bourgeois virtue of frugality and a synonym of Catholic ostentation and idolatry. What could be a better symbol of this sinfulness than Henri's dogs, the little dogs that are said to share his bed and to be catered to by special governesses and driven around in fancy carriages?

Indeed, D'Aubigné's biting satire of the later Valois's court life in Book II of *Les Tragiques,* "Princes," really heats up when, after an initial and rather traditional critique of the malicious role of flatterers, the poet turns to Henri's animal obsessions. In fact, the turn to the bestial in the text is what allows D'Aubigné to move from the common and undaring critique of evil counselors to the more direct and trenchant depiction of a depraved monarchy. Furthermore, it is the monarchy's sinfulness itself that leads to a horrific inversion of the social hierarchy and to the catastrophe of civil war. At the same time, though, the sinful nature of the Valois kings is itself the manifest work of divine retribution: "Dieu veut punir les siens quand il leve sur eux, / Comme sur des meschans, les princes vicieux"[5] ("God wants to punish his own when he raises over them / as over the wicked, vicious princes"). This conclusion is prepared, a hundred verses earlier, when the subject of the king's attitude to animals and its possible inversion/perversion of the norm are first introduced:

> Il est permis aux grands, pourveu que l'un ne face
> De l'autre les mestier et ne change de place,
> D'avoir renards, chevaux et singes et fourmis,
> Serviteurs esprouvez et fideles amis.[6]

> [It is permissible for the great, so long as one does not
> do the other's job and changes places,
> to have foxes, horses and monkeys and ants,
> proven servants and loyal friends.]

The great are permitted to indulge in the pleasures of petkeeping as long as they do not allow for any change in the hierarchy of domestication: animals must be their servants, not the other way around. However, their characterization as "proven servants and loyal friends" allows the entire following passage to be read as an allegory of the proper relations between a king and his human underlings. In such a way and in a manner typical of D'Aubigné, the passage on royal petkeeping reads as a true syllepsis, at once literal and figural:

> Mais le mal-heur avient que la sage finesse
> Des renards, des chevaux la necessaire adresse,
> La vistesse, la force et le coeur aux dangers,
> Le travail des fourmis, utiles menagers,
> S'employe aux vents, aux coups; ils se plaisent d'y estre.[7]

[But the misfortune occurs by which the wise finesse
of foxes, the necessary dexterity, speed
force and courage of horses,
the hard work of ants, useful managers
is cast to the winds, to chance; they are content just to be there.]

The perversion of Henri's rule means that everything is out of order, and the good qualities of beasts/servants (wisdom, dexterity, courage, hard work) are left to waste, whereas that most useless and exotic of pets, the monkey, actually overturns the relations of domination and rules the ruler:

Tandis le singe prend à la gorge son maistre,
Le fait haïr, s'il peut, à nos princes mignons
Qui ont beaucoup du singe et fort peu des lions.
Qu'advient-il de cela? Le bouffon vous amuse,
Un renard ennemi vous fait cuire sa ruse,
On a pour oeconome un plaisant animal,
Et le prince combat sur un singe à cheval.[8]

[While the monkey grabs his master by the throat,
makes him hated, if he can, by our mignon princes
who have much of the monkey and very little of the lion.
What gives from this? The buffoon amuses you,
an enemy fox makes you swallow his ruse,
you have a joker of an animal for making economies,
and the prince fights riding horseback upon a monkey.]

Deceit, cowardice, and wastefulness are the vices the monkey brings in the place of the other animals' virtues. These vices are also used to describe the infamous "mignons" of Henri's court, who are also accused of taking over the royal governance at the expense of faithful lords and hard-working civil servants. Very much hated by many people, the mignons were seen as unscrupulous social climbers whose ambitions were realized though sexual favors, as the last line just quoted indicates through its oblique reference to anal intercourse or as D'Aubigné makes more explicit a thousand lines later in the same book, when through the voice of Fortune he describes the mignons "faisans . . . par le cul d'un coquin chemin au coeur d'un Roy" ("making way to the king's heart by way of a rogue's ass").[9] Very quickly, then, the totality of D'Aubigné's satire of late Valois court society, which he continues to elaborate in every sordid detail for another 1,200 lines, has been skillfully and concisely sketched in just over a dozen lines. By arguing that petkeeping is perverse, D'Aubigné's critique becomes a synecdoche for the generalized perversion of Henri's rule, where

les desirs, *comme des bestes fieres,*
Desirs, dis-je, sanglants, grondent en devorant
Ce que l'esprit volage a ravi en courant.[10]

[desires, *like fierce beasts,*
desires, I say, dripping with blood, growl while devouring
what a flighty mind has ravished on the run].

An inversion of the moral order takes place and becomes a veritable world turned upside down,[11] where beasts rule men when men are not ruled by their own (bestial) desires, mignons run the government, foreigners (under the aegis of the Italian and very Catholic queen mother, Catherine de Medicis) drive out native Frenchmen, vice trades places with virtue, and men dress as women and vice versa.

The point of D'Aubigné's monkey example is to demonstrate the folly of Henri's ways: by elevating the simian mignons to high status, he not only undercuts his own ruling nobility and retainers but also jeopardizes himself because these unscrupulous upstarts can just as easily conspire against him ("le singe prend à la gorge son maistre, le fait haïr"), foreshadowing Henri's eventual murder, not by a Huguenot but a discontented monk. For D'Aubigné, unleashed depravity knows no bounds, and the king must pay dearly for his not keeping pets and subjects in their proper places. The passage that follows just after the one about the monkey reinforces this theme by evoking the animal whose magnanimity and courage makes it the antithesis of the monkey, namely the king of the beasts, the lion:

Qu'ai-je dit des lions? Les eslevez courages
De nos Rois abaissoyent et leur force et leurs rages,
Doctes à s'en servir; les sens effeminez
De ceux-ci n'aiment pas les fronts determinez,
Tremblent de leurs lions, car leur vertu estonne
De nos coulpables Rois l'ame basse et poltronne.
L'esprit qui s'employoit jadis à commander
S'employe, degenere, à tout apprehender.[12]

[What did I say about lions? The haughty courage
of our kings lowered both their force and their rage,
wise to make use of them; the effeminate senses
of these ones do not like determined brows,
tremble before their lions, for their virtue astonishes
the lowly and cowardly soul of our guilty kings.
The spirit that once upon a time would command
is used, now degenerate, to fear everything.]

The lions quite clearly refer to the nobility whose (masculine) force and virtue, instead of providing strength to the very heart of the realm, constitute a threat to the low, cowardly, and effeminate Valois kings who, in another example of inversion and "degeneration," learn to fear everyone and everything over which they are empowered to command. This inversion is inscribed into the heart of the monarch himself, whose traditional "highness" and courage are overturned in a "low and cowardly soul" and who thereby bears responsibility for the more widespread inversion of values that afflict the body politic as a whole. The ensuing "guilt" that is here specifically attributed to the Valois kings, and not just to evil flatterers or bad company, is a move D'Aubigné dares to make for the first time.

This inversion that explains royal paranoia is then portrayed as the source of irrational violence, not against the metaphorical lions of the nobility but against the literal lions of his palace menagerie, who are hysterically slaughtered in the aftermath of a "premonitory" dream:

> Pourtant ce Roy, songeant que les griffes meurtrieres
> De ses lions avoyent crocheté leurs tanieres
> Pour le deschirer vif, prevoyant à ces maux
> Fit bien mal à propos tuer ces animaux.
> Il laissa le vrai sens, s'attachant au mensonge.[13]

> [But this king, dreaming that the murderous claws
> of his lions had burst through their lairs
> in order to rip him alive, very inappropriately
> had these animals killed to forestall such harm.
> He left the true meaning behind and attached himself to the lie.]

This incident is not D'Aubigné's satirical invention (although it certainly seems made to order) but is historically authenticated by other sources, particularly Pierre de L'Estoile, who relates the story in his journal under the date of January 21, 1583:

> [Le Roy] s'en revint au Louvre, où arrivé il fist tuer à coups de harquebuzes les lions, ours, taureaux et autres semblables bestes qu'il souloit nourrir pour combattre avec les dogues; et ce, à l'occasion d'un songe qui lui estoit advenu, par lequel il lui sembla que les lions, ours et dogues le mangeoient et dévoroient. Songe qui sembloit présager ce que depuis on a veu advenir, lorsque ces bestes furieuses de la Ligue, se ruans sur ce pauvre prince, l'ont déchiré et mangé avec son peuple.[14]

> [The king returned to the Louvre, where upon his arrival he had the lions, bears, bulls and other such beasts he would nurture for combat with his mastiffs killed by blunderbuss shots; and all this, on the occasion of a dream that came

to him, by which it seemed that the lions, bears and mastiffs were eating and devouring him. A dream that seemed to foretell what we have since seen come about, when those enraged beasts of the League, hurling themselves upon that unfortunate prince, tore him to pieces and ate him along with his people.]

D'Aubigné concurs with L'Estoile that Henri misreads literal for figural lions, thus massacring the royal zoo at the expense of his own throne:

Un bon Joseph eust pris autrement un tel songe.
Et eust dit: "Les lions superbes, indomptez,
Que tu dois redouter, sont princes irritez,
Qui briseront tes reins et tes faibles barrieres
Pour n'estre pas tournez aux proyes estrangeres."[15]

[A good Joseph would have taken the dream otherwise,
and would have said: "The proud, untamed lions
that you must fear, are angry princes,
who will break your back and weak frontiers
for not being directed towards foreign prey."]

But D'Aubigné, ever the didactic preacher, relates Henri's inability to deal with recalcitrant nobles back to his personal vices: pet dogs, cross-dressing, and religious decadence.

Apren, Roy, qu'on nourrit de bien divers moyens
Les lions d'Afrique, ou de Lion les chiens:
De ces chiens de Lion tu ne crains le courage
Quand tu changes des Rois et l'habit et l'usage,
Quand tu blesses des tiens les coeurs à millions,
Mais tu tournes ta robbe aux yeux de tes lions
Quand le royal manteau se change en une aumusse,
Et la couronne au froc d'un vilain Picque-Puce.[16]

[Learn, o king, that there are very different means of nurturing
African lions and the dogs of Lyon:
You need not fear the courage of these Lion dogs
when you change the costume and habits of kings,
when you wound by the millions the hearts of those who belong to you,
but you turn your robe in the eyes of your lions
when the royal mantle is traded for an amice,
and the crown for the shabby frock of Pique-Puce.]

Once again, the satire of Henri's vices is triggered by the instance of the toy dogs. In this case, these toy dogs are none other than the Little Lion Dogs, so called from their being bred in Lyon, where, in the passage quoted earlier from the *Histoire Universelle,* we saw him shopping for dogs. The reintroduction of these toy dogs into the narrative coincides with the return of syllepsis and thus confounds again the literal versus figural distinction that L'Estoile blames for Henri's problems. At the most literal level, we are told a training banality: that one must not raise African lions like little Lion dogs, the unstated but obvious assumption being that the African lions need much more skill and attention than the Lion dogs, who implicitly remain nothing more than cuddly objects of fetishistic pleasure requiring no particular force of domestication. On one metaphorical level, then, the lesson would be that the king should pay more attention to his seditious Catholic lords than to his hundreds of lapdogs. At another level, we can read the "chiens de Lions [dont] tu ne crains le courage" as once again a reference to his cowardly mignons who, earlier on, were caricatured by their simian affinities. The mignons are not upset by the king's strange habits or dress, nor by his bouts of devotion, where they would join in Henri's penitent processions wearing the "aumuce" and flagellating themselves. Or they would accompany him in his monastic "retreats" such as at the Franciscan abbey of Picpus (which D'Aubigné humorously links back to the canine theme as the abbey of Picque-Puce, or flea picking, and of course Saint Francis is well known in Catholic iconography for his love and care of animals). On the other hand, the "lions" of the Catholic League were very incensed by what they understood—rightly or wrongly—as a hypocritical masquerade and as the king's near-treasonous abandonment of his royal duties in a time of national crisis. Catherine de Medicis, the king's own mother, is said to have made this same complaint to the papal nuncio, while the former charge appeared in satirical verses such as the following:

> Mignons qui portez doucement
> En croupe le sang de la France
> Ne battez le dos seulement
> Mais le cul qui a fait l'offense.[17]

> [Mignons who softly bear
> The royal blood in your crotch
> Don't just beat your back
> But also the ass, which committed the offense.]

If Henri's actions were intended to give a few strokes to the savage beasts of Catholic orthodoxy, they backfired. The "African" lions, so D'Aubigné seems to say, need firm discipline to maintain their respect and loyalty, not the indulgent pats one gives little Lion dogs.

Historically, though, it seems that Henri's actions were inspired by a sentiment quite close to D'Aubigné's own, that the kingdom's troubles were to be explained by the wrath of God falling on France. In the Catholic reading, this is not just an example of God's mysterious ways and hidden actions that, in the Calvinist understanding, require an even greater act of sheer faith on the part of the righteous. Rather, causes are induced (human moral depravity) and remedies prescribed in the form of good deeds: appease God's anger through acts of public penitence and self-immolation. As Henri writes in a 1582 letter to his ambassador in Venice, "Notre seigneur veut étendre son ire sur nous et nous admonester par ce châtiment de changer de voies et avoir recours à sa bonté par bonnes oeuvres" ("Our Lord wants to cast his ire upon us and admonish us by this punishment to change our ways and have recourse to his goodness by doing good deeds").[18] To think that one could change God's mind by the ostentation of ritualized masochism, while appearing hypocritical to Henri's Catholic opposition, could only come off as absurd superstition or madness for Huguenot commentators such as François Hotman.[19] For D'Aubigné, as we have seen, far from being a response to God's wrath, Henri's actions, general conduct, and weakness of character are themselves *signs* of it.

Chief among the signs of Henri's viciousness is the dog obsession, to which D'Aubigné returns at the close of this opening passage in the long invective against the Valois court that makes up the bulk of "Princes:"

> Les Rois aux chiens flatteurs donnent le premier lieu,
> Et, de cette canaille endormis au milieu,
> Chassent les chiens de garde.[20]

> [The kings give first place to the flattering dogs,
> and chase the watchdogs out
> from that riff-raff asleep in the middle.]

Again, the sylleptic reading tells us that Henri has unconscionably elevated his untrustworthy mignons while foolishly exiling powerful protectors of the realm *and* has also abandoned the large breeds traditional of masculine power to collect instead the small toy breeds associated with ladies, and wanton ones at that. It is said that he developed a miniature breed of spaniel, the papillon, small enough to be carried around in basket or pocket and to be placed in the royal bed by the dozen. And if the cross-dressing might invite a reading of Henri as desiring to appropriate a certain femininity, his keeping of lapdogs certainly moved, as L'Estoile notes, from being simply a symbolic appropriation of feminine habits and styles to the literal seizure of women's pets:

> [Le Roi] va en coche, avec la Roine son epouse, par les rues et maisons de Paris, prendre les petits chiens damerets, qui à lui et à elle viennent à plaisir; va semblablement, par tous les monastères de femmes estans aux environs de Paris, faire pareille queste de petits chiens, au grand regret et desplaisir des dames ausquelles les chiens appartenoient.[21]

> [The king rides by carriage, with the queen his spouse, along the streets and houses of Paris, to get little ladylike dogs, which give pleasure to both him and her; he goes in the same way, to all the monasteries for women in the vicinity of Paris, carrying out a similar quest for little dogs, to the great regret and displeasure of the ladies to whom the dogs belonged.]

From his desire not for women but for "les petits chiens *damerets*," to his forcible taking of such dogs from the "dames" to whom these dogs belonged, we see how the beastliness of desire has crossed over into an uncontrollable desire for the beast.

For D'Aubigné, of course, whatever is bestial, or approximates it in his metaphorical arsenal, is consistently linked with what is abject, degenerate, evil, or simply "monstrous." To no surprise, Henri III comes off as a monstrous beast: "Ce Roy donc n'est plus Roy, mais monstrueuse beste."[22] Catherine de Medicis is described at length in bestial terms: "savage et carnaciere beste," "ce serpent monstrueux," "Cette Hydra renaissant," "de basilique veuë," and so on.[23] The horrors of religious war are emblematized by beasts run amok and feasting on human cadavers in the aftermath of battle.[24] Should we be surprised that monstrous bestiality is also in association with femininity and foreignness? The Italian Catholic queen, Catherine de Medicis, egregiously condenses all of these attributes in her sole person, thereby sharply cathecting the energy of D'Aubigné's invective. The exchangeability of these traits in myriad combinations supplies an unlimited amount of fuel for the metaphorical engines that drive *Les Tragiques*. The evil Italian influences of the "faux Machiavel" and "la beste de Rome" are relayed and amplified by "les hermaphrodites, monstres effeminez" who inhabit the court, dominate the state, and corrupt the nation.[25]

In a sense, there is nothing particularly surprising about such animal metaphors in the derogatory rhetoric of texts understood to be "humanist" in orientation, although there does exist in the same period a contrary tradition of theriophilia among the later humanists, such as Montaigne's famous panegyrics to animal intelligence and morality over and against human presumptuousness.[26] Perhaps of greater interest in our context is that the court mentality under Henri III, although obviously more favorable to little dogs, monkeys, cross-dressing monarchs, and perfumed mignons, does not differ appreciably from D'Aubigné's assessment in terms of the metaphorical hierarchies in question. Femininity, animality, and cultural alterity remain linked together in a paradigm that invests petkeeping with an erotic fascination that stems from the unpredictable and pluridirectional quality of desire[27] associated with the nonutilitarian domestic animal, or household beast, consistent with this associative network. Certainly the African lion deserves to be feared more than a Lion dog, but nothing seems to compare with the Little Lion Dog's capacity, far out of proportion to its miniature stature and status, to scramble the very foundations of social, sexual, and gender identity. In fact, if one reads D'Aubigné with close attention, it seems that the lapdog is a much greater threat to the realm than the figural wild beasts of the League or the literal ones of the Louvre's menagerie. After all, in the first passage that we read by him, D'Aubigné was quick to attribute the king's puppy mania as having a direct consequence on the realm's "great sterility and destruction of finances." On the other hand, Henri's own attraction to swarms of little creatures is motivated by their relation to femininity ("les petits chiens *damerets*") and the exotic (monkeys ordered by the boatload).[28] All in all, the pet turns out to be an extraordinary bearer of cathected desire whose consequences are not only psychological but social and political as well.

NOTES

1. See A. Lytton Sells, *Animal Poetry in French and English Literature and the Greek Tradition* (Bloomington: Indiana University Press, 1955), 3–16.

2. Agrippa D'Aubigné, *Les Tragiques*, ed. A. Garnier and J. Plattard (Paris: Marcel Didier, 1966–67), II, 795–96.

3. Pierre de Bourdille, Seigneur de Brantôme, *Oeuvres complètes*, ed. Ludovic Lalanne (Paris: Renouard, 1849), tome 5: *Grands capitaines françois, Couronnels François*, 104–5. All translations in this chapter are mine unless otherwise noted.

4. D'Aubigné, *Histoire Universelle*, ed. Le Baron Alphonse de Rublé (Paris: Renouard, 1893), tome 7: 1585–88, 102.

5. D'Aubigné, *Les Tragiques*, II, 391–92.

6. Ibid., 285–88.

7. Ibid., 289–93.

8. Ibid., 294–300.

9. Ibid., 1317–18.

10. Ibid., 382–84, emphasis added.

11. See D'Aubigné, *Les Tragiques*, I, 235: "comme au monde à l'envers."

12. D'Aubigné, *Les Tragiques*, II, 301–9.

13. Ibid., 309–13.

14. Pierre de L'Estoile, *Journal du règne de Henri III*, ed. M. Lazard and G. Shrenk (Geneva: Droz, 1992), II, 99.

15. D'Aubigné, *Les Tragiques,* II, 314–18.

16. Ibid., 319–26.

17. Cited in Pierre Chevalier, *Henri III, roi shakespearien* (Paris: Fayard, 1985), 546.

18. Ibid., 543.

19. Ibid., 550.

20. D'Aubigné, *Les Tragiques,* II, 327–29.

21. De L'Estoile, *Journal,* Nov. 1575, 93.

22. D'Aubigné, *Les Tragiques,* II, 485.

23. D'Aubigné, *Les Tragiques,* I, 783–992.

24. Ibid., 461–94.

25. Ibid., 1047 and 1213; II, 667.

26. Michel de Montaigne, *Essais,* ed. P. Villey (Paris: PUF, 1924), II, xii, 449–86; on Renaissance theriophilia, the classic reference remains George Boas, *The Happy Beast in French Thought of the Seventeenth Century* (Baltimore: Johns Hopkins University Press, 1933).

27. On this pluridirectionality of desire, see Teresa de Lauretis, *The Practice of Love: Lesbian Sexuality and Perverse Desire* (Bloomington: Indiana University Press, 1994).

28. Chevalier, *Henri III,* 413.

Hairy on the Inside: Metamorphosis and Civility in English Werewolf Texts

S. J. Wiseman

WILD AND DEGENERATE

"Her feet were bare: her body was covered with rags and skins: her hair with a gourd leaf; and her face and hands were of the same colour as a negroe's. . . . Those who saw her first, run away, crying out, 'There is the devil.' And indeed her dress and colour might very well produce such thoughts in the country people . . . one of them, thinking probably that the devil was afraid of dogs, set loose upon her a bull dog with an iron collar."[1] This is the description of a wild girl found in 1731 in France. Discovered to be civilizable, her face reshaped by her acquisition of the French language, and even able to embrace religious faith, Mademoiselle le Blanc is transformed in the narrative from her devilish seeming into a civil Parisienne, living by the sale of her story, which is offered as a drama of the wild being subject to the law and made obedient to social and political process. But this tale is built from materials that might also suggest that, instead of being wild, she was a figure cast out of the civil and so she was in some sense *re*discovered. We might ask where she got her clothes and why she wanted them. Where did the idea for a gourd-leaf hat come from? Most significant, why is it the "country" people, living with the civil at its most intimate (the village) but also at the border with the wild (the forest), who interpret her as "the devil"?

I begin with this tale because, even as it presents the savage girl as the benevolent object of charity (the characteristic that has situated it as part of the history of education), it rewrites another narrative genre in which the creature-human returning from the fields vividly embodies the hostility within the village or city from which she was cast out. Wildness exists in two ways in this story. It can be read as signifying an uncompromised quality out of which the social and civil human can be built, but, equally, it might represent the failure of the civil community. Some of the ways in which the wild is used to figure civil crisis in seventeenth-century English stories, specifically in writings on the werewolf, are my subject here. As I shall argue, although the theological context and that of disease and melancholy are crucial to the understanding of the werewolf, they overlap with other ways of understanding this border creature, ways that are strongly tied to ideas and experiences of the social and the civic.

WOLVES AND WEREWOLVES

In the genealogy of the wild child, the werewolf is a close relative. A tension between apprehension of the wild as a category completely other than the social and its existence as the dangerous product of civil discontents permeates early modern narratives of transformation. Generated by several distinct and overlapping aspects of early modern English culture, narratives of wolf transformation (perhaps because the problem of lycanthropic transformation did not appear to be on the writers' or readers' doorstep because wolves were long gone from England, save those Edward Topsell describes as being "kept at the Tower of London to be seene by the Prince and people, brought out of other countries") articulate theological concerns but also, in their interpretation of metamorphosis, assess the relationship between the wild and the civil, the human and its others.[2] Therefore, the status of the werewolf becomes a little clearer when set against its truly wild cousin, the wolf. As Hayden White argues, the wild (which the werewolf is not) functions mythically: "The notion of wildness (or its Latinate form, 'savagery') belongs to a set of culturally self-authenticating devices . . . used . . . to confirm the value of their dialectical antitheses." White, locating civilization as the mythic and dialectical opposite of wildness, goes on to discuss a specific form of degenerate wildness in which humans have fallen below the level of the human (or the differently set standard for the animals), such as those who have confused species by copulating with animals (as prohibited in Leviticus 18:23–30).[3] Discussions of early modern wolves put them in a literal but also a figurative relationship to wildness. Accordingly, tracing the associations and significances of the wolf with a view to their symbolic significance rather than consistency, Topsell repeatedly distinguishes the power of the wolf from that of the lion and reminds us that not only is the wolf savage and ravening but "it cannot be safe for strangers to live with them in any league or amity, seeing that in their extremity they devour one another" (although, characteristically, he gives narrative examples of such leagues).[4] Having no claim to be human, such creatures are not actually degenerate (a human quality), but in the discussions of their collective personality, they are perceived as sharing some of the characteristics of the degenerate and reprobate. And, of course, in figurative terms wolves consistently represent those who had fallen so far from God that it was safe to assume that they were damned.

All this adds up to representations of wolves in early modern England as drawing on a rich and partially contradictory, imagistic vocabulary. In Topsell's account, the wolf is not exactly the opposite of the human but represents an animality so extreme that human society cannot mix with it. Moreover, besides being irredeemably antipathetic to the human, the wolf displays some of the characteristics that caused human degeneracy, particularly a willingness to mix species by breeding with other kinds, including with other species understood as having abilities peculiarly hostile to humanity, such as the hyena, who could kill a man by merely lying on him.[5] The wolf stands in a contradictory relation to the rules of civilized human behavior. He is understood as refusing all forms of reciprocity, amity, or brotherhood, yet, simultaneously, humans are represented as strengthened (though also in some narratives subject to the degeneration associated with species mixture) if they can draw on the qualities of wolves. In the story of Romulus and Remus, though not only there, the acquisition of these ambivalent and powerful qualities is figured by suckling.[6]

Does the blending of human and wolf in early modern writing precipitate a crisis of meaning and representation? Yes and no. Certainly the werewolf renders the implications of the wolf vivid and problematic (and so fascinating and debatable) by locating them directly in a human. In such a mixture it is far from clear where the animal is and where the human is. In Ovid's *Metamorphoses,* the dominant classical text of animal transformation, the animal or human status of the figure produced by metamorphosis remains to an extent a paradox; in the case of the werewolf transformation of the tyrant Lycaon, he becomes a wolf while retaining "human" characteristics such as his ironically "savage" face: "His look still grim with glaring eyes, and every kind of way, / His cruell heart in outward shape doth well it selfe bewray."[7] Such paradoxical transformations as that of Lycaon, simultaneously changed into an animal expression of his crime and remaining ambiguously human and so responsible for his actions, were not readily tolerated in early modern thought, where God was understood to have created animal-human distinctions and hierarchy. As Hayden White notes, in formal writings the issue of whether God could have assigned a human soul to an animal body was resolved as an impossibility: to decide otherwise would be to imply that God might make a mistake or, worse, to suggest that he might wish ill on humanity.[8] Yet in many writings God's relationship to human-animal metamorphosis is not the sole or main focus, and in the sixteenth and seventeenth centuries, werewolf narratives canvass the meanings of transformation in other ways.[9] What do these stories tell us? Specifically, what do they suggest about the civil and the wild in human-animal transformation?

HUMAN IN WOLF LIKENESS: WOLF SHAPES IN NARRATIVE

Two separate printed English narratives of the German werewolf "Stubbe Peeter" differently indicate the need to resolve the question of the soul, exploring wolf transformation as an index of the presence of the human. They also register the association between the werewolf and civic discontent. The first narrative, a pamphlet of English composition, analyzes the question of the wild and the civil, of what might be met in the fields, and of in what way a man might become a beast: "The Devill . . . gave unto him a girdle which, being put about him, he was straight transfourmed into the likenes of a greedy devouring Wolf, strong and mighty, with eyes great and large, which in the night sparkled like brandes of fire, a mouth great and wide, with most sharpe and cruell teeth, A huge body, and mightye pawes: And no sooner should he put off the same girdle, but presently he should appeare in his former shape, according to the proportion of a man, as if he had never beene changed."[10] Stubbe Peeter's Faustian compact with the devil means that he, "a most wicked Sorcerer," is given twenty-five years to pursue the "divelish practice" of werewolf transformation. Having a "tirannous hart, and a most cruell bloody minde" he becomes a werewolf of his own volition, as one who had "followed the imagination of his own harte" without thought of redemption because the "shape fitted his fancye." No sooner would someone he hated or desired "walke abroad in the feeldes or about the Cittie, but in the shape of a Wolfe he would presently encounter them, and never rest till he had pluckt out their throates." So he continues, "sometime in the habit of a man, sometime in the Townes and Cities, and sometimes in the woods and thickettes to them adjoyning"; sometimes human and sometimes in the "likeness of a greedy devouring Wolf" he rages in the fields outside the city.[11]

The narrative enlarges Stubbe Peeter's doings beyond the most energetic criminal career. The authenticating signatures of four named witnesses and "divers others that have seen the same" are scarcely sufficient to retain these extraordinary and exciting events within the boundaries of the criminal yarn or trial narrative. When he found "a Maide, Wife or childe" that he lusted after, "if he could by any meanes get them alone, he would in the feeldes ravishe them, and after in his Wolvish likenes cruelly murder them." While in wolf form he is presented as having a complex relationship to sexuality and to children (he had "murdered thirteene young children"), mutilating his victims with an epicurean savagery. He killed "two goodly young women bigge with Child, tearing the Children out of their wombes, in most bloody and savedge sorte, and after eate their hartes panting hotte and rawe, which he accounted dainty morsells and best agreeing to his Appetite." In his human guise he has sex with his daughter (and the narrative notes that mere fornication, unrepented, is enough to warrant damnation), corrupts a previously upstanding woman to become his concubine, and finally needs a "she-Devil"—a fully supernatural and diabolic figure—to serve his lust.[12]

As the narrative emphasizes, he remained at home in the city, rubbing neighborly shoulders with those who were to fuel his solitary cannibal feasts: "sundry times he would go through the streetes of *Collin, Bedbur,* and *Cperadt,* in comely habit, and very civilly as one well knowen to all the inhabitants therabout, & oftentimes was he saluted of those whose freendes and children he had buchered, though nothing suspected for the same."[13]

Inviting the reader to imagine fantastic danger ready to erupt in the heart of the civic order, the narrative is also careful to lodge moral responsibility firmly in Stubbe Peeter himself. In this narrative the decision to change shape remains one of will. That the human underlies the wolf is made absolutely clear in the denouement that, even as it restages a scene of magic transformation in Stubbe Peeter's return to human form, insists on the human agency of the wolf.[14] Men out hunting "espye him in his wolvishe likenes" and attack him so severely that

> presently he slipt his girdle from about hym, whereby the shape of a Wolfe cleane avoided, and he appeared presently in his true shape & likenes, having in his hand a staff as one walking toward the Cittie; but the hunters, whose eyes was stedfastly bent upon the beast, and seeing him in the same place metamorphosed contrary to their expectation: it wrought a wonderfull amazement in their mindes, and had it not beene that they knew the man so soone as they saw him, they had surely taken the same to have been some Devill in a mans likenes, but for as much as they knewe him to be an auncient dweller in the Towne, they came unto him and talking with him they brought him by communication home to his owne house.[15]

The metamorphosis to human form indicates an underlying humanity throughout his wolf behavior and shape.

What happens to Stubbe Peeter, and what does the text ask us to believe? The cartoon accompanying the text picks him out in his true and false shapes: an upright wolf wearing the girdle and then a man broken on the wheel (fig. 3.1). Stubbe Peeter may look like a wolf but never completely sheds his humanity, signaled by his girdle and upright posture. Moreover, as Erica Fudge has observed, Stubbe Peeter's crimes committed in wolf form are darkly human: deceit, incest, rape, violent and potentially sexual assault on children. To eat human flesh is natural for wolves, cannibal for humans, and Stubbe Peeter's activities are those of a depraved or degenerate human.[16] In this telling of his story, the border between the wolf and Peeter, between animal and human, remains, and, it seems, being a werewolf rather than a wolf names the desire to appear like a wolf (possibly in different ways in the text and the illustration) while being human. Ultimately, this crisis of the coincidence of the natural and the human is resolved with Stubbe Peeter located in the human, and species difference—which the text strives to maintain—is reconfirmed. We are not required to believe that Stubbe Peeter became a wolf, onl y that he took on the likeness of a wolf, for in the various incidents of the text, the putting on of the girdle remains an act of will. Stubbe Peeter has the likeness of a wolf, but becoming a werewolf does not involve the magical dissolution of the border between man and animal in this story. Rather, it suggests the coexistence of the wolf's likeness with the soul and reason of the man.

Before we begin to think of this werewolf as hardly distinguishable from Ovid's Lycaon in his melding of wolf and human, the text's ending reminds us of the hierarchy of species and the supernatural implications of transformation. In the monument to the events erected by the authorities, we are told, the wheel on which he was broken is set on a pole; above that "the likeness of a wolf was framed in wood, to show to all men the shape wherein he executed those cruelties," and "on the top of the stake the sorcerer's head it selfe was set up."[17] Thus, Stubbe Peeter's consciousness is set over all and determines all.

In a summary version of the story, Roman Catholic compiler of ancient lore Richard Verstegan is contrastingly careful to elucidate the implications of werewolf transformation for human status. Verstegan raises the question of human responsibility for wolf actions, asserting that "*were-wolves* are certain sorcerers" who

> having annoynted their bodyes, with an oyntment which they make by the instinct of the devil; and putting on a certaine inchanted girdel, do not only unto the view of others seeme as wolves, but to their own thinking have both the shape and nature of wolves, so long as they wear the said girdel. And they do dispose th'selves as very wolves, in wurrying and killing, and moste of humaine creatures.
>
> Of such sundry have bin taken and executed in sundry parts of *Germanie*, and the *Netherlands*. One Peeter Stump for being a *were-wolf*, and having killed thirteen children, two women, and one man; was at *Bedbur* not far from *Cullen* in the yeare 1589 put into a very terrible death. The flesh of divers partes of his body was pulled out with hot iron tongs, his armes thighs & legges

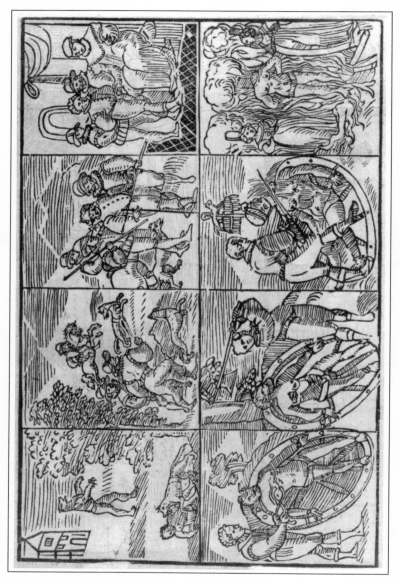

Figure 3.1. From *A True Discourse Declaring the Damnable Life and Death of One Stubbe Peeter, A Most Wicked Sorcerer* (London, 1590). By permission of The British Library, classmark C 27 a 9.

broke on a wheel, & his body lastly burnt. He dyed with very great remorce, desiring that his body might not be spared from any torment, so his soul might be saved. The *were-wolf* (so called in Germanie) is in *France,* called *Loupgarou.*[18]

Verstegan's synopsis condenses and interprets the earlier, more discursive narrative to offer an assertion about how werewolf transformation is effected, to pinpoint the question of animal-human transformation in the more specific terms of body and soul, and in doing so to turn the meaning of transformation definitively toward the question of salvation. Whereas in the earlier text we are told Peeter confessed because of "fearing the torture," here the question of soul-body relations and repentance are used to moralize (and justify, or explain) the violence and "terrible death" to which he was subject. Verstegan's highly condensed interpretation limits its interest in the narrative of killings to numbers ("thirteen children, two women, and one man") and privileges the means and meanings of werewolf transformation and its effects on the being of the transformed, who—in his slightly ambiguous phrase—"to their own thinking" (is this wolf or human thought? human, presumably) "have both the shape and nature of wolves, so long as they wear the said girdle."[19]

In Verstegan's tangled apprehension of werewolf transformation and werewolf consciousness, Stubbe Peeter seems not to be wholly responsible once transformed. Although he enters into hallucinatory wolfishness voluntarily, the resultant wildness combines human agency and animal compulsion: the wolf shape compromises the human status of the shape changer so that only after his return to human form can he recognize and repent of the atrocities he committed. The synopsis has a religious emphasis absent in the first version and thereby (for a reader of both) illuminates the hollowing out of what perhaps should have been a theological core to the first text by reminding us that that earlier text has taken the debate a long way from any theological ground. In the two versions we have attention to shape and likeness on the one hand, and on the other to soul, blame, and repentance. The two tales contrast in the power they give wolfishness, with Verstegan understanding it as a power in itself that takes over once the act of transformation is initiated. Each text analyzes the point at which human becomes animal, but they resolve that distinction differently. Both narratives belong to a rich seam of witchcraft narratives in which the theologically determined status of the soul of the perpetrator is not the sole, or even main, narrative focus. Such narratives, meditating in religious, political, and social ways on wolfishness, though theologically dubious, form a significant part of the werewolf corpus. And such discussions of the werewolf repeatedly canvass the relationship between the werewolf and the human ("civi-lized") world that has fostered it.

HAIRY ON THE INSIDE: DISEASE AND IDENTITY

As the treatment given to the werewolf in each of these texts might suggest, demonologically speaking, lycanthropy is a borderline case: much theoret-ical material (with significant exceptions such as Jean Bodin) asserts that actual human-animal transformation is impossible. When theologians and demonologists asked themselves whether the devil is able to transform the human shape, almost all answered "no," though with qualification. In *The Discoverie of Witchcraft* (1584) Reginald Scot comments ironically on Bodin's acceptance of shape changing: "I mervell, whether the divell createth him-selfe, when he appeareth in the likenesse of a man; or whether God createth him, when the divell wisheth it."[20] Or as John Cotta put it, although the devil could override "some particular natures" he cannot "command over gen-eral Nature"; although "the Devill as a Spirit doth many things, which in re-spect of our nature are supernaturall, yet in respect of the power of Nature in universall, they are but naturall unto himselfe and other Spirites, who are also a kind of Creature contained within the generall nature of things cre-ated: . . . against or above the generall power of Nature, hee can do noth-ing."[21] Unable to alter the natural world, the devil makes "seeming and jug-gling transformations." The devil's inability to create fresh forms means that lycanthropy is understood in other, more ambiguous terms and gen-erates "a gamut of explanatory languages" in some texts.[22] Explanations in-clude the possibility that transformation is suggested to the lycanthrope by the devil inducing hallucination ("glamour") and that the devil (taking ad-vantage of dream states induced by unguents applied to the body) super-imposed hallucinated shapes on the lycanthrope's body to deceive the vic-tim and observers.[23] Thus, in witchcraft texts the focus of discussion often is on the nature of metamorphosis as true or illusory, and what is much can-vassed is how the illusions are produced and where the devil is in that pro-cess.[24]

Such discussions of illusion and hallucination have a focus on what is human and what is not, what is and is not transformed in the werewolf. This is something that is shared between theological and other werewolf texts. The debate was unresolved but heated, and it facilitated the circula-tion of European werewolf stories for English readers. However, the am-biguous theological status of werewolf transformation meant that to con-sider the werewolf was to speculate about state of mind, as well as soul, and led toward the humoral vision of lycanthropy as melancholy, mania, and frenzy. Thus, in the case of lycanthropy rather than possession, as Stuart Clark indicates, psycho-physiological and social meanings are important on one hand, and on the other demonological debate is connected to "scientific" testing.[25]

Related to theological discussion but not wholly inside it, the lycanthropy debate is made up of many-layered vocabularies and meanings. Ambiguously like possession without being possession, the idea and stories of werewolves concretized issues of wider purchase than the narrowly defined theological. One such text, John Webster's *The Duchess of Malfi* (performed 1613/14, printed 1623), explores the melancholic werewolf. Yet the literary text that is best known for an exploration of the diseased, hallucinatory dimensions of lycanthropy also, crucially, binds that question of hallucinatory consciousness to the civic and even political implications of metamorphosis. *The Duchess of Malfi* foregrounds the social and psychic dimensions of wolf transformation that are implicit in the Stubbe Peeter narratives. But here lycanthropy is also framed by two other strains of language: the vocabulary of animal annihilation (in which, as mentioned earlier, the hyena figures as a woman who can draw all the breath out of a man's body merely by lying on him) and the opposition between transformation and fixity in which geometry and mathematics are opposed to other malleable textures, particularly femininity. And like the question of animal significances, metamorphosis permeates the text.[26]

Bosola, whose malcontent alignment with Ferdinand is the product of compromise after partial release from slavery, uses the language of animal-human relations to illuminate human monstrosity:

> But in our own flesh, though we bear diseases
> Which have their true names only ta'en from beasts,
> As the most ulcerous wolf, and swinish measle;
> Though we are eaten up of lice, and worms,
> And though continually we bear about us
> A rotten and dead body, we delight
> To hide it in rich tissue: all our fear—
> Nay, all our terror—is lest our physician
> Should put us in the ground to be made sweet.[27]

Voicing anxiety about inevitable physical decay, Bosola transforms this into a kind of degeneration. Truly animal in being both of the body and with the power of diminishing human status, the animal diseases here are shown as feeding off the human that they also replace. The disease of the ulcerous wolf ambiguously combines the wolf as preying on human flesh and as a characteristic of human degeneracy. Lycanthropy, in which Ferdinand first projects wolfishness and then identifies with it, makes the connection between human and wolf more firmly than in Bosola's animated clichés because Bosola makes it psychic or conscious as well as physical. Ferdinand sees wolves everywhere, saying of his sister's language, "the howling of a wolf is music [compared] to thee," and calling her children "young wolves." Visiting his sister in prison, he asks, "where are your cubs?" And in the next scene, seeing them strangled, he comments that "the death / Of young wolves is never to be pitied."[28] It is in his ascription of wolfishness to others that Duke Ferdinand comes initially to appear lupine to the audience. At the death of the duchess, Ferdinand's perception of his deeds is transformed and realigned with that of the audience. He says, "She and I were twins: / And should I die this instant, I had liv'd / Her time to a minute." His language shifts to become perversely identificatory, climaxing: "The wolf shall find her grave, and scrape it up: / Not to devour the corpse, but to discover / The horrid murder."[29] And this, it seems, is what Ferdinand does:

> Doctor: In those that are possess'd with't there o'erflows
> Such melancholy humour, they imagine
> Themselves to be transformed into wolves,
> Steal forth to churchyards in the dead of night,
> And dig dead bodies up: as two nights since
> One met the duke, 'bout midnight in a lane
> Behind Saint Mark's church, with the leg of a man
> Upon his shoulder; and he howl'd fearfully;
> Said he was a wolf, only the difference
> Was, a wolf's skin was hairy on the outside,
> His on the inside; bade them take their swords,
> Rip up his flesh, and try: straight I was sent for,
> And having minister'd to him, found his grace
> Very well recovered.[30]

The recovery is short-lived, and in the same scene Ferdinand presents himself in a state of furious hallucination:

> Ferdinand: I will throttle it
> [*Throws himself upon his shadow*]
> Malateste: O, my lord: you are angry with nothing.
> Ferdinand: You are a fool: how is't possible I shall catch my shadow unless I
> fall upon it? When I go to hell I mean to carry a bribe; for look you, good
> gifts evermore make way for the worst persons.

Ferdinand, tormented psychically by his hairy inside, now identifies himself *and* others as wolfish. He is a "like a sheep-biter," but in his eyes his physician is worryingly hairy, needing his "beard sawed off, and his eyebrows filed

more civil."[31] Ferdinand and his doctor finally, in different ways, acknowledge his disease: "possess'd with't . . . they imagine / Themselves to be transformed into wolves." Ferdinand is not "possessed" with devils, although the
play's language toys with this possibility, but "out of his princely wits." Certainly, *Malfi* uses lycanthropy to signify deathly mental decay. Yet Ferdinand
is not just out of his wits but out of his "princely wits" and perceives the
healer, always of resonant politicized status, as uncivil. The play uses Ferdinand as lycanthrope to suggest both the ambiguous power of wolfishness
and its crucial association with rule—with tyranny, and specifically with the
threat to social relations. The play's language and Ferdinand's actions suggest that the understanding of Ferdinand's lycanthropy as melancholy or disease is accompanied by a sense of its social and civic implications. He is tormented by internal hairiness, he murders his sister and her children, and he
is also the violent—not so much animalistic as specifically wolfish, untam-
able, degenerate, possibly cannibal—heart of the civil system. Ferdinand's
lycanthropic frenzy is specifically a mania generated by the court and overtly
an index of its moral crisis. And although the play's representation of the
marriage of Ferdinand's sister to Antonio may offer a progressive moral and
political counterweight, albeit compromised, to Ferdinand's regressive, ar-
chaic court, there is no doubt that the play's animal transformations, centrally that of the wolf, constitute its dominant political language. Indeed, the
emotional dynamic of the play turns on Ferdinand's failure of self-diagnosis
in the first part of the play, where he attributes his wolflike preying and secrecy to others, and in the second part of the play, where his self-recognition
as a wolf simply presses him into fully acting out despotism.

It is possible to trace a more specific genealogy of the importance of civic
crisis and tyranny in early modern representations of werewolf transformation. *The Duchess of Malfi* is an example of werewolf representation in a
text that, as a play for the stage, consciously addresses diverse constituen-
cies. Like that of the other English texts discussed here, *Malfi*'s representation of wolves is characterized by the primacy of textual relations—of texts
both popular and elite—in its representation of wolves. The textual quality
of such werewolves is illuminated by the contrasting body of material can-
vassed by Caroline Oates in her fascinating analysis of the connections between werewolf trials and encounters with wolves in Franche-Comté.[32]
Oates's material is textual but is shaped by its direct address to the problem
of actual wolves or werewolves, and accordingly she discusses narratives of
encounters with suspect wolves, the sudden appearance of people in the forest just after the disappearance of the wolf, and the nature of testimony. Although the printed material I have discussed is clearly bound to such con-
tacts and draws its frisson from them, it has other, textual contexts.

Thus, it seems possible, at least, that part of the reading context of the Stubbe Peeter stories was the interest in witchcraft from the 1590s witch trials onward. Although, as James Sharpe notes, many English witches were involved in "personal and local" disputes, Lawrence Normand and Gareth Roberts, discussing the 1590 trials, illuminatingly argue that with regard to the North Berwick witch hunt, "elite and popular culture interacted" with printed explorations of the witchcraft embracing both domestic disputes and "elite fears" of "demonic conspiracy" against James I.[33] The printed material Normand and Roberts examine brings together worlds that appear different but, as the texts reveal, share strikingly similar concerns. Whether or not these or other witch trials influenced purchasers and readers of werewolf material, Normand and Roberts's insight about the effect of printed accounts in shifting between or mixing together different discourses on a supernatural subject is very helpful in thinking about werewolf metamorphosis in early modern English culture, for it invites us to recall classical writing on the werewolf, particularly the fascination with Ovidian metamorphosis that so clearly marks elite culture and, through translation, vernacular readers. And, unsurprisingly perhaps, these texts take us back to civic and political crisis—specifically, to tyranny and fratricide. In early modern England werewolf stories themselves were discursive hybrids signifying within overlapping modes of thought—folkloric, religious, and classical. What happens if we look at *Malfi* from the perspective of circulating classical narratives of werewolves?

LYCAON AND LUPUS

Two aspects of the werewolf stories—the nature of the animal-human border and the implications of the civic, political dimension of the werewolf—are illuminated by classical werewolf texts, texts that are intermittently in a relationship to early modern writings. Classical writing on the werewolf, translated and to an extent popularized, adds a further dimension to the imaginative place occupied by lycanthropy. The qualities I have found in the werewolf—of a border-creature powerful and violent in a problematically inward, recursive, cannibalistic, infanticidal, and ultimately civic sense—are differently articulated in the two classical stories of wolfishness circulating in fairly readily available forms for some contemporaries: those of Romulus and Remus and of Lycaon. The lupine ingestion in the story of Romulus and Remus and the stories of "actually" transformed forms in the *Metamorphoses* are significantly different from the theologically inflected fascination of the other texts that we have looked at in that they locate the significance of transformation in the physical being of the wolf rather than in any hallucinatory change (as in *Malfi*) or in a crisis of the soul. The story of the punishment of the tyrant Lycaon and Zeus's punitive visit is retold in Golding's translation. Zeus speaks to describe Lycaon's conduct:

> And yet he was not content: but went and cut the throte
> Of one that lay in hostage there which was an *Epyrote:*
> And part of him he did to roste, and part he did to stewe.
> Which when it came upon the borde, forthwith I overthrew,
> The house with just revenging fire upon the owners hed.
> Who seeing that slipt out of doores amazed for feare and fled
> Into the wilde and desert woods, where being all alone,
> As he endeavorde (but in vaine) to speake and make his mone,
> He fell a howling: wherewithal for very rage and mood
> He ran me quite out of his wits and waxed furious wood [mad]
> Still practising his wounted lust of slaughter on the poore
> And silly cattel, thirsting still for blood as heretofore.
> His garments turned to shaggie haire, his armes to rugged pawes
> So is he made a ravening Wolfe: whose shape expressely drawes
> To that the which he was before: his skin is hory gray,
> His look still grim with glaring eyes, and every kind of way,
> His cruell heart in outward shape doth well it selfe bewray.
> Thus was one house destroyed quite, but that one house alone
> Deserveth not to be destroyd.[34]

This description is part of the narrative of human degeneracy prefacing the body of the text, and Lycaon's crime fulfills an exemplary function in the naming of events. Golding's interpretation emphasizes the reciprocity between wolf and Lycaon: the shape of the wolf he has become registers, in its very wolfishness, his earlier nature and even appearance. Although Lycaon struggles for some time to articulate his grief and rage in language, this is definitively taken from him, and although he might (reversing Ferdinand's condition) continue to experience himself as human on the inside, as a wolf he is "thirsting for blood as heretofore," and to others he has always been beastly. As this extract indicates, if Golding, famously, reshapes Ovid to fit his Calvinist views, the relationship is not one way. An Ovidian sense of metamorphosis, with its survival of human characteristics in strangely appropriate animal form, comes in a reciprocal exchange to inhabit Golding's translation.[35]

The second story is that of Romulus and Remus, first the story of the ingestion of wolflike qualities and then the story of fratricide. Wolves and werewolves in this story figure the character of the polis, the establishment and also the cannibalistic or fratricidal falling off of civil government. As Topsell reminds us, the linguistic and other hygiene of the story of Romulus and Remus suckled by a wolf is troubled by the double meaning of *lupa* as wolf and prostitute.[36] Moreover, the never-to-be-trusted nature of the wolf and the wolf's power seem to be registered in the fratricide, which leaves Romulus as the founder of Rome. The ambiguity inherent in the story of the founding of Rome (was it the triumph of the institution, government, and order or a sequence of fratricidal crimes?) has been recently explored by Michel Serres but was also troubling to Topsell and his contemporaries.[37]

Topsell registers the calculated ambiguity of the Romulus and Remus story by giving both the "natural" (lupine) and the whorish versions. More significantly, he ends his discussion of the wolf with an apparently unrelated comment on the wearing of wolfskin: "The skins of wolves after they were dressed by Curriers, we do read that there were garments made wherewithal great princes and Noblemen were cloathed, the bare being inward next to their bodies, and the rough being outward, these were used in journies and huntings, and they were the proper garment of the guard of Tyrants."[38] In early modern culture, where clothes were felt to be so steeped in the significant traces of a person that they were used in magic, such a comment is significant. In using this as his conclusion, Topsell registers strongly the link between wolves and tyranny made by both these classical stories, and it is this particular feature of classical narrative that, when mixed with other discourses on the werewolf, reshapes the stories as about tyranny as the most frightening form of civic collapse.

Topsell's mixed account also illuminates the way in which the classical werewolf narratives, in intermittent but transformative contact with early modern stories, were also important in the minds of the readers and formed a significant context against which plays such as *The Duchess of Malfi*, even narratives such as those of Stubbe Peeter, might readily be set. If some early modern werewolf texts draw consciously on the civil crisis figured by wolf transformation in Ovid's tale of Lycaon, then we might imagine that readers, too, put their classical as much as their theological knowledge to work in interpreting these texts. Both inside and outside ostensibly popular werewolf texts, these historical and Ovidian stories provided a catalyst to the interpretation of other werewolf writings. The textual or readerly recollection of classical narratives formalized the charge of such stories as political, but most intensely civic, figuring civil government as a struggle not with nature or the wild but with the discontents of civic power itself.

A further aspect of the Lycaon narratives registered by Topsell imbues early modern texts. Topsell writes, "There was another *Lycaon*, the son of Pelagius, which built the Citty *Lycosra*, in the Mountaine *Lycaus*, this man called *Jupiter Lycaeus*. On a time he sacrificed an infant upon his altar, after which sacrifice he was presently turned into a wolf."[39] So Topsell tells us in his section on infanticidal wolves. And it is in this figuration of tyranny and civil crisis that the Christian implications of the werewolf and Ovidian transformation are brought together. Jonathan Bate tells us that Christian allegorizations of Ovid read Lycaon's plot to make Zeus a cannibal as Herod's plan to murder the infant Jesus.[40] Herod, like Ferdinand, is hairy on the inside: he holds within himself the Ovidian werewolf. But can we say that Webster's Ferdinand is tickled by the same hair that covered Lycaon and was absorbed by Herod? Or do the infanticidal desires of Stubbe Peeter and Ferdinand register a less genealogical aspect of early modern anxiety? The evidence of the texts examined here suggests that to choose between the two might be to exclude the contexts of reading from consideration. *Malfi* is evidently knowing in its blending of Ovid and melancholy, and the readers of Stubbe Peeter stories also might have read Ovid. Less immediately, the folkloric and popular ideas of metamorphosis have relationships far back, as Caroline Walker Bynum notes, with Ovid's sources.[41] Moreover, as I have argued, besides the theological implications of werewolf transformation it is also possible to see in these stories a reciprocal dynamic between three related terms: the civic, the wild, and the human. As I have suggested, werewolf narratives freed from restraining theological discipline blend uncannily into their apparent opposites: the stories of the acquisition of animal characteristics for the strengthening of the civic virtues of the human, such as the story of wolfish suckling of Romulus, fratricide (like the werewolf) and founder of Rome.

CIVIL SHAPES AND EDUCABLE BODIES

The werewolf is not the only evidence that the wild in early modern culture was not always the opposite of the civil but might also serve to tell an audience about the crisis or pain of that civilization. It was not only Christian writing that might be both drawn to and resistant to shape shifting.[42] Concomitantly, the place of Ovid's *Metamorphoses*—with its apparently endless versions of human-animal transformation—at the heart of Renaissance culture is only the most vivid of the signs that the wild can signify the crisis of the civil or of the scapegoat's return to visit vengeance on the scene of injustice. Thus, above the fireplace in a bedroom of Haddon Hall in Derbyshire a relief shows Orpheus taming the beasts. Peacocks and boars, among the animals being tamed, represent the families of Vernon and Manners. But what Orpheus is doing in Derbyshire, at the center of a lord's house, and what the penalties of disharmony might be—what might happen if the animals were not tamed—is, though differently inflected, present in this bedchamber story of civil harmony, as it is in the early modern wolf stories. The wild's ability to signify civility, in or out of crisis, permeates high and domestic early modern representational modes.

Indeed, as Kate Soper notes, the "natural" devolves easily into colloquial discourse, so that the poet's nature is and is not "the kind of thing we eat for breakfast."[43] Yet what is humanly cultivated still in such colloquial discourse lodges itself in the realm of "nature," as in Milton and Jonson's gardens. Though not concerned with historical discourses, Soper enables us to recognize that the early modern figuration of the werewolf involves an expansion of the categories of culture and civility—including religious belief—to be understood as generating wildness and wolfishness at the heart of culture. At the same time, the imagination of the transformation into a wolf expands the category of the natural, more particularly the wild, from the waste around the city to its governmental heart. The simultaneous quality of these expansions—the secret incorporation of the human (civil) in the wolf and the natural (wild) in the citizen—is only one of the meanings of these narratives of human transformation.

These wolf narratives tell us something about the way this specific form of metamorphosis calls on distinct, overlapping, sometimes melding ways of thinking about the world to provide a shape to think with that resonates as fantasy, theology, marvel, and a discourse on the discontents of the civil. They tell us why this shape is culturally important. And as the longer narrative of Stubbe Peeter shows, *shape* and *likeness* are the significant terms, besides *body* and *soul.* Certainly, these stories configure the human very differently from the way in which Descartes was to split mind and body. These wolves are neither humanists nor things that think, and therein lies their value. Such stories offer insights into the cultural circulation of questions about the designation of the border between the human and the animal that humanism and Descartes do not.

Clearly, early modern werewolf narratives articulate and resolve a crisis in where the border of the human is to be placed. And wherever that border is drawn, implied, or imagined, they offer a way of thinking through civil discontents. How does this relate to my opening analysis of discovery of the civilizable savage, Mademoiselle le Blanc? The two are related, genealogically connected. Yet the first thing that strikes one is that although they are connected, Mademoiselle le Blanc is offered as diabolic only for that whole possibility to be dispelled as a peasant's fantasy: it seems she is the wild thing of the Enlightenment and made in the Enlightenment's own image with an educable body and mind, whereas the werewolves have shapes and seemings. And these shapes are, overlappingly, likenesses, bodies, and souls. Just as there are important distinctions to be made about the way the werewolf and wild child express the civic and social orders that made them, there are more connections to be explored in the wild child's reconfiguration of animal-human metamorphosis. Yet a few things are clear: werewolves disappear narratively around the 1660s, and wild children begin to be "found," as Rousseau notes, in the 1640s.[44] And something written many years later about a wild child reinforces my point: in "the savage horde most vagabond, . . . man is only what he is made to be by his external circumstances. . . . We ought, then, to seek elsewhere the model of a man truly savage."[45] Part of the pleasure of the narrative of the eighteenth-century wild child successfully or unsuccessfully civilized is that inside each narrative there is a werewolf, secretly incorporated, just waiting to get out.

NOTES

1. *The History of a Savage Girl, Caught Wild in the Woods of Champagne* (London: R. Dursley et al., 1760), 5–6.

2. Edward Topsell, *The Historie of Foure-footed Beastes* (London, 1607), 735. As Caroline Oates notes in her fascinating discussion of werewolf trials in Franche-Comté, trials offer a contrasting context. For them to happen, there had to be wolves in the area: "where there were no wolves, there were no werewolves." Caroline Oates, "Trials of Werewolves in the Franche-Comté in the Early Modern Period," unpublished Ph.D. thesis, University of London, 1993, 11. Topsell also recounts the forced species mixture between a wolf and a mastiff at the Tower.

3. Hayden White, "Forms of Wildness," in *The Wild Man Within: An Image in Western Thought from the Renaissance to Romanticism,* ed. Edward Dudley and Maximilian E. Novak (London: University of Pittsburgh Press, 1972), 3–38, quote on p. 3.

4. Topsell, *Historie,* 737–48, quote on p. 744. On leagues, see 741 and 748; on lions, see 746. In a discussion of the relationship between discourses enunciating the symbolic significance of the animal and an "emerging" emphasis on factually true and empirically testable statements about animals, William B. Ashworth Jr. carefully places Topsell's collection of animal lore in terms of its significant departures from Conrad Gesner in importing variously symbolic information. See Ashworth's "Natural History and the Emblematic World View," in *Reappraisals of the Scientific Revolution,* ed. David C. Lindberg and Robert S. Westman (Cambridge: Cambridge University Press, 1990), 303–32, especially 306 and 316. I am grateful to Kevin Killeen for bringing this article to my attention. Readers interested in a fuller discussion of Topsell than space permits here will find it in Erica Fudge, *Perceiving Animals: Humans and Beasts in Early Modern English Culture* (Basingstoke: Macmillan, 2000), 11–13, 93–96.

5. Topsell, *Historie,* 737, compares the wolf and the hyena, and 745 discusses the progeny of wolves mated with hyenas and panthers: "Wolves do engender not only amongst themselves."

6. Ibid., 748–49. He also discusses the magical properties "about the partes of wolves"—"heads, teeth, eares, tails & privy parts"—but does not give details "because I cannot tel what benefit shal come to the knowledge of them by the English Reader" (748).

7. *The XV. Bookes of P. Ovidius Naso, Entituled, Metamorphosis,* trans. Arthur Golding (London, 1593), B4r–v. See also Frederick Ahl, *Metaformations, Soundplay and Wordplay in Ovid and Other Classical Poets* (Ithaca, N.Y.: Cornell University Press, 1985), 69–74, 81–86. I am grateful to the University of Illinois Press reader for this suggestion.

8. White, "Forms of Wildness," 5, 18.

9. In her fascinating discussion of twelfth-century werewolf texts, Caroline Walker Bynum notes what seems an intriguingly similar way in which a large range of discourses, not simply theological, canvass and are skeptical about the status of werewolf transformation. See Bynum, *Metamorphosis and Identity* (New York: Zone Books, 2001), 82–111. She concludes that medieval explorations of "body-hopping" "reflect less a desire to shed the body than an effort to understand how it perdures, less an escape into alterity than a search for the rules that govern change" (109).

10. *A True Discourse Declaring the Damnable Life and Death of One Stubbe Peeter, A Most Wicked Sorcerer* (London, 1590), 4. Subsequent references are all to this edition. There is also a modernized edition in Charlotte F. Otten, *A Lycanthropy Reader: Werewolves in Western Culture* (New York: Syracuse University Press, 1986), 69–76.

11. Ibid., 4–5, 5, and 10.

12. Ibid., 19, 5–6, 7, 7–9, and 9.

13. Ibid., 5.

14. Caroline Oates presents a different woodcut of the arrest (Augsburg, 1589) showing the arrester slicing off the wolf's paw in a scene reminiscent of many other stories of lycanthropic transformation and witchcraft transformation more generally, where the human agent is found to have a wound in the same place as the animal wounded after an attack. Caroline Oates, "Metamorphosis and Lycanthropy in Franche-Comté, 1521–1643," in *Fragments for a History of the Human Body Part I,* ed. Michael Feher, Ramona Naddaff, and Nadia Tazi (New York: Zone Books, 1989), 315–16, fig. 3.

15. *Stubbe Peeter,* 15–16.

16. Fudge, *Perceiving Animals,* 51–55.

17. *Stubbe Peeter,* 19.

18. Richard Verstegan, *A Restitution of Decayed Intelligence in Antiquities* (London, 1605), 237.

19. *Stubbe Peeter,* 16.

20. Reginald Scot, *The Discoverie of Witchcraft* (London, 1584), book V, chapter I, 89.

21. John Cotta, *The Triall of Witch-Craft* (London, 1616), 34. Also quoted by Stuart Clark, "The Scientific Status of Demonology," in Otten, *Lycanthropy Reader,* 181.

22. Clark, "Scientific Status of Demonology," 179. Clark is discussing Jean de Nynauld. On possession, see Stuart Clark, *Thinking with Demons, the Idea of Witchcraft in Early Modern Europe* (Oxford: Oxford University Press, 1997), 190–94, 396, and passim.

23. Clark, "Scientific Status," 177–81.

24. Clark, *Thinking with Demons,* 166–67, 172–73, and passim.

25. Clark, "Scientific Status," 176–79.

26. John Webster, *The Duchess of Malfi*, ed. John Russell Brown (Manchester: Manchester University Press, 1974), III.1.25–33.

27. Ibid., II.1.52–60.

28. Ibid., IV.1.34 and IV.2.256–57.

29. Ibid., IV.2.267–69 and II.2.309–11.

30. Ibid., V.2.7–21.

31. Ibid., V.2.38–43 and V.2.59–60.

32. Oates, "Metamorphosis and Lycanthropy," 305–61.

33. James Sharpe, *Instruments of Darkness: Witchcraft in England, 1550–1750* (London: Hamish Hamilton, 1996), 65; Lawrence Normand and Gareth Roberts, eds., *Witchcraft in Early Modern Scotland: James VI's Demonology and the North Berwick Witches* (Exeter: University of Exeter Press, 2000), 1–2.

34. Golding, *Metamorphosis*, B4r–v.

35. See Louis Thorn Golding, *An Elizabethan Puritan* (New York: Richard R. Smith, 1937).

36. Topsell, *Historie*, 734; Michel Serres, *Rome: The Book of Foundations* (Stanford, Calif.: Stanford University Press, 1991), 9: "Romulus and Remus, the abandoned Alban twins, nurse at the dry breast of a she-wolf; I say 'dry breast' because in Latin the she-wolf, *lupa*, refers to a prostitute from a brothel. . . . False sons of a prostitute, true sons of a vestal and Mars, legendary sons of violence and rape, sons of the God of war and a chaste, primitive priestess, Romulus and Remus are also grandsons of enemy brothers. Murder between brothers was not born yesterday. Romulus, then, kills Remus, and founds Rome."

37. See Serres, *Rome*, 9.

38. Topsell, *Historie*, 749.

39. Ibid., 735.

40. Jonathan Bate, *Shakespeare and Ovid* (Oxford: Clarendon Press, 1993), 26. See also Jean Seznac, *The Survival of the Pagan Gods* (New York: Pantheon, 1953), 84–95. For a selection of the identifications of Lycaon and for the different ways in which *Metamorphoses* was interpreted in relation to the Bible, see Ann Moss, *Ovid in Renaissance France* (London: Warburg Institute, 1982), 30–35.

41. Bynum, *Metamorphosis and Identity*, 178.

42. Ibid., 96.

43. Kate Soper, *What Is Nature?* (Oxford: Blackwell, 1995), 1.

44. Lucien Malson, "Wolf Children," in Lucien Malson and Jean Itard, *Wolf Children and the Wild Boy of Aveyron* (1964) trans. Edmund Fawcett, Peter Ayrton, and Joan White (London: New Left Books, 1972), 40. Malson quotes Nicolas Tulpe, *Observationes Medicae* (Amsterdam, 1672), fifth edition, 296.

45. Jean Itard, "Preface" to *The Wild Boy of Aveyron*, (1799), translated in 1802 as *An Historical Account of the Discovery and Education of Savage Man* (London: Richard Phillips, 1802), 6; reprinted, with some alterations, in Malson and Itard, *Wolf Children*, 91–93.

4

Saying Nothing Concerning the Same: On Dominion, Purity, and Meat in Early Modern England

Erica Fudge

> God, who art the giver of every good and perfect gift, sanctifi wee beseech thee these thy Creatures now prepared for us, make them wholesome for our bodies: and our soules and bodies serviceable unto thee for them, through Jesus Christ our Lord, Amen.
>
> —Anon., *A Good Companion for a Christian* (London, 1632), n.p.

If bear-baiting is the most spectacular display of human dominion over animals in England in the early modern period, then the dinner plate might be figured as the least dramatic. The meal is a place where humans interact with animals on a day-to-day basis, and it seems obvious that this recurring event should form a part of any history of animals. The very domesticity of flesh eating is what makes it interesting. It is almost invisible in its power, but unthought anthropocentrism is more significant and more powerful than any dominion that has to be constantly defended, and it is for this reason that meat is important. Animal flesh exists, historically, at a conjunction of two significant and related ideals: that of order and that of anthropocentrism. As such, meat epitomizes all that should be in human-animal relations: there is harmony, and there is dominion. But, of course, it is never as simple as this, and in this chapter I attempt to highlight some of the paradoxes that surround conceptualizations of meat eating in early modern England by tracing the journey of meat from its ideal form in the mind to its physical manifestation in the body of the eater. The chapter follows a digestive route. Through the paradoxes inherent in meat thinking and eating I want to argue that what appears to be made secure in the eating of meat—human dominion—may actually be deeply, dangerously fragile. By consuming an animal the human does not necessarily enact his or her superiority.

THE TROUBLED ORIGINS OF MEAT EATING

To begin to piece together some of the problems that can be traced in early modern thinking about meat eating, we need to return to the origin: Eden. Genesis 1:29–30, the first mention of food in the Bible, reads, "And God said, Behold I have given you every herb bearing seed, which is upon the face of all the earth, and every tree, in the which is the fruit of a tree yielding seed; to you it shall be for meat. / And to every beast of the earth, and to every fowl of the air, and to every thing that creepeth upon the earth, wherein there is life, I have given every green herb for meat: and it was so." According to the scriptures, meat eating was not introduced until after the flood. In Genesis 9:2 God tells Noah, "Every moving thing that liveth shall be meat for you: even as the green herb I have given you all things." This representation of meat eating as a product of the Fall and the flood makes the dominion of the dinner plate a part of human corruption. The biblical narrative states that humanity's original sin led to the wildness of animals, which led in turn to the need for dominion, a replacement of a more egalitarian cohabitation: Francis Bacon wrote, "being in his creation invested with sovereignty of all inferior creatures, [man] was not needy of power and dominion."[1] After the Fall, however, dominion was necessary when animals and humans began to live at odds with each other, and man—the God on Earth—had to enforce his position. With this enforcement came the eating of meat.

It seems that paradise was vegetarian, and this may be the thinking of Thomas Bushell and Roger Crab, a couple of the vegetarians who wrote down their ideas in the period. But it is worth noting two things when thinking about the position of what might now be called an ethical diet. First, a nonmeat diet clearly was regarded as bizarre, something that can be traced when Bushell's eating habits are called his "strange diet" and when Crab writes that he has "become a gazing stock to the Nation."[2] The implication here is that meat eating was perceived to be the norm. Second, as Carole Shammas has shown, meat and fish were a "constantly cited" commodity in the bills of fare and account books of southeastern English poorhouses between 1570 and 1650. Shammas argues that this inclusion "indicates that a commodity is firmly entrenched in the diet of the general population." The only other commodities always cited in this period are bread, cheese, peas and beans, beer, and salt.[3] We need very clearly to place the nonmeat diet against the absolute dominance of meat eating then, but we also need to look to the wider historical and theological context to understand why Bushell and Crab turned away from animal flesh.

The Reformation was in part about a return to what was viewed as a purer theology (St. Paul and St. Augustine rather than the darkened minds of Thomas Aquinas and Duns Scotus) and about a return to a purer way of living (the word instead of the image, the book rather than the theater). For this reason a movement that might take the believer closer to original innocence might be something to aspire to. As the great Elizabethan Calvinist William Perkins wrote, "man by creation was made a goodly creature in the blessed image of God: but by *Adams* fall men lost the same, and we are now become the deformed children of wrath: our dutie therefore is, to labour to get againe our first image, and indeavour our selves to become new creatures."[4] If vegetarianism is part of the original, innocent order of things, a vegetarian diet might be an obvious way for Reformed thinkers to begin their own quest for purification. A few people did follow this logic.

Thomas Bushell responded to the demise of his master, Francis Bacon, in what seems to be an absolutely theologically logical way. He retired from court (and from excess) and lived as a hermit on the Calf of Man (an island just off the Isle of Man).[5] In his recollection of this time Bushell wrote that he lived on "a Diet of Oyle, Honey, Mustard, Herbs and Bisket, my Drink Water, like those long-lif'd Fathers before the flood."[6] His repentance for former excesses takes the form of a return to an original order of consumption: where there had been overindulgence, there was perfection.

Thirty years after Bushell, Roger Crab offered another version of the importance of a vegetarian diet. In fact, Crab made the case for vegetarianism even stronger. He wrote, "if naturall Adam had kept to his single naturall fruits of Gods appointment, namely fruits and hearbs, we had not been corrupted."[7] Rather than seeing the consumption of animal flesh as evidence of human corruption, he argued that it had caused it. In this sense it is logical that in his attempts to be truly pure Crab should avoid meat.

But this kind of abstinence is notable for its rarity, and this fact begs a question: why, when a theological logic can be traced that would support vegetarianism, were there so few vegetarians in England? To answer this question we need to look at an alternative Reformed debate about meat that was taking place at the same time.

Early modern theologians were not always content to accept the possibility of a vegetarian paradise at face value. For William Perkins antediluvian vegetarianism held only parenthetical problems: "Before the flood," he wrote, "the Patriarches (in all likelihood) were not allowed flesh, but onely hearbs, and the fruit of the ground."[8] However, this was not the only position taken by Protestant theologians. John Calvin wrote of Genesis 1:29, "Hereof some gather, that untill the time of the floude, men were contented with hearbes & fruit, and that it was not lawfull for them to eate fleshe. And this seemeth to be the more probable, bycause God after a sorte shutteth up the sustenance of man within certeine boundes and limites. Furthermore, after the floud he granteth expressly the eating of flesh." This seems to be a straightforward interpretation of the verses. However, Calvin goes on, "Howbeit these reasons are not strong ynoughe. For on the contrarie parte it may be alledged, that the men of the firste age offered sacrifices of beastes. For this is the lawe of true sacrificing, to offer unto God nothing else but those thinges, whiche he hath graunted unto our use. Furthermore they were cloathed with skinnes: therefore it was lawfull for them to kill beastes. Therefore I thinke it shall be better if we say nothing concerning the same."[9] Spoken and unspoken, the possibility of antediluvian vegetarianism is clearly a theological problem too far for Calvin, and in this refusal of the straightforward interpretation of the verse he was not alone. In 1605, for example, Andrew Willett, the great English biblical scholar, took an even more explicit stance on the same scriptural passage: "we refuse the opinion . . . that neither man nor beast did eate of any flesh, but onely of the fruits of the earth before the flood."[10]

This quibbling about the (apparently) straightforward meaning of the scriptures dealing with meat eating may seem strange, but there is a possible reason, and it has to do with important meanings that were associated with flesh in Reformed theology. It appears that eating meat is a moment when many of the main tenets of Reformed theology are brought to the fore; in fact, meat eating is almost a necessary part of Reformed theology.

THE PRESENT REFERENT

The animal—as animal—is never present at the meal table, or so says Carol Adams in *The Sexual Politics of Meat.* She writes, "Live animals are . . . the absent referents in the concept of meat." She goes on to argue that this "permits us to forget about the animal as an independent entity; it also enables us to resist efforts to make animals present."[11] It is our ability to forget the source of the flesh we consume, to repress the real animal, that allows meat to be eaten, she argues, and that supports the continuation of meat eating. The implication of Adams's work is that if the animal could be made once again present—if the meat eater was reminded of the source of the meal—then the consumption of flesh would be unbearable and would therefore cease.

But to say with Adams that meat eating relies on the absence of the animal, the distinction between flesh and living being, is to assume a very modern notion of the experience of the meal. For one thing, in preindustrial culture the death of the animal did not take place only in the slaughterhouse,

away from the eaters' eyes; it was also very much a part of domestic activities.[12] But this is not the only way in which the animal made its individual
presence felt at the meal table. In fact, early modern readings of meat eating seem to work in absolute opposition to the model Adams sets up. It is
in its very visibility that meat can be eaten. This can be shown in a number
of ways.

In the first interpretation we return to religion and can begin to piece
together why Calvin had nothing to say about vegetarianism. In 1617 the
Leicestershire divine John Moore wrote,

> Our life is as a garment that weares of it selfe, and by itselfe; for we weare out
> our life in living; the more we live, the lesse we have to live, and still approach
> nearer death: whatsoever we are cloathed with, is a mortall and perishing mer-
> chandise; our garments weare upon our backs, and we in our garments; they
> are eaten with mothes, and we with time. So in our meates (as in a looking-
> glasse) we may learne our own mortalitie: for let us put our hand into the dish,
> and what doe we take, but the foode of a dead thing, which is either the flesh
> of beasts, or of birds, or of fishes, with which foode wee so long fill our bod-
> ies, untill they themselves be meate for wormes? All this we see by experience,
> we feele it and we taste it daily: we see death (as it were) before our eyes: we
> feele it betwixt our teeth, and yet can wee not cast our accompt, that we must
> die.[13]

In Moore's reading, meat is a *memento mori,* something that, of course,
figures it as very visible. In a daily diet of flesh humans experience a reminder of the corruption of humanity, corruption that is reiterated in the
failure to read the sign. Without the presence of animal flesh, Moore seems
to be arguing, humans might forget their position in God's universe, and
so meat becomes central to Reformed thinking.

Moore's interpretation is reiterated in other works of the period: William
Perkins proposed that "both we & our meate are but perishing; and therefore when we feede thereon, it may serve to stirre us up, to seeke for the
foode of the soule, that nourishment to life everlasting."[14] There is a circu-
lar movement: meat is postlapsarian, evidence of humanity's corruption,
and humans eat meat to remind themselves of their status as fallen beings
so that they can refuse any possibility of self-aggrandizement, Adam's original sin. Reformed theologians did not promote vegetarianism, then, because they argued for the need for humans to remind themselves constantly
of their own pitiful status. Looking in the bowl is part of a religious act of
self-loathing.

But as Gervase Babington, the bishop of Llandaff, argued in 1592, food itself is a sign of human frailty. Adam and Eve's need for food before the Fall
shows that they were immortal in a different way from God: they "may live

for ever," he wrote, "a condition being observed," that is, food being consumed.[15] For the nature of that food to be changed after the flood was to further distance humanity from God. The attempt at total knowledge, an attempt at the godhead (performed, of course, by an act of eating), actually worked to instigate change that took humans further from God. Calvin wrote of Genesis 9:2, God's permission to eat flesh, "Wild beastes in verie deede do ravage, & many wayes are noysome unto men. And no marvell: for seeing we are disobedient unto God, why should not the beastes rebell against us?" Eating with blood on our hands and with death in our bowls is an appropriate reminder of humanity's state. The link between food and pleasure is not one that persists in this aspect of Reformed theology. But Calvin does add another sentence to his discussion that is important here: "Neverthelesse, the providence of GOD is a secrete bridle to restraine [animals'] outrage."[16] Even at the moment of humiliation—the breakdown of humanity's natural control of animals—there remains a sense of human power and dominion, but it is God who reiterates human centrality. Humans themselves can do no such thing; this is dominion by faith alone.

So the dinner plate daily offers some of Reformed theology's central tenets: humanity is fallen and corrupt ("wretched" is a favorite term of Calvin), and dominion is God-given. It is perhaps for this reason that Calvin wanted to say nothing about the possibility of an antediluvian vegetarianism. The eating of meat held a more powerful position in theological terms than any attempt to regain the vegetarian innocence of Eden. A return to purity—a refusal of meat—would take away a point of humiliation for humans that was vital to their understanding of their place in the universe. But Calvin reminds his readers that despite this humiliation humans are still the most powerful creatures on Earth. Eating meat, then, is double-edged. It represents both death (human mortality) and power (human dominion).

This interpretation of animal flesh can be traced in other areas of early modern culture, and the cultural ambivalence about the status of humanity in the face of meat that can be traced hints at not only the extensive reach of Reformed theology but also the very powerful symbolic qualities of flesh in the period. It is not only in the mind but also in the mouth that meat holds meaning.

LIFE COOKING

Where the Fall created the need for dominion—for human control of the natural world (however violent that might be)—the preparation of animals for consumption followed a similar pattern. Violence and eating meat were inextricably linked. Thomas Dawson made this clear in 1597. The following is his list of "Tearmes of a Carver," and they describe the movement from creature to cut, from fish to fillet.

> Breake that Deare, Leach that Brawn, reare that Goose, lift that Swan, sauce that Capon, spoyle that Hen, fursh that chicke[n], unbrace that Malard, unlace that connie: dismember that Heron, display that Crane, disfigure that Peacock, unjoynt that Bitture, untach that Curlew, alay that Fesaunt, wing that Partrich, wing that Quaile, mince that Plover, thie that Pigion, border that passtie, thie that Wodcock, thie all manner of small birds.
>
> Timber that fire, tire that egge, chine that Salmon, string that Lampry, splat that Pick, sauce that place, Sauce that Tench, splay that Breme, side that Haddock, tusk that Barbel, culpon that Troute, finne that Chevine, transen that Eele, traunch that Sturgion, undertraunch that purpes, tame that crab, barde that Lobster.
>
> Heere endeth the goodly Tearmes.[17]

The terms used here—*break, leach, lift, unbrace*—are the "proper verbs" for each specific animal. For example, one would never "break" a swan, nor would one "untach" a rabbit. Michel Jeanneret has noted that in the early modern period carving was a specialized skill; he writes of the techniques presented in manuals, "Such precise control of gesture and posture and such demanding physical training are paralleled at the time in treatises on fencing and riding."[18] It is almost as if, in carving, humans declare war on animals, a war begun at the Fall and ended at the table.

But we can go further even than this linguistic and gestural link between cookery and dominion. In early modern gastronomic texts the meaning of meat that can be traced in religious ideas emerges once again. In one recipe recorded by Dawson he advised those in the service of "a Prince or any other estate" to "Take up a capon, and lift the right leg and the right wing, and so array foorth and lay him in the platter as he should fly, and serve your soveraigne."[19] And similarly, in the same year, A.W. advised the housewife when "boyl[ing] a Conie with a pudding in his bellie" to "leave on the eares."[20] There is no attempt at disguising the animal origin of these meals. The power of humanity requires a display of humanity's absolute power, and, once again, this is found at the meal table. The live creature is being recreated in order that it can be consumed, finally destroyed, without effort. The difficulty of the first conquest is eradicated in the spectacle of the second.

But alongside this desire for life cooking, cookery manuals of the time also recognize linguistically the presence of death at the table. Just as John Moore scans his bowl for the image of his own mortality, so the terminology of cookery recreates mortality in language. In 1617 (the same year Moore's text was published), John Murrell advised his readers that, to bake a swan, the parboiled, seasoned bird should be placed with pepper, salt, and ginger "in a deepe Coffin of Rye-paste with store of Butter." Similarly, twelve years later, the anonymous *Booke of Cookerie* provided a recipe for a baked turkey that included the direction that the turkey, seasoned with cloves, should be laid in "the coffin."[21] The *Oxford English Dictionary* traces the use of the word *coffin* for a pie dish or mold, noting that its first appearance was in 1580 and its last in 1662. The meal, a reminder of human status, was also at this time the symbolic burial of the animal. So as the simultaneous use of the term *coffin* for burial chest and pie crust and the reading of meat as a *memento mori* shows, early modern writers emphasize in a variety of ways the very important visible presence of the animal. As a reminder of mortality and human dominion, the animal had to be seen to be eaten.

In this sense, meat eating simultaneously replicates and reverses the Reformed understanding of the Eucharist. As in meat eating, in the taking of Holy Communion recipients are reminded both of their own special status (only humans take Communion) and of their frailty (only because of the great mercy of God do humans gain salvation; they can do nothing for themselves). But there is also a reversal. In the consumption of animal flesh its literal presence serves a vital function: it is a real death that John Moore feels betwixt his teeth, and it is this that serves his Reformed purpose. However, the debates over transubstantiation in the sixteenth and seventeenth centuries work in opposition to this and refuse the literal interpretation that sees the real flesh and blood of Christ being consumed in Communion. As Theodore Beza, Calvin's successor in Geneva, argued, the bread given in Communion is not mere bread, nor is the wine mere wine; the latter "is the sacrament of the precious blood spilled for us." Beza continues, "Nevertheless, we do not say that this change is to the material of the sign itself but that the change relates to the use and goal which each has been given."[22] The denial of the literal sets the flesh of the Savior apart from the flesh of the swine (a crucial separation), and it also sets Protestant apart from Catholic. As the Huguenot pastor Jean de Léry argued on his mission to Brazil, the less Reformed members of his missionary group, in their faith in the actual presence of Christ, were worse than the cannibalistic "savages nommés Ouetecas."[23] In this instance, the refusal to countenance the literal presence of Christ enforces the divinity of Léry's position. He knows the difference between a cow and Christ, and cannibalism, a "merely physical" encounter with flesh, becomes less uncivil than Catholicism, which is a form of "spiritual cannibalism."[24]

The ambivalent status of humans at the meal table—the constant shifting between humans as corrupt and humans as all-powerful—also emerges in a number of other places in early modern English culture. Visibility comes up again as a way into the issue, and this time we find not an ambivalence about so much as the destruction of human status.

HORSE PIES

In the 1660s the ballad "Newes from More-lane" staged the danger of the absence of the animal at the meal table; that is, it made the invisibility of the animal a problem rather than a reason for the eating of meat. The ballad tells the tale of a tapster who "made his Neighbours [a pie] and bid them all to Supper." We are told that this pie is filled not with the flesh of a chicken but with the flesh of a horse. The eaters, however, do not know this:

> The Car-mans Wife cry'd out and said
> troath 'tis good Meat indeed,
> So likewise said the chamber-maid,
> when she on it did feed . . .
> The Glovers Wife was in a heat,
> and did both pout and mump,
> Because they would not let her eate
> the Buttock and the Rump.
> As for the merry Weavers Wife,
> I will give her her due,
> She spent her coyne to end the strife,
> among the joviall Crew.

The pleasure of the neighbors turns to disgust when they realize what they have been eating, and the ballad traces—in a couplet—the shift:

> Some say it eate as mellow then
> as any little Chick;
> But I tell thee good-fellow then,
> it made the Neighbours sick.[25]

The unknown meat—meat that looked like meat but not like animal—is made known, and in knowledge comes the realization of what has been done: the wrong flesh has been eaten. The ballad represents a problem. There are limits to the dominion of the meal table: horses exist on one side of a conceptual boundary where they, alongside certain other animals, are not for consumption. But these differences are lost in the act of eating. It is the animal's absence from the meal—the fact that horse meat looks like any other meat—that has allowed this gastronomic faux pas. Absence does not only make the meal easier to consume; it also makes a border un-knowable, and this has implications for the eater.

Anthony Pagden writes of European interpretations of New World na-tives, "the Indians not only ate men, who were too high in the scale of being to be food, they also ate creatures which were too low." This, he goes on, "was a sure sign of their barbarism because by such unselective consump-tion the Indian revealed . . . his inability to recognise the divisions between species in the natural world and the proper purpose of each one."[26] "Newes from More-lane" takes us closer to home and shows that the dominion of the meal table brings with it problems for English humanity. If the animal is absent, humans cannot truly know what they are eating, and without this knowledge humans potentially animalize themselves.

In fact, the issues raised in this ballad place in a comic frame an idea voiced by Thomas Cogan in 1584. In his *Haven of Health,* Cogan noted that "the flesh of a swine hath such likenesse unto mans flesh, both in savour and tast, that some have eaten mans flesh in steede of porke."[27] The existence of horse pies and humans as accidental replacements for pigs are one logical outcome of the consumption of flesh, and cannibalism becomes simultaneously an act of barbarity and a genuine mistake; in fact, it is hard to tell the difference be-tween the two. The outcome of this ambivalence is that the line between ci-vility and barbarity, between human and inhuman, is lost.

So the ballad about the horse pie shows that dominion, that is, an asser-tion of human status, can exist at the meal table only when the consumed animal is visible, when one contemplates the nature of one's meal. If we can-not see what we are eating, we may as well eat each other. Without the pres-ence of the animal, meat has lost its religious, moral, cultural, and natural significance. To be human (truly human) humans must eat animals, know-ingly.

But it is not only the presence of the flesh on the plate that is important; also significant is what happens after consumption, and here a different version of visibility emerges. And just as the ambivalent status of human-ity is played out in consumption, so questions of digestion also raise issues about dominion and purity—this time, species purity.

GREAT EATERS

In his sermon *The Bread of Life* (1616), Thomas Granger offers a lengthy description of the processes involved in the consumption of flesh:

> The bodies of beasts, foules, and fishes (that they may be meate) must be
> mortified: I. By the shedding of their bloud, and other actions pertayning to

that trade, separating the grosest impure from the pure. II. Their flesh must be further mortified by water and fire, and other actions pertaining to that trade. III. Their flesh must be further mortified by mostication, or chewing in the mouth. IIII. They must be mortified by generall digestion in the common stomach, and from thence must they passe into innumerable parts of the body: All which doe mortifie the meat that is sent unto them, separating the impure from the pure; converting the one into their owne substance and property, but expelling the other, as an unprofitable excrement. So that mans body is the grave, and destruction of all things, though in another consideration it be the perfection of all things; for as much as it is the Centre of all things, and for the sustenance and maintenance whereof, the world, with the fulnesse thereof, was created.[28]

Here can be traced many of the ideas that have already been raised. Man as center of the universe destroys and perfects nature in one movement: the animal's death is the completion of the animal's function on Earth, a completion represented in the burial of the animal in the gut of humanity. However, what I am particularly interested in is Granger's belief that meat is converted "into [man's] substance and property," that is, that in the process of eating humans take on the animal.

This is not a new idea. Early Christians recognized the paradoxical possibilities of the consumption of animals: Dianne M. Bazell argues that "not only was meat considered inappropriately delicate [by early Christians,] it was also seen . . . as a potent and forceful stimulant of lust,"[29] that is, as a source of human bestialization. Centuries later Thomas Aquinas argued, as Joyce E. Salisbury puts it, that "animal flesh is converted into human flesh." But this scholastic belief can be taken the wrong way: Salisbury goes on to point out that "the medieval texts much more often reveal a preoccupation with the belief that one becomes what one eats, rather than one transforms what one eats."[30] This is a problem that remains present in the early modern period. For Cogan, this can have almost comic possibilities: "Wherefore," he writes, "Rammes mutton I leave to those that would be rammish."[31]

In contemporary writings on diet a clear link is made between consumption and identity more generally. Leonard Lessius spends a great deal of time expanding on his belief that "a *Sober life* or *diet*" is vital, and what is important here is that life and diet are regarded as alternative terms: you are what you eat.[32] Central to Lessius's and others' writings on diet is the ideal of temperance, moderation: "a constant measure is to be kept." This moderation in consumption leads to a development of the faculties that are regarded as truly human. Lessius writes, "And hence it comes to passe, that men given to Abstinence are watchfull, circumspect, provident, of good forecast, able to give good counsel, and of sound judgement: and for matters of learning, they do easily grow to excellencie in those things whereunto they apply themselves."[33] The implication here is that human status is not a given, constant thing but is something—like Adam and Eve's original immortality in Babington's reading—that entails certain conditions to be met and that, by extension, can be lost if those conditions are not met. However, Lessius's tract does not propose a nonmeat diet; in fact, he gives advice on what meat is best for each constitution. What is important is moderation. To resist temptation, lust, is to turn away from the pleasures of the flesh to the pleasures of the mind. Judgment comes with temperance, and judgment is something animals—and some humans—lack. But moderation has its opposite, overindulgence, and where human status can be encouraged through temperance, it can be blotted out through intemperance. A couple of instances display this in its most visible manifestation, and it is through meat that the greatest danger is traced.

In 1630 John Taylor, the Water Poet, recorded the fame of *The Great Eater of Kent.* In this pamphlet Taylor celebrates the feats of Nicholas Wood, "the absolutest man of mouth, and the most renowned stifgut in this Westerne Angle of the World." It should come as no surprise that Taylor had planned, he writes, "to have [Wood] to the Beare-garden, and there before a house full of people, he should have eaten a wheele barrow full of Tripes." This is an offer Wood turned down, fearing arrest, but what is shown is that great eating is a spectacle, and the dominion of cruelty represented in the Bear Garden seems to slide all too easily into the dominion of eating.[34]

Placed within a lineage of other greats—Pompey, Alexander, Tamburlaine, Charlemagne, Arthur—Wood is celebrated for his voracious appetite: "He hath (within himselfe) a stall for the Oxe, a roome for the Cow, a stye for the Hogge, a Parke for the Deere, a warren for the Coneies, a storehouse for fruit."[35] But this historic and histrionic status is not the only one in Taylor's pamphlet; the Water Poet also presents Wood as achieving a postapocalyptic perfection: "his guts are the Rendez-vous or meeting place of Burse for the Beasts of the fields, the Fowles of the Ayre, and Fishes of the Sea; and though they be never so wild or disagreeing in Nature, one to another, yet hee binds or grindes them to the peace, in such manner, that they never fall at odds againe."[36] Isaiah 11:6 foretold the perfection brought by the seed of Jesse, when "the wolf also shall dwell with the lamb, and the leopard shall lie down with the kid," and it is this end of natural, fallen enmity that also takes place in Wood's stomach. The consumption of animal flesh is central once again, and here humanity's status as the gods on Earth is given a physical embodiment: the great eater.

But Taylor's mock-heroic prose undercuts the status of its hero, and Wood's position as a manifestation of God on Earth is to be read alongside the other version of the great eater. This is the man who takes on the flesh of a whole herd of beasts:

> All men will confesse that a Hogge will eate any thing, either fish, flesh, fowle, root, herbe, or excrement, and this noble *Nick Nicholas,* or *Nicholas Nick,* hath made an end of a Hogge all at once, as if it had bin but a Rabbet sucker, and presently after, for fruit to recreate his palate, he hath swallowed three peckes of Damsons, thus (Philosophically) by way of a Chimicall Infusion, as a Hogge will eate all things that are to be eaten, so he in eating the Hogge, did in a manner of extraction distill all manner of meates thorow the Limbeck of his paunch.[37]

By his excessive eating—his excessive enactment of dominion—Wood (philosophically at least) becomes like the hog he consumes. His human status is undercut by the very thing that seems to prove it.

The philosophical nature of the degeneration of Wood is taken to further extremes in another ballad from the 1630s. This time it is a physical transformation that is wrought, and the link between diet and life, between food and identity, is taken to its logical extreme. The ballad "A Monstrous shape, Or A shapelesse Monster" (1640) tells the story of the "hog-faced gentlewoman" who was then on exhibition in London. The body of the gentlewoman is human, but "she has a dainty white swine's face." And the reason that the writer of the ballad gives for this deformity is simple: "she came of a race / that loved fat porke and bacon."[38] The link made between physique and food in the ballad fits into contemporary ideas about diet, and, like Wood, the hog-faced woman loses her humanity because of her excessive enactment of the most domestic of human dominions. Her power over pigs turns her—physically, rather than philosophically—into a human pig.

POSTPRANDIAL

So what does this tell us about the meaning of meat in the early modern period? There are a number of issues that must be seen as making up a continuum of ideas. In Reformed thought, dominion—the belief in the centrality of humanity and the instrumentality of animals—is a representation of humanity's corruption, and from this perspective meat eating is to be celebrated (if that is the right word) in order that humans should remain aware of their wretchedness. So human power and human frailty are two sides of the same coin, inseparable from and meaningless without each other. But the absence of the real animal on the dinner plate, what Carol Adams argues has allowed for the continuation of meat eating, destroys the moral meaning of consuming flesh in early modern writing, and mealtime becomes merely a physical act rather than an act of devotion. This is something that leads logically to the destruction of certain boundaries: between horse and chicken, for example, but also, and even more dangerously, between human and animal. In turn, this physical side of meat eating finds its way into the dietary regimens of the period, in which what is eaten becomes of extreme importance to the nature of the eater. Moderation can improve human status (thus proving the latter to be an achieved rather than an essential thing), but even in moderation the consumption of meat forces an acknowledgment that humans constantly take on the being of another species, that animal flesh can be transformed into human flesh. Further developments of this argument would propose another reading: human flesh can be transformed into animal. Just as human dominion and human weakness are revealed as inseparable, so at the meal table, it appears, are human and animal.

Ultimately, it is this that interests me about meat in the early modern period; it seems to undercut the very thing that it might be assumed to do. By writing about meat, by placing it as a topic of discussion, early modern writers reveal an anxiety about dominion. If the most unthought, apparently natural of humanity's exercises of its power—the consumption of meat at the meal table—is being offered in a way that makes dominion problematic, as I think it is in a number of works from the period, then the possibility emerges that human dominion more generally was not as assumed or natural as our vision of the early modern period might have us believe. What appears to be other is no longer so, and eater and eaten are revealed to be more akin than is comfortable.

There are two possible conclusions here: one silent and longing to hide, perhaps, the dangerous implications of meat eating, and the other staging it. The first is one that has already been considered. Looking at the status of meat eating in paradise, Calvin unwittingly offers what can be read as a more general comment on human-animal relations: "I thinke it shall be better if we say nothing concerning the same." Similarly, the destruction of otherness must be silenced for human status to be maintained, and, in passing, we might argue that this is what we have been doing ever since.

The alternative conclusion, one that spectacularly blows apart this apparent stability of status, comes from perhaps the most canonical representation of ambivalent meat eating in the period, Shakespeare's *Titus Andronicus*. Like many of Shakespeare's plays—*King Lear* is another example—*Titus Andronicus* is full of images of animals, images that, by their frequency, begin to upset the normal distinction that is made between human and animal. Bassianus is likened to a slaughtered lamb; Titus's sons are called whelps and curs; Rome is a "wilderness of tigers"; Lavinia is likened to a deer, wounded in the hunt; Chiron and Demetrius are "bear-whelps," no doubt licked into shape by their mother; and the nurse dies, in Aaron's rendition, with "wheak, wheak," the noise of a pig.[39] But these animal images might be purely conventional without the staging of species confusion in III.3. Marcus kills a fly, and Titus responds with a speech that bespeaks the uncertainty about human-animal difference:

> Titus: Out on thee, murderer! Thou kill'st my heart.
>   Mine eyes are cloyed with view of tyranny.
>   A deed of death done on the innocent
>   Becomes not Titus' brother. Get thee gone.
>   I see thou art not for my company.
> Marcus: Alas, my lord, I have but killed a fly.
> Titus: "But?" How if that fly had a father, brother?
>   How would he hang his slender gilded wings
>   And buzz lamenting dirges in the air!
>   Poor harmless fly,
>   That with his pretty buzzing melody
>   Came here to make us merry—and thou hast killed him!

In Titus's eyes the fly is not a mere insect; rather, it is a son, a maker of melody. But Marcus distinguishes between fly and son, between animal and human, and reclaims the safety of secure humanity by stating that the death is purely symbolic. This fly is never really a fly at all. Marcus states, "Pardon me, sir, it was a black ill-favoured fly, / Like to the Empress' Moor. Therefore I killed him." "O, O, O!" says Titus, "Then pardon me for reprehending thee, / For thou hast done a charitable deed."[40] The animal is secure only as a symbol of the human. A real animal would be too threatening, as real humans are hard to find.

It is no surprise, then, that it is at a meal table that the question about order is raised once again. This time there are no symbols, and the line between human and animal appears to have vanished completely. In V.3, when Titus invites Tamora and Saturninus to eat with him, the antagonisms of the struggle for power appear to be set aside as Titus acts as overzealous host and Tamora as grateful guest. But the new-found harmony is short lived; the revelation that the pie Titus has served contains Tamora's sons destroys all notions of order.

But the play does not only show that the disruption of the meal equates to the disruption of civil order. At the moment of the revelation of the contents of the pie, one question is being asked, and it is a question that pervades the whole of the play: where is the human? In this scene the sons are mere flesh, mistaken for animals; Titus is a murderer and dismemberer of all values and order; and Tamora is a cannibal, or worse, the eater of her own children. In III.3 symbolism was claimed as a way of asserting difference—Aaron is *like* a fly, but other humans are human. By Act V no such escape is found. Where Calvin requested silence, Shakespeare presents a spectacle, but the outcome appears to be the same. The culmination of the culinary chaos of *Titus Andronicus* reveals the logical outcome of both: the stage direction reads "Confusion follows."[41]

NOTES

1. Francis Bacon, *Valerius Terminus of the Interpretation of Nature* (1603), in *The Works of Francis Bacon,* ed. James Spedding, Robert Leslie Ellis, and Douglas Denon Heath (1859. Reprint. Stuttgart: Friedrich Frommann, 1963), III, 217.

2. William Blundell, *A History of the Isle of Man* (1648–56), in *The Manx Society* XXIII (1876): 34; Roger Crab, *The English Hermite, Or, Wonder of this AGE* (London, 1655), 1.

3. Carole Shammas, "Food Expenditures and Economic Well-Being in Early Modern England," *Journal of Economic History* 43:1 (1983): 97–98.

4. William Perkins, *An Exposition of the Symbole, or Creed of the Apostles* (1595), in *The Works of that Famous and Worthie Minister of Christ . . . M W Perkins* (London, 1616–18), I, 153.

5. For a biography of Bushell see J. W. Gough, *The Superlative Prodigal: A Life of Thomas Bushell* (Bristol: Bristol University Press, 1932).

6. Thomas Bushell, "Post-script to the Judicious Reader," in *Mr Bushell's Abridgement of the Lord Chancellor Bacon's Philosophical Theory in Mineral Prosecutions* (London, 1659), 8.

7. Crab, *English Hermite,* "To the Impartial Reader," n.p.

8. Perkins, *A Golden Chaine* (1590), in *The Works,* I, 129.

9. John Calvin, *A Commentarie of John Calvine, upon the first booke of Moses called Genesis* (London, 1578), 48.

10. Andrew Willet, *Hexapla in Genesin* (Cambridge, 1605), 18.

11. Carol J. Adams, *The Sexual Politics of Meat: A Feminist-Vegetarian Critical Theory* (Cambridge: Polity Press, 1990), 40.

12. See Robert Malcolmson and Stephanos Mastoris, *The English Pig: A History* (London: Hambledon Press, 1998), 89.

13. John Moore, *A Mappe of Mans Mortalitie* (London, 1617), 40.

14. Perkins, *The Second Booke of the Cases of Conscience,* in *The Works,* II, 133.

15. Gervase Babington, *Certaine Plaine, briefe, and comfortable Notes upon everie Chapter of Genesis* (London, 1592), f7r.

16. Calvin, *Commentarie,* 218.

17. Thomas Dawson, *The Booke of Carving and Sewing* (London, 1597), A2r–v.

18. Michel Jeanneret, *A Feast of Words: Banquets and Table Talk in the Renaissance,* trans. Jeremy Whiteley and Emma Hughes (Cambridge: Polity Press, 1991), 60.

19. Dawson, *Booke of Carving,* B2r.

20. A.W., *The good Huswives hand-maid for Cookerie in her Kitchin* (London, 1597), 6.

21. John Murrell, *A New Booke of Cookerie* (London, 1617), 47; Anonymous, *A Booke of Cookerie And the order of Meates to bee served to the Table* (London, 1629), 28.

22. Theodore Beza, "Colloquy of Poissy" (1561), in *Documents on the Continental Reformation,* ed. William G. Naphy (Basingstoke: Macmillan, 1996), 77.

23. Jean de Léry, *Histoire d'un Voyage* (1580), cited in Janet Whatley, "Food and the Limits of Civility: The Testimony of Jean de Léry," *The Sixteenth Century Journal* 15:4 (1984): 389.

24. Ibid.

25. Anonymous, "Newes from More-lane" (n.d.).

26. Anthony Pagden, *The Fall of Natural Man: The American Indian and the Origins of Comparative Ethnology* (Cambridge: Cambridge University Press, 1982), 87.

27. Thomas Cogan, *The Haven of Health* (London, 1584), 116. This similarity is voiced again in almost exactly the same terms by Henry Buttes, *Dyets Dry Dinner: Consisting of eight severall Courses* (London, 1599), I5r.

28. Thomas Granger, *The Bread of Life* (London, 1616), 7.

29. Dianne M. Bazell, "Strife among the Table-Fellows: Conflicting Attitudes of Early and Medieval Christians toward the Eating of Meat," *Journal of the American Academy of Religion* 65:1 (1997): 76.

30. Joyce E. Salisbury, *The Beast Within: Animals in the Middle Ages* (London: Routledge, 1994), 44.

31. Cogan, *Haven of Health,* 116.

32. Leonard Lessius, *Hygiasticon: or, the right course to preserving Life and Health unto extream old Age* (first published 1613, English translation, London, 1636), 15.

33. Ibid., 16, 170–71.

34. John Taylor, *The Great Eater of Kent* (London, 1630), 16.

35. Ibid., A2v, 9, 11–12.

36. Ibid., 12.

37. Ibid., 6.

38. Anonymous, "A Monstrous Shape Or A shapelesse Monster," in *A Pepysian Garland: Black-Letter Broadside Ballads of the Years 1595–1639,* ed. Hyder E. Rollins (Cambridge: Cambridge University Press, 1922), 453–54. This is a different interpretation of the gentlewoman from that given in a pamphlet written in the same month that states that her hog face resulted from her being "bewitched in her mother's womb." Anonymous, *A certaine Relation of the Hog-faced Gentlewoman called Mistris Tannakin Skinker* (London, 1640), title page.

39. William Shakespeare, *Titus Andronicus* (c. 1592), in *William Shakespeare: The Complete Works,* ed. Stanley Wells and Gary Taylor (Oxford: Clarendon Press, 1988), II.3.223 and 281; III.1.53 and 89; IV.1.95; V.2.145.

40. Ibid., III.1.54ff.

41. Ibid., V.3.65.

5

"Why should a dog, a horse, a rat, have life, and thou no breath at all?": Shakespeare's Animations

Erica Sheen

When I first read Stephen Greenblatt's essay "Shakespeare and the Exorcists" in the mid-1980s, my eye was caught by his discussion of Samuel Harsnett's use of the word *corky* in his *A Declaration of Egregious Popish Impostures:* "It would (I feare mee) pose all the cunning Exorcists that are to this day to be found, to teach an old corkie woman to writhe, tumble, curvet, and fetch her morice gamboles."[1] Assuming this "unusual" word to mean "sapless, dry, withered," Greenblatt follows editorial tradition in assuming that *Egregious Popish Impostures* was the source for Shakespeare's use of the word at *King Lear* III.7.31, where Cornwall and Regan seize Gloucester and "bind fast his corky arms" before gouging his eyes out. Greenblatt's account of the process of textual transmission at work here was central to New Historicist methodology in the 1980s and early 1990s: "Harsnett's arguments are alienated from themselves when they make their appearance on the Shakespearean stage. This alienation may be set in the context of a more general observation: the closer Shakespeare seems to a source, the more faithfully he reproduces it on stage, the more devastating and decisive his transformation of it. . . . This one-word instance of repetition as transvaluation may suggest in the tiniest compass what happens to Harsnett's work in the course of *Lear*."[2]

The reason *corky* caught my eye was that I knew it means something completely different from "sapless, dry, withered." Quite the opposite, in fact: *corky* is a technical term used to describe dogs, and in that context it means buoyant, lively, and springy. The question presented itself: could this reading possibly apply to Shakespeare's play? If so, Greenblatt's account of *King Lear*'s relation to Harsnett's book as "a reiteration that signals a deeper and unexpressed institutional exchange" between Shakespearean theater and the Church needs substantial revision. Such a revision is what I undertake in this chapter. First, I offer a contrasting reading of the meanings the word *corky* brings into *King Lear* and then, in a discussion of animal metaphors in *Hamlet* II.2, I offer an alternative account of the process of institutional exchange it records.

❦

The Renaissance already had a well-developed account of textual transmission, and it's noticeable that Stephen Greenblatt did not use it. Studies of imitation, not to mention the related interest in "source studies"—described by Greenblatt as "the elephant's graveyard of literary history"[3]—offered a formalist account of literary production that all but disappeared in the 1980s and 1990s under the onslaught of New Historicism. Yet theories of imitation situate the Renaissance literary text more decisively not only within its historical context but also within the awareness of that context displayed by its own contemporaries. When Francis Bacon defended Sir John Hayward's *The First Part of the Life and Raigne of King Henrie the IIII* against accusations of treason with the assertion that Hayward was guilty only of the lesser crime of felony because "he had stolen many of his sentences and conceits out of Cornelius Tacitus," it was from the theory of imitation that he drew his argument.[4] Imitation provided the conceptual basis for what later emerged as a concept of literary property. As G. W. Pigman III has shown, Renaissance writers identified, contrasted, and evaluated modes of authorial appropriation ranging from gathering, collecting, and borrowing to theft and outright expropriation.[5] These forms of agency were conventionally identified by a range of animal metaphors, notably bees, apes, and crows. The bee metaphor draws on a humanist discourse of an ideal productivity based on Homer, Virgil, and Lucretius; apes and crows are associated with slavish imitation and theft, the latter via the Aesopian fable of the crow and his stolen plumage.

This kind of thinking allies Renaissance theories of imitation with burgeoning interest in the laws of personal property. As John Baker points out, "Readers who chose to lecture on theft were particularly fond of the finer points relating to the ownership of beasts and fish."[6] Filow's Case, an action of trespass brought to the Court of Common Pleas in 1520, provides us with a demonstration of some of those finer points in action.[7] The case was brought by Sir William Filow against Ashley, a servant who was alleged to have stolen one of his bloodhounds and who subsequently pleaded estray in defense. The account we have of this case in the yearbooks is important because it presents a type of argument known as a demurrer, a form of pleading that acknowledges the facts of the case but denies that they are such as to entitle the plaintiff to legal relief. In other words, the participants in this case are initially concerned mainly with the question of whether the action can be brought at all, and as a result they produce a range of speculative arguments that are highly indicative of the status of animals, and ideas about animals, in a society coming to terms with a historical shift from a land-based economy to one based in chattels, or personal property.[8] The crucial argument, advanced by Justice Anthony Fitzherbert, was the common law position that a dog was "a thing of pleasure" and therefore had no value and could not be stolen. However, this position was countered by Justice Richard Broke with a statement of the principle of occupation, the process by which things held in common, like animals, wood, and water, become property when someone enters the territory they inhabit and reduces them into possession:[9]

> At the beginning of the world all beasts were obedient to our first father Adam, and all the four elements were obedient to him; but after he broke the command of our lord God all beasts began to rebel and be wild, and this was punishment for his crime. And now they are in common, *et occupanti conceduntur:* as fowls in the air, fishes in the sea, and beasts upon the land. And when I have taken a fowl, and by my industry I have made it tame by restraint of its liberty, now I have a special property in it, inasmuch as it is made obedient by my own labour, and then it is not legal for anyone to take it.

Justice Richard Elyot responded with a distinction between property and possession. Because the dog has no quantifiable value—unlike a farm animal—it is held in possession, not a property, and if it strays from the place where it is so held it is deemed to have reverted to the wild and to be available to someone else for occupation: "If my horse or cow goes into another county, and a stranger takes it, I would have an action of trespass against him . . . but if my dog goes into another county, and someone takes him, I would not have an action for him because when he is out of my possession I have no property in him." Dogs are thus an exemplary instance of the anxieties of ownership in a changing, uncertain society. Poised unpredictably between liberty and restraint, wildness and obedience, they are defined above all by an Ovidian potential to revert from one to the other. All of which brings me back to Stephen Greenblatt, Samuel Harsnett, and *corky.*

Corky is a technical term associated with dog breeding standards, particularly those of terriers. What it refers to might be seen precisely as the dog's "Ovidian potential": according to international terrier authority Tom Horner, "it describes the type of terrier that is full of life and interest, bouncing with energy and inquisitiveness—in fact like a cork on a rough sea."[10] I have not found examples of the word being used to describe dogs in the sixteenth century, but since this meaning—glossed by the *Oxford English Dictionary* as "buoyant, lively, springy"[11]—is the one the word carries in every instance of its use from 1601, when it was used in that sense by John Marston in *Pasquil and Katharina,* this hardly constitutes a problem for my argument. In fact, the only references for *corky* meaning "sapless, dry, withered" are Harsnett and Shakespeare, and the only reason this meaning rather than the other is allocated to Shakespeare is that his editors have decided he was following Harsnett, so Greenblatt's reading is already weaker than mine.

Could Shakespeare's reproduction of this word be less faithful to Harsnett than Greenblatt suggests? Or has the word *corky,* like Filow's bloodhound, strayed out of Harsnett's possession to become Shakespeare's "special property"? To answer this, we need to look in detail at the episode into which Shakespeare inserts the word, shortly after the beginning of III.7:

> *Corn.* Who's there? the traitor?
> Enter GLOUCESTER, *brought in by two or three.*
> *Reg.* Ingrateful fox! 'tis he.
> *Corn.* Bind fast his corky arms.
> *Glos.* What means your Graces? Good my friends, consider
>   You are my guests. Do me no foul play, friends.
> *Corn.* Bind him, I say.
> *Servants bind him*
> *Reg.* Hard, hard. O filthy traitor!
> *Glos.* Unmerciful lady as you are, I'm none.[12]

The fox reference is followed twenty lines later by Gloucester's identification of himself as a dog-baited bear: "I am tied to the stake and I must stand the course." Nine lines later, Gloucester says, "If wolves had at thy gate howl'd that dern time / Thou shouldst have cried, good porter, turn the key," and then at line 74 Cornwall addresses the servant who tries to protect Gloucester, "How now, you dog!"[13]

Two things can be said about this from the outset. First, even if we suppose that Shakespeare meant Cornwall to describe Gloucester's arms as "sapless, dry, withered" in the spirit of Harsnett, as an insult to his age, the dramatic context ensures that the opposite meaning is also fully active. Gloucester is not a passive victim: he has just returned from helping Lear to find shelter in a night he himself describes as so wild that wild animals would voluntarily submit to occupation in order to escape it, and his own bear metaphor suggests that he has the vigor and strength to resist it.[14] Second, in light of the sheer intensity of reference that clusters around this episode, it is perverse *not* to see *corky* as part of the play's extended system of canine connotation.

Jonathan Bate suggests that dog imagery in *Lear* is presided over by Ovid's version of the story of Hecuba, the wife of Priam, King of Troy. Hecuba witnesses the slaughter of her family when the city falls, runs mad with grief, and is finally transformed into a howling dog.[15] The actions immediately before her metamorphosis parallel and invert the events of *Lear* III.7:

> Upon him speaking so,
> And swearing and forswearing too, she looked sternly then,
> And being sore inflamed with wrath, caught hold upon him, and
> Did in the traitor's face bestow her nails, and scratched out
> His eyes: her anger gave her heart and made her strong and stout.
> She thrust her fingers in as far as could be, and did bore
> Not now his eyes (because his eyes were pulled out before),
> But both the places of his eyes berayed with wicked blood.
> The Thracians at their Tyrant's harm for anger waxing wod,
> Began to scare the Trojan wyves with darts and stones. Anon
> Queen Hecuba running at a stone, with gnarring seized thereon,
> And worried it between her teeth. And as she oped her chap,
> To speak, instead of speech she barked.[16]

It is hard to avoid the conclusion that it was this "old corky woman" who came to Shakespeare's mind when he was working on the Gloucester sub-plot. Her implicit presence in *Lear* opens up the full potential of Ovidian reversion in the story of Gloucester's "taming" and associates that potential with a representation of femininity that contrasts strongly with that provided by Harsnett.

Pace Jonathan Bate, this is not imagery in any conventional sense.[17] Like Filow's Case, it builds up an argument *in utramque partem* that uses animals not just as a metaphorical illustration of a set of particular circumstances but also to embody an investigation of the ethical principles that inform them. Gloucester's point about wolves—"If wolves had at thy gate howl'd that dern time / Thou shouldst have cried, good porter, turn the key"—is repeated, but reworked, by Cordelia later in the play: "Mine enemy's dog / Though he had bit me, should have stood that night / Against my fire."[18] These two related arguments, which one might easily read as different versions of the same case, express a benign version of the principle of occupation that echoes Broke's reading of the process as a recuperation of the Fall. But the possibility that an animal's wildness might function as an expression not of its own nature but of that of its owner exposes the dark side of that reading. John Baker records Inner Temple readings that indicate that "to kill by means of a vicious dog was just as felonious as to kill in person."[19] The legal principle articulated here, known as the fiction of identity of principal and agent, is one that consistently interests Shakespeare and one that he consistently uses dogs to act out in his plays.[20]

Throughout Shakespeare's plays, this fiction emerges as a way not just of thinking about masters and servants but also of prizing open the traditional instrumentality of the relationship. In an earlier play written in 1590–91, well before the formation of the Chamberlain's Men and their move into a permanent home at the Theatre and then at the Globe, Shakespeare had already begun to explore its possible application to the theater profession itself. Lance's monologue about his dog Crab in *The Two Gentleman of Verona*, IV.4, probably was written to showcase the skills of the famous clown Will Kempe, a real-life owner and trainer of performing animals. Lance's relationship of servant to his faithless master, Proteus, is paralleled and inverted in his own relationship to Crab: "When a man's servant shall play the cur with him, look you, it goes hard." Despite his master's training ("I have taught him, even as one would say precisely 'Thus I would teach a dog'") Crab's nature is ultimately, and paradoxically, beastly: "I would have, as one should say, one that takes upon him to be a dog indeed, to be, as it were, a dog at all things." His distinctly corky behavior—stealing a capon's leg from Sylvia's plate while she is eating, pissing underneath the Duke's table—nearly gets him hanged, but for the fact that Lance takes the blame, and subsequent whipping, himself: "How many masters would do this for his servant?" The extremely favorable comparison between dog and master and master and servant is evident only a few lines later, when Proteus asks how Sylvia has received a little lap dog he had sent her, and Lance is forced to admit that he lost it and tried unsuccessfully to give her Crab instead. His explanation comically discredits the fiction of the identity of principal and agent (it's clearly impossible to pass Crab off as Proteus's "little jewel") and in doing so, like Filow's Case, exposes the gap opening within the master-servant relationship under the historical pressure of changes in the laws of property: "The other squirrel was stolen from me by the hangman boys in the market place, and then I offered her mine own, who is a dog as big as ten of yours, and therefore the gift the greater." Proteus's response to his servant is as nasty, within the play's own generic parameters, as the later cruelties of *Lear:* "Go get thee hence, and find my dog again / Or ne'er return again into my sight."[21] And just as Lear's "poor fool" is later to disappear from the action of *Lear* after his or her encounter with a hangman, we never see either of them again.[22]

Like the dogs in *Lear*, Lance's monologue derives its affective power from the fact that, however beastly their own behavior, these animals are not only innocent in comparison with the human beings who take them into possession but also mortally endangered by them. Cordelia's argument about how to treat "mine enemy's dog" has a strong explanatory relation not just to the events of the play but also to the questions of principle, or "reason," they raise. In this respect it recalls the "special cases" that illustrate the dialogues between Christopher St. German's Doctor and Student, like the one that opens a discussion of "the law of secondary reason," so called because "it is founded not only upon reason, but also upon the aforesaid law or custom of property, and upon the reason derived from property." In response to the Doctor's request, the Student expounds an example concerning a distress for rent service in which a tenant's animals are impounded until the arrears are settled but then allowed to die: "And thereupon may be asked this question, that if the beasts die in pound for lack of meat, at whose peril die they; whether die they at the peril of him that distreined or of him that oweth the beasts?"[23] At whose "peril" is it that Cordelia dies in prison? That of the dutiful servant whom Lear finds hanging her? Or Lear himself, who deprives her of her property in the kingdom and thus puts her in the position of having to enter the country as a foreign invader and suffer the consequences of military defeat? When Lear and Cordelia are taken away to prison, Cordelia reminds us that she is a Queen, not just a daughter: "For thee, oppressed King, am I cast down."[24] Her last words invite an appropriately courtly interview with her captors: "Shall we not see these daughters and these sisters?" But Lear brushes it aside, imagining instead that the space they are about to occupy is domestic, intimate and safe. In doing so, he helps seal her fate:

> No, no, no, no. Come, let's away to prison.
> We two alone will sing like birds i'th' cage.
>   . . . so we'll live
> And pray and sing and tell old tales and laugh
> At gilded butterflies, and hear poor rogues
> Talk of court news, and we'll talk with them too. . . .
> He that parts us shall bring a brand from heaven
> And fire us hence like foxes.[25]

His bird metaphor is indicative. In Filow's Case, sergeants-at-law John Newport and John Newdiegate counter the argument that a thing of pleasure is without value with the example of singing birds: "Although this dog is a thing of pleasure, it is also profitable for hunting, or for my recreation. For if I have a popinjay or thrush, which sings and refreshes my spirits, that is a great comfort for me, and if anyone takes it away from me, he does me a great wrong, and for that it is required that he be punished." The fact that singing birds have value because they are a "comfort" reminds us of Lear's intentions toward Cordelia at the beginning of the play. Despite the fact that he is about to give her away in marriage, he tells Kent that he had "thought to set my rest / On her kind nursery."[26] Lear's division of the kingdom thus reveals itself as a way of securing a property in his daughter rather than endowing her as a wife, and his metaphor of singing birds suggests that these fatal intentions remain essentially unchanged. His fox metaphor, a last glimpse of dogs driven violently from their homes by humans, evokes the cycle of dispossession he has released into the play.

❧

What is the connection between the way animal metaphors bring ideas about property into Shakespeare's plays and the part they play in Shakespeare's creation of his own special property in theater? I've glanced at this question in the previous discussion, but to answer it more fully we can look back to an earlier engagement with the Hecuba story: a monologue, like Lance's, in which we are invited to witness a demonstration of the player's art and to think about the professional status of Shakespearean theater in its contemporary society. By 1601 Shakespeare's status as the leading writer for a company generally acknowledged to be "the best in this kind" was well assured.[27] In *Hamlet* the skills he showcases are those of the First Player, not the Clown, and his concern is not to draw comic capital from the audience's recognition of the player's social position as a servant but to assert the Player's mastery within the theater and his profession.

When the Tragedians of the City enter the Danish court in II.2, Hamlet asks the First Player to perform "Aeneas' Tale to Dido," the story of the Fall of Troy and the death of Priam: "We'll e'en to it like French falc'ners, fly at anything we see. We'll have a speech straight. Come, give us a taste of your quality. Come, a passionate speech."[28] The hawking metaphor is indicative from the outset: unlike a bloodhound that strays from its territory, "if a tamed bird of prey were let fly at a quarry, not only did the bird remain the property of its owner, but the quarry if taken also became his."[29] But Hamlet himself cannot make this material obedient to his labor: he has to hand it over to a superior performer. Appropriately for one who has repudiated the uses of memory, he doesn't remember his lines and is forced to correct himself before conceding the stage to the First Player. However, the line he "gets wrong"—"The rugged Pyrrhus, like th'Hyrcanian beast"—brings to the fore the theory of imitation, its animal imagery and the issues they both raise about questions of property. As such, it marks the beginning of the First Player's performance with an assertive statement of ownership. This "accidental" reference to the Hyrcanian beast is one of the first markers of the presence in this speech of a source text: Marlowe and Nashe's *Tragedie of Dido,* in which Dido berates Aeneas for his hard-hearted decision to leave her and sail for Italy:

Thy mother was no goddess, perjured man,
Nor Dardanus the author of thy stock:
But thou art sprung from Scythian Caucasus
And tigers of Hircania gave thee sucke.[30]

Dido was published in 1594 with a title page that claims it was acted by the Chapel Children, the children's company that became fashionable in London at the turn of the century, which Hamlet discusses with Rosencrantz and Guildenstern earlier in the scene. There is thus much at stake when Shakespeare refers to this source in a speech intended to vindicate the superior quality of an adult company. The reference encapsulates a complex self-consciousness about its own process of appropriation: it glances back at Robert Greene's famous use of Aesop's fable of the crow to describe Shakespeare's invasion of the London theater: "An upstart Crow, beautified with our feathers, that with his Tiger's heart wrapt in a Player's hide, supposes he is as well able to bombast out a blank verse as the best of you and being an absolute Johannes *fac totum,* is in his own conceit the only Shake-scene in the country."[31] Here, Greene parodies Shakespeare's line from *3 Henry VI,* "O tiger's heart wrapped in a woman's hide!," which was itself followed eighteen lines later by a less ambitious earlier borrowing from *Dido:* "But you are more inhuman, more inexorable / O, ten times more than tigers of Hyrcania."[32] Because Greene's attack on Shakespeare is generally held to be addressed to Marlowe, Nashe, and Peele, it's clear that what we are looking at in *Hamlet* is not just an appropriation of a source but a reflection on that process of appropriation as it institutionalizes across time into a competitive mode of production. From Shakespeare's innocent first "borrowing" to Greene's aggressive accusation of theft and Shakespeare's subsequent act of outright expropriation, this process marks the entire range of authorial agency identified by Pigman.[33] Shakespeare is not just flying at the work of his fellow dramatist; he has taken his quarry. By supplying the source as a mistake that is immediately eliminated, Shakespeare gives not just an example but a performance of the process by which he takes into possession things that stray from other people's theatrical space. It is from this confident and assertive position that the Player's narrative moves toward its focus on Hecuba:

But who, O who had seen the mobbled queen— . . .
Run barefoot up and down, threat'ning the flames
With bisson rheum; a clout upon that head
Where late the diadem stood, and for a robe,
About her lank and all o'er-teemed loins,
A blanket in th'alarm of fear caught up—

Who this had seen, with tongue in venom steep'd
'Gainst Fortune's state would treason have pronounc'd.
But if the gods themselves did see her then,
When she saw Pyrrhus make malicious sport
In mincing with his sword her husband's limbs
The instant burst of clamour that she made
Unless things mortal move them not at all,
Would have made milch the burning eyes of heaven
And passion in the gods.[34]

Analyzing this part of the speech as if it were film helps us identify its complex internal structure of visualization and to convey how conceptually advanced this structure is within the simple spatial resource of early modern theater. It presents something like an embedded point-of-view sequence that combines a range of subjective and objective positions within a general position of spectatorship.[35] Hecuba is visually placed by an unspecified point of view ("who had seen") but is herself both the subject of a point of view on Pyrrhus ("when she saw"), and the object of one by "the gods themselves" ("did see her then"). The speech thus sets up a theatrical deep focus that maps the internal spatial relations within the speech and the agencies of performance and spectatorship that produce them. The Player's occupation of this space and its inhabitants is predicated on his ability to "tame" Hecuba—to put her before his audience's imagination and keep her there. However, his property in her is predicated not on her obedience but rather on her Ovidian potential to revert to wildness. At the center of this complex visual field is her "burst of clamour." If Hecuba's naked frenzy recalls a terrified stray, her cry brings into the text an anticipation of what she would finally become: an old abandoned dog howling in sorrow in the wilds of Thrace. Her movement out of language and beyond is followed by the Player himself. He breaks off, in tears, and Hamlet excuses him the rest of the speech.

In what sense, then, does this speech constitute a demonstration of "quality"? As a form of master-servant relationship, the acting profession was both an exemplary instance of the fiction of identity of principal and agent and, particularly in the hands of Shakespearean theater, one of the institutional means by which this social narrative was progressively discredited in the social and economic revolution of the late sixteenth and early seventeenth centuries. Conventionally, early modern theater based its pleasures and comforts on a safe balance between the two: a level of skill convincing enough to sustain the equivalence of actor and character, accompanied by a facile exposure of the underlying difference between the two,[36] as in the comic "woman's part" of the 1590s, with its structural insistence on its own "lack." But this speech provides a blueprint for an approach to female characterization that refuses to be dutiful, refuses to collapse back onto a servant's acknowledgment that he is, after all, only a servant. It does this in two ways. First, it uses a literary mode that does not have to replace a woman with a man; second, it emphasizes the potentiality thus released in the female character by aligning her with the animal rather than the human. As Crab so eloquently shows, animals were the only performers in early modern theater whose "characters" could not short-circuit back into a male actor's position of enunciation. "Aeneas' Tale to Dido" thus offers an identity between a female third person that bypasses the limitations of the "woman's part" and pure theatrical presence.

We might approach this technique of characterization in terms of the cinematic concept of special effect, a parallel that is strengthened by the fact that, in contemporary Hollywood as in Shakespeare, this approach to representation extends the agencies of theatrical performance beyond the institutionally defined limits of what counts as human. Indeed, I might follow my earlier reservations about the term *imagery* and suggest that when Shakespeare uses animals in the way I have been discussing in this chapter, what he is doing might more appropriately be seen as a kind of animation. These animations supply an alterity that is fundamental to Shakespeare's innovative female characterization. To the extent that he addresses the animal as a potential within the human, he is also able to address women as a potential for Shakespearean theater rather than a lack within it.

From a contemporary perspective, such a conclusion may encourage us to assimilate our readings of Shakespeare's animals into ethical critical approaches, just as his characterizations of women have long been assimilated into feminist approaches. But my argument here has been that they must, at least in the first instance, be approached in institutional terms. For Shakespeare, their function was, above all, to elicit a quality of performance that distinguished the theatrical experience available to members of Shakespeare's audiences from that offered by his competitors. As the Tragedians of the City could testify, success in the precarious profession of early modern theater depended on developing skills that would convince customers to prefer one play, one company, to another. In Filow's Case, Broke's argument that human industry is the basis of personal property leads to an acknowledgment that such industry will inevitably result in some people being more successful than others: "If an artificer acquires for himself more customers than another of the same art, for instance a Scrivener, or a Schoolmaster who has more pupils than another because he is more erudite, this is damage to the other but not an injury, because each man should prefer himself, and it is not punishable." Shakespeare's adaptation of contemporary debates about animals to create a "special property" in theater helps us understand how the case of a stolen bloodhound might inevitably lead to a discussion of monopoly.[37] Yet the passion and sympathy they unfailingly evoke would soon begin to relocate these values from the economic sphere to that of the modern discipline of philosophy, which Shakespeare seems so unfailingly to anticipate. From *Hamlet* and *Lear*, with their complex legal arguments about liberty and property, we might look forward to Enlightenment thinkers such as John Locke and David Hume and glimpse an expanded understanding of human life as part of a larger nature and "reason" as evidence of the animal in us rather than the god. It is in Shakespeare that this understanding begins to be animated. When Lear asks "Why should a dog, a horse, a rat, have life, / And thou no breath at all?" our sense that Cordelia has a "life," that her character does not collapse onto the limited historical stylizations of a squeaking boy, depends to a considerable extent on the perception that the space of Shakespearean theater is occupied by dogs, horses, and rats as well as people.

NOTES

1. Stephen Greenblatt, "Shakespeare and the Exorcists," in *Shakespeare and the Question of Theory*, ed. Patricia Parker and Geoffrey Hartman (New York: Methuen, 1985), 178.

2. Ibid., 178.

3. Ibid., 163.

4. This comment is recorded in *Apophthegms New and Old*, in *Letters and Life*, ed. James Spedding (London: Longman, Green, Longman and Roberts, 1861–74), III, 150.

5. G. W. Pigman III, "Versions of Imitation in the Renaissance," *Renaissance Quarterly* 33:1 (Spring 1980): 1–32.

6. J. H. Baker, "Introduction," in *The Reports of Sir John Spelman*, ed. J. H. Baker (London: Selden Society, 1977), II, 212. See also 317–18.

7. All references to Filow's Case are from the entry for 1520 in *The Reports del Cases, De Termino Trinitatis*, 3–4 (my translations). These yearbooks, which ended on Michaelmas in 1535, were frequently reprinted in the Elizabethan period. After 1558, they were printed by the law printer Richard Totell as single-year volumes and by other printers between 1590 and 1610 as collections. J. H. Baker comments on this case in *Reports*.

8. As Anthony Fitzherbert, one of the justices involved in Filow's Case, acknowledged seven years later, "common law and common reason consider goods, chattels and money, as highly as land, for many people who do not have lands have goods and money of as great value as land" (cited in Baker, *Reports*, 209).

9. For an account of the principle of occupation, see J. H. Baker, "How Personal Property Arises," in Baker, *An Introduction to English Legal History*, 3d ed. (London: Butterworths, 1990), 429.

10. From a letter to me by Tom Horner. See also Horner, *Terriers of the World* (London: Faber and Faber, 1983).

11. The word does not appear in early modern dictionaries.

12. William Shakespeare, *King Lear,* III.7.27–33. All references to Shakespeare plays are from *The Norton Shakespeare,* ed. Stephen Greenblatt, Walter Cohen, Jean E. Howard, and Katherine Eisaman Maus (New York: W. W. Norton, 1997). For convenience, references to *King Lear* are taken from their Conflated Text.

13. Ibid., III.7.53, 62, 74.

14. In an earlier reference that appears to encapsulate both positions, the Gentleman describes the night as one "wherein the cub-drawn bear would couch, / The lion and belly-pinchèd wolf / Keep their fur dry." Ibid., III.1.12–14.

15. Jonathan Bate, *Shakespeare and Ovid* (Oxford: Clarendon, 1993), 191.

16. W. H. D. Rouse, ed., *The XV Bookes of P. Ovidius Naso, entytuled Metamorphosis translated oute of Latin into English meeter, by Arthur Golding Gentleman* (London: Centaur Press, 1961), Book 13, 669–81 (my modernization).

17. Bate, *Shakespeare and Ovid,* 191.

18. Shakespeare, *King Lear,* IV.7.36–38.

19. Baker, *Reports,* 308.

20. This fiction is expressed in the Latin maxim "qui facit per alium, facit per se": "He who acts through another acts for himself." Its primary force is to identify legal liability in actions undertaken by someone on behalf of someone else. In an early modern context, it had a particular bearing on the actions of wives and servants because they were not held to have legal capacity in their own right.

21. Shakespeare, *Two Gentlemen of Verona,* IV.4.3–4, 5, 11, 25, 47–50, 51–52.

22. Shakespeare, *King Lear,* V.3.303. The ambiguity of the reference—does he mean his fool, or Cordelia?—has been noted.

23. Christopher St. German, *Doctor and Student* (English editions, 1531–32), ed. T. F. T. Plucknett and J. L. Barton (London: Selden Society, 1974), Dialogue I, 35. Writing only a year or so later, Protestant preacher Hugh Latimer recorded the fact that human prisoners could suffer a similar fate: "I had rather be in Purgatory than in the bishop of London's prison; for in this I might die bodily for lack of meat; in that I could not." From "Articles Untruly, Unjustly, Falsely, Uncharitably Imputed to Me" (1533), in *Sermons and Remains,* ed. G. E. Corrie (London: Parker Society, 1845), 236, cited in Stephen Greenblatt, *Hamlet in Purgatory* (Princeton, N.J.: Princeton University Press, 2001), 34.

24. Shakespeare, *King Lear,* V.3.5.

25. Ibid., V.3.8–23.

26. Ibid., I.1.123–24.

27. Shakespeare, *A Midsummer Night's Dream,* V.1.208.

28. Shakespeare, *Hamlet,* II.2.413–14.

29. Baker, *Reports,* 210.

30. Christopher Marlowe and Thomas Nashe, *Tragedie of Dido* (1594), in *The Works of Christopher Marlowe,* ed. C. F. Tucker Brooke (Oxford: Clarendon, 1966), V.1., 1564–67.

31. Robert Greene, *Greenes Groats-worth of Wit* (1596), in *Life and Complete Work,* ed. A. B. Grosart (New York: Russell and Russell, 1881–96), XII.

32. Shakespeare, *3 Henry VI,* 1.4.138, 155–56.

33. In "The 'Upstart Crow,' Aesop's Crow, and Shakespeare as a Reviser," *Shakespeare Quarterly* 35: 2 (Summer 1984): 205–7, Peter Berek adduces the evidence of parallel passages to suggest contrasting readings of the "upstart crow" as a mere actor, speaking lines written for him by someone else, and a plagiarist trying to pass off as his own the work of other writers. He provides additional evidence for the latter and concludes that "this 'plagiarism' may have come about by Shakespeare's working as an adapter or reviser." Useful as these distinctions are, they can all be subsumed into the process of institutional appropriation I describe earlier.

34. Shakespeare, *Hamlet,* II.2.482, 485–98.

35. For an account of "point of view" in film see Edward Branigan, *Point of View in the Cinema: A Theory of Narration and Subjectivity in Classical Film* (New York: Mouton, 1984).

36. Shakespeare's comic representations of theater—as in Hal and Falstaff's improvisations in the Eastcheap Tavern and the Mechanical's rehearsals and performance of "Pyramus and Thisbe"—invariably play on the contradictory relationship between the two.

37. By the time of *Hamlet,* legal debate about monopoly was no longer as restrained as it was in 1520. The period from the mid-1590s to the end of Elizabeth's reign, during which the Chamberlain's Men consolidated their leading status in the profession, was characterized by an aggressive proliferation of monopolies. They were attacked as a grievance in the parliaments of 1597 and 1601, and in a decisive case in 1602 a patent for sole right to make and sell playing cards was declared void on the basis that it transgressed precisely the principle identified by Broke, that it was an "injury" to others already engaged in this business. Monopolies continued to cause offense until Coke's bill of 1621, enacted in 1624, declaring all monopolies void except those that could genuinely be presented as a defense of innovation. In approaching Shakespearean theater as monopolistic, I seek to situate it specifically within this historical context.

❧ 6

Government by Beagle: The Impersonal Rule of James VI and I

Alan Stewart

To James VI and I, his principal secretary and later lord treasurer Sir Robert Cecil, earl of Salisbury, was almost invariably "my little beagle."[1] Thirty-five surviving letters from king to minister open with the greeting,[2] and in them James elaborated on the theme, praising his "little cankered beagle," "my patient beagle," the "king's best beagle if he hunte well now in the hard ways," and "the little beagle that lies at home by the fire."[3] James was notorious for providing epithets and nicknames for his counselors; he also had a "fat chancellor," a "little, saucy constable," and a "tall, black and cat-faced keeper," who together made up a "trinity of knaves."[4] Cecil himself shifted moniker "from Beagle to Tom Derry, from Tom Derry to Parrot";[5] when he balked at being dubbed the king's "littell foole," the earl of Worcester reminded him that he was also known as "a parrot-monger, a monkee-monger, and twentee other names."[6] Despite his annoyance, Cecil played along with his master's name games, dutifully referring to himself as James's beagle, as when he protested to Sir Thomas Lake that the king's "monkey loves him not better than his beagle, nor his Great Commissioner in Scotland more than his little Secretary."[7] Frederick Henry Marcham, who first collected what he dubbed the "Little Beagle Letters," saw them as no more than a piece of whimsy on the part of a characteristically trivial sovereign: "The name 'Little Beagle,' like the 'Little Beagle' correspondence, was not a mark of special friendship or favor; it was nothing but a product of James' frivolous and trifling manner."[8] In this chapter, by contrast, I shall take seriously James's characterization of Cecil as "my little beagle" and suggest that through this "frivolous and trifling" nomenclature we might understand something of the very particular nature of James's chosen style of government in the first decade of his English reign, a style in which hunting played a significant role.

❧

It is now a historiographical commonplace to note that James's accession to the English throne produced an important shift in the constitution of the offices nearest to the sovereign and therefore to the style of government.[9] In a 1977 essay, David Starkey argued that the Privy Chamber's power was founded in its access to the king's body; therefore, Starkey argued, there was "a coherent and developed system of symbolism, centered on the human body: the king's person was the most expressive symbol of his office; the persons of his body servants were the fullest representation of their master; and finally, the mechanism by which this latter representation was achieved—the symbolism of intimate attendance—was a kind of body symbolism as well."[10] Starkey's arguments for body symbolism were influentially developed in the collection of essays *The English Court,* where shifts of personal rule by sovereign are registered.[11] Under Henry VIII, the functions of the royal household were crucially divided at the door of the Privy Chamber, and within the Privy Chamber, there were the more private Privy Lodgings centering on the king's Bedchamber. By contrast, Elizabeth's gender meant that the Privy Lodgings, where she spent much of her time, were divided from the Privy Chamber by a Withdrawing Chamber, and as a result the Privy Chamber became more formal. With James's accession to the throne, however, came what Neil Cuddy influentially dubbed "the revival of the entourage."[12]

Under the new king, "the Bedchamber displaced the Privy Chamber as the focus of the monarch's private life. . . . The balance of power swung away, increasingly, from the Privy Council and a bureaucrat-minister toward the Bedchamber and the royal favourite." The Bedchamber "took over the whole of the king's intimate, informal service," and the Privy Chamber was "left only with the formal and the ceremonial—and not even very much of that." Whereas attempts were made to keep the Privy Chamber roughly half Scots and half English, the Bedchamber was made up almost entirely of Scottish courtiers, with the sole exception of Sir Philip Herbert.[13]

It was the absolute dominance of Scots in the Bedchamber that particularly galled English commentators such as Gervase Holles, who wrote of James bringing with him "a crew of necessitous and hungry Scots" and filling "every corner of the Court with theis beggarly blew caps."[14] His kinsman Sir John Holles complained in 1610 that "the Scottish monopolize his princely person, standing like mountains betwixt the beams of his grace and us," urging that "his Majesty his Bedchamber may be shared as well to those of our nation as to them."[15] The exclusion from the Bedchamber had serious administrative implications. Because the household ordinances stated that "no person of what condition soever do at any time presume or be admitted to come to us in our Bed-Chamber, but such as . . . are . . . sworn of it, without our special licence, except the Princes of Our Blood,"[16] as Cuddy points out, "this effectively excluded on a routine basis the greater and lesser officers of state and the Privy Council from that access to the king which the Bed-chamber's own personnel exclusively and routinely enjoyed." Even Secretaries of State were granted audiences in the (outer) Privy Chamber or Withdrawing Chamber, with the king emerging from his (inner) Bedchamber for the purpose.[17] In summary, Cuddy writes, "With the institution of the Bedchamber, even the inner councillors no longer had an automatic claim to the nearest access to the monarch; and even if the *entrée* were granted, it was enjoyed in much greater measure by the Bedchamber's staff. . . . Now . . . the Bedchamber did possess special advantages of contact with the king; Bedchamber and Council were now separate entities with, for the most part, separate membership; Council and minister now revolved in a different orbit from the king and Bedchamber."[18] This state of affairs would have been aggravating enough but manageable if James had remained in his Bedchamber at Whitehall. But the king was more often than not somewhere else. When James made the journey south to London upon his accession in 1603, expectations were high. "Our vertuous Kinge makes our hopes to swell; his actions sutable to the tyme and his natural disposition," wrote Thomas Wilson enthusiastically in June. But it was soon discovered that James's "natural disposition" led him away from what many regarded as his kingly duties. "Sometymes he comes to Counsell," Wilson continued, "but most tyme he spends in fieldes and parkes and chaces, chasinge away idlenes by violent exercise and early risinge, wherin the Sune seldom prevents him."[19] Or as a less partisan commentator, the Venetian ambassador, put it, "The King, in spite of all the heroic virtues ascribed to him when he left Scotland and inculcated by him in his books, seems to have sunk into a lethargy of pleasures, and will not take heed of matters of state. He remits everything to the Council, and spends his time in the house alone, or in the country at the chase."[20]

Hunting had been a passion for James since his adolescence. He recommended a range of sports to his son Henry in his *Basilikon Doron,* but it was hunting to which he gave special praise, deeming it "martial" and "noble," "speciallie with running hounds, which is the most honorable and noblest sort thereof," although he acknowledged that he might well be considered "a partiall praiser of this sport."[21] Not that James was necessarily adept at the sport: the Lancashire gentleman Nicholas Assheton reported one afternoon of royal hunting during the August 1617 progress. James, he recorded in his journal, "went and shott at a stagg, and missed. Then my Lord Compton had lodged two brace. The King shott again, and brake the thigh-bone. A dogg long in coming, and my Lord Compton shott again and killed him."[22] Nevertheless, hunting was James's passion.

Within months of his accession, James had established small hunting lodges at Newmarket and Royston—not far from London, but far enough for him to be distant from the mechanics of government. For whereas Elizabeth on her lengthy summer processes was followed, albeit with reluctance, by her entire court including the Privy Council, James took off for the fields with only what Dudley Carleton dismissed as "his hunting crew" in tow,[23] a crew the Venetian ambassador described as "a few persons only, and those always the same, people of low degree, as is usual in that exercise."[24] It has been calculated that throughout his entire reign in England, James spent "about half his time" either at his hunting lodges or on progress, and at the lodges he took with him only "a small household composed of one or two clerks, the Guard, the Privy Chamber, and, above all, the Bedchamber."[25] This was not the English way, as the Venetian ambassador noted: James was "more inclined to live retired with eight or ten of his favourites than openly, as is the custom of the country and the desire of the people."[26]

When challenged, James cited his health as the reason for hunting—to escape the unhealthy environs of London and the sedentary life it entailed. "I shall never take longer vacancy from them," he told Cecil to assure his Council, "for the necessary maintenance of my health, than other kings will consume upon their physical diets and going to their whores."[27] In February 1605, the Venetian ambassador Nicolo Molin reported in cipher how James had written a letter to his Privy Council

> in which he tells that having been recently for nearly three weeks in London he finds this sedentary life very prejudicial to his health for in Scotland he was used to spend much time in the country and in hard exercise, and he finds that repose robs him of his appetite and breeds melancholy and a thousand other ills. He says he is bound to consider his health before all things, and so he must tell them [the Council] that for the future he means to come to London but seldom, passing most of the time in the country in the chase; and as he will thus be far away from Court he cannot attend to business, and so he commits all to them, relying fully on their goodness and polity.

According to Molin, James went on to conclude "by announcing that he will approve all their resolutions. In this way the King has virtually given full and absolute authority to the Council, and has begun to put his plan in practice, for many who went to him with petitions and grievances have been told to go to the Council, for they are fully authorized to deal with all business public and private."[28]

James imagined that he had struck a perfect trade-off: the Privy Council would be given a free hand, and he would be allowed to get his country exercise. But in practice the Privy Council was not confident of its power to bypass the king and was forced constantly to attempt to win the king's

attention while he was on hunting trips—no mean feat. The earl of Worcester, one of James's inner sanctum, attended the hunting crew at Royston in
December 1604. Writing to Shrewsbury, he complained,

> I think I have not had two hours of twenty-four of rest but Sundays, for in
> the morning we are on horseback by eight, and so continue in full career from
> the death of one hare to another, until four at night; by that time I find at my
> lodging sometimes one, most commonly two packets of letters, all which must
> be answered before I sleep, for here is none of the Council but myself, no, not
> a Clerk of the Council nor Privy Signet, so that an ordinary warrant for post
> horse must pass my own hand, my own secretary being sick at London.[29]

James's absences thus caused huge problems for his principal counselors,
especially because he often refused to deal with any official paperwork.
Henry Howard, earl of Northampton, had to beg Sir Thomas Lake to persuade the king to deal with a grant to appoint a new keeper of Carlisle Castle while understanding that "the king is reluctant to sign grants during his
recreations."[30] Very early in the new reign, Cecil lamented the change of
regime from the time of Elizabeth: "I wishe I waited now in her presence-
chamber, with ease at my foode, and reste in my bedde. I am pushed from
the shore of comforte, and know not where the wyndes and waves of a court
will bear me."[31] In time, Council and king came to an agreement. Sir Thomas
Lake recalled how James sent for him in 1608 "in a very pleasant humour"
and told him "that he had kept his word with his Council, by being parsi-
monious, and not troubling them with directions, and they had performed
their part by leaving him quietly to his sports."[32]

Whereas the Privy Council encountered administrative problems, James's
hunting was increasingly unpopular with the wider public for other reasons. Molin, the Venetian ambassador, recorded how James's trips were "the
cause of indescribable ill-humour among the King's subjects, who in their
needs and troubles find themselves cut off from their natural sovereign, and
forced to go before Council, which is full of rivalry and discord, and frequently is guided more by personal interest than by justice and duty."[33] By
May 1606, the people were making their feelings felt. "The people desire to
see their sovereign," wrote another Venetian envoy. "The discontent has
reached such a pitch that the other day there was affixed to the door of the
Privy Council a general complaint of the king, alleging that his excessive
kindness leaves his subjects a prey to the cupidity of his ministers. The king
read it with some annoyance, and showed it to those who were about him.
The expressions did not go beyond a paternal warning to the king not to
give his subjects further cause for acting so that he should have to complain
of them."[34]

While those at court condemned his absence, those near him in the country mourned his presence. The royal trampling of local farmers' fields was a constant source of contention. One Thetford farmer, "highly offended at the liberty his majesty took in riding over his corn, in the transport of his passion threatened to bring an action of trespass against the king," a threat that led to a permanent withdrawal of royal favor from the town.[35] Samuel Calvert was grateful when the weather denied the king "his common Exercise" and therefore lessened "somewhat the ordinary Complaints of poor Country Farmers to endure continual Wrong, by the hunting Spoyls, and Misgovernment of the unruly Traine."[36] The Venetian ambassador noted that "whenever he goes a-hunting the crops are mostly ruined."[37] Even Godfrey Goodman, chaplain to Queen Anna, singled out hunting as an evil in his 1616 sermon *The Fall of Man,* identifying the damage done to the poor tenants of farmland: "the high waies cannot alwaies containe them, but over the hedges and ditches; here begins the crie and the curse of the poore tenant, who sits at a hard rent, and sees his corne spoyled."[38]

In December 1604, the accusations reached the king. Matthew Hutton, archbishop of York, wrote to Cecil, charging James with neglecting his duties, undue extravagance, and an over-liberal use of his privilege of purveyance. At length, he came to the subject of the king's hunting: "As for other thinges (as I confesse) I am not to deale in State matters, yet as one that honoreth, & loveth his most excellent majestie with all my hart, I wish lesse wastinge of the treasure of the realme, & more moderacion in the lawfull exercise of huntinge both that poore mens corne may be lesse spoiled & other his Majesties subjectes more spared."[39] While carefully admitting that hunting was "lawfull," Hutton gave voice to the complaint of James's people that their crops were being ruined by the king and his "hunting crew" galloping across their fields.

When James read Hutton's letter, the earl of Worcester recorded, "he was merry at the first but when he came to the wasting of the treasure and the immoderate exercise of hunting began to alter countenance and said it was the foolishest letter that ever he read."[40] Cecil's response, which he had written even before the king saw the first letter (presumably knowing what his reaction would be concerning this delicate subject), was firm:

> for your last poynt in your lettre concerninge huntinge, seinge I perceive you have so unsecret clarkes, as they are like to make my lettre as common as your owne; my ende beinge only now in serious thinges to shew you in private what I am to you as well as to my selfe. I thinke it impertinent to spend any tyme in discourse of it. least men that see the passages betwixt us, may thinke that yow & I doe, both of us forgett our accoumpt for our other talents, we have in keep-

einge. And this shalbe my conclusion, that it was a praise in the good Emper-
our Trajan: to be disposed to such manlike & active Recreacions. so ought it
to be a joy to us to beholde our kinge of so able a constitucion, promisinge so
longe life, & blessed with so plentifull a posteritie, as hath freed our mindes
from all those feares which had besiedge this potent Monarchie; for lacke of
publique declaracion of his lineall & lawfull succession to the same, whilest it
pleased god to continew to the fullnes of dayes our late soveraign of famous
memorie. And so for this tyme I conclude.[41]

James praised Cecil for this response: "I am thoroughly pleased with your
answer," he wrote, "and specially concerning my hunting ye have answered
it according to my heart's desire, for a scornful, answerless answer became
best such a senseless proposition."[42] Yet York's "senseless proposition" evidently chafed the king nonetheless. In a later letter, he acclaimed a "miracle" that he had noticed: "Notwithstanding that the ancient, reverend father of York hath reprehended the king's hunting, yet hath the king lately
received out of York House [which belonged to the archbishop of York but
was traditionally leased to the lord chancellor] the allowance of his hunting by very many hands, and so it is like the miracle of Balaam's Ass that
the house is wiser than the great prophet that is owner thereof."[43]

Complaints about James's hunting were almost always complaints about
James's style of government—or, more properly, his failure to govern because of his absence. At the same time, with his characteristic delight in accentuating the traits that most annoyed those around him, James adopted
hunting as the overarching metaphor for his activities. In March 1605, he
defined his kingly activities as the hunting of "witches, prophets, puritans,
dead cats and hares." Time was measured by the successfully tracked quarry:
James signed off, "so going to bed, after the death of six hares, a pair of fowls,
and a heron."[44] His new favorites were those who distinguished themselves
at the hunt, not at court or in government. It was no accident that Sir Philip
Herbert, the first Englishman to be admitted to the Bedchamber, was remarked, in Clarendon's words, for "his skill, and indefatigable industry in
hunting" and that he "pretended to no other qualifications than to understand horses and dogs very well."[45] Robert Carr, later earl of Somerset,
grabbed the king's attention by falling off a horse and for "his great perfection in loving field-sports";[46] George Villiers, later duke of Buckingham, first
entered the royal orbit as he joined the king hunting at Apethorpe.[47]

In this economy, being the master's top dog was the highest compliment:
James's last favorite, Villiers, wrote wistfully of "the time which I shall never
forget at Farnham, where the bed's head could not be found between the
master and his dog," and he signed himself "Your majesty's most humble

slave and dog."[48] The seventeenth-century dog, like his twenty-first-century descendant, could easily be man's best friend. Edward Topsell opined in *The Historie of Foure-footed Beastes,*

> There is not any creature without reason more loving to his Maister, nor more serviceable . . . then is a Dogge induring many stripes patiently at the hands of his maister, and using no other means to pacifie his displeasure, then humiliation, prostration, assentation, and after beating, turneth a revenge into a more fervent and whot love. In their rage they will set upon all strangers, yet heerein appeareth their Noble spirit, for if any fall, or sit downe on the ground & cast away his weapon, they bite him not; taking that declining for submissive pacification. They meete their maister with reverence and joy, crouching or bending a little, (like shamefast and modest persons:) and although they know none but their maisters and familiars, yet they will help any man against another Wilde beast. They remember voyces, and obey their leaders hissing or whistling.[49]

It might be objected to this rosy picture that the early modern dog, as Mark Jenner has shown, was easily vilified. Dogs were the first scapegoats in any clampdown against plague in London: the preliminary steps, according to one Venetian envoy, were "to kill the dogs and mark the houses."[50] A summer 1563 mayoral proclamation prohibited unleashed dogs in the street, on pain of a fine of three shillings and fourpence for the owner and death for the dog.[51] A proclamation from 1592 laid out the terms more starkly: "Noe person . . . shall kepe any dogg, or bitche, but such as they will keepe within there owne doores, withowt suffering them to goe loose in the streets, not ledd in slippe or lyne, nor within there owne doores making howling or other annoyaunce to there neyghbours. And that the Common hunts man shall have speciall chardge to kill every dogg or Bitch, as shalbe found loose in any streete or lane. . . . And if he be remisse and negligent, and wittingly spare and shewe favour in not killing any such dogge or Bitche, he shall loose his place and service, and suffer Imprisonmente."[52] But, as Jenner notes, "crucially it was *dogs* that they slaughtered, not other members of the canine commonwealth. Ladies lap-dogs and the hounds of the gentry were specifically excluded from these regulations," so in 1590 London aldermen granted "greyhounds [and] spanyelles" immunity from the general dog-cull.[53] Of course, the canines with whom James hunted were very definitely hounds, not dogs.

When his queen, Anna of Denmark, wanted to gain the upper hand over the king, she knew where to aim. John Chamberlain records an incident in 1613 at Theobalds, when "the Quene shooting at a deere mistooke her marke and killed Jewell the Kings most principall and speciall hound, at which he stormed excedingly for a while, but after he knew who did yt, he was soone pacified, and with much kindnes wisht her not to be troubled with yt, for he shold love her never the worse, and the next day sent her a diamond worth 2000 £ as a legacie from his dead dogge. Love and kindnes increases dayly between them, and yt is thought they were never in better termes."[54] Soon after, Chamberlain reported that "the Quene by the late pacification hath gained Greenwich into her joynter."[55] James remembered the incident well. When George Abbot, the archbishop of Canterbury, out hunting deer, killed a keeper by mistake, James responded to the news with "a gracious aunswer that such an accident might befall any man, that himself had the yll lucke once to kill the kepers horse under him: and that his Quene in like sort killed him the best brache ever he had, and therefore willed him not to discomfort himself."[56] Erica Fudge, writing on this letter, notes that "the servant, the horse and the bitch are the same thing to the King. Their deaths are equally insignificant."[57] This is a generous interpretation: for James, the hunter's death is far less traumatic than that of his favorite bitch. If he could survive that, why should the archbishop discomfort himself about the keeper?

So what does it mean that, in this royal economy of hunting, his principal secretary and foremost minister became "my little beagle?" Though ostensibly affectionate, the casting of Cecil as an animal allowed James to imply an absolute distance between them, as was seen in March 1605, when the king and Cecil were both asked to be sponsors to the newborn son and heir of the earl and countess of Southampton. James pretended to be insulted at being treated as Cecil's equal: if Southampton "had matched him with a Christian [i.e., a human being], he could have believed my lord had good meaning in it; but having coupled him with a hound, he thinketh my lord did it only to flatter him, because he knoweth his Majesty loveth hunting and the beagle as well as any of the company at least."[58]

Most obviously, the beagle was a small hound and therefore an appropriate canine analogy for the diminutive Cecil. But Gervase Markham distinguishes the beagle from other hounds in other ways. After the stow-hound, "a large great dogge, tall, and heavy," there is the "middle siz'd dogge, which is more fit for the Chase, being of a nimble composure" and "the light, nimble, swift slender dog," each originating from particular counties and terrains. Then he comes, "lastly," to "the little *Beagle,* which may bee carried in a mans glove, and are bred in many countries for delight onely; being of curious sents, and passing cunning in their hunting."[59] As this suggests, the beagle was one of the "smelling Dogges"[60] known for its abilities to track by scent, like the basset hound, foxhound, harrier, and bloodhound and unlike the "gaze-hounds" such as the greyhound, gazelle hound, Afghan hound, and whippet, which hunt by sight.[61] Francis Quarles refers to "quick-scented beagles," and Edward Halle in his *Chronicles* refers to French soldiers as being "like good begeles, folowyng their preye."[62] Topsell tells of how "Terriors or Beagles . . . will set upon Foxes and Badgers in the earth, and by biting expell them out of their Denns; whereof *Aristotle* reporteth a wonder, that one of them followed a Foxe under the ground in *Boetia,* and there made so great a noyse by barking, that the hunters went also into the cave, where they saw many strange things which they related to the chiefe magistrate."[63] As a result, the term *beagle* could be used to describe a person who sniffed out or hunted down people or information. Barnaby Googe writes of Roman Catholic bishops having "preetie Begles . . . That hunt out Prebendes fatte for them, and follow fresh the chace,"[64] and Sir Walter Raleigh's *Maxims of State* suggests that "a Barabarous and professed Tyranny" should have its "Beagles, or listeners in every corner, and parts of the Realm; especially, in places that are more suspect, to learn what every man saith, or thinketh, that they may prevent all attempts, & take away such as mislike their *State.*"[65] Cecil's inheritance of the intelligence networks created by Sir Francis Walsingham and his own father, Lord Burghley, made him the nation's lynchpin beagle.

But the beagle's relationship to the hunt was very particular. His "cunning," according to Markham, lay in his tendency "for the most part tiring but seldome killing the prey, except at som strange advantage." His main use was cosmetic: to add a high-pitched sound to a pack of dogs, for those who want their kennel to possess "sweetenesse of cry": "You cast in a couple or two of small slinging Beagles, which as small trebles may warble amongst them: the cry will bee a great deale the sweeter."[66] In fact, Markham concludes, the beagle is an ideal hunting hound only for people who "have infirmities, which detaines them from running a foot, or labouring like lackies or drudges, yet they can endure ordinary and orderly walking, such as shal bee fit for any moderate exercise, and therefore they would hunt on Foote." The beagle will appeal to those for whom a large hound is too expensive and troublesome, especially in a small house: "To these I answere that it is good for them to keepe the little small mitten *Beagle,* which may be companions for a Ladies Kirtle, and in the field wil hunt as cunningly as any hound whatsoever, onely their musique is very smal, like reeds, and their pace like their body, onely for exercise, and not for slaughter."[67] So the beagle is a hunting hound for those who can't hunt properly, a little, cunning, "smelling dogge" who is best lodged in a glove or a mitten. Cecil was constantly made aware of his failure as one of James's chosen intimates. In one missive, the secretary was urged to send back the bearer promptly: "Haiste him bake I praye you for our matche againse sondaye at nichte, for he is secretarie of oure corporation, that is, of fooles, horses, & doggis, & darre sweare he is more qualified for that office then ather ye, or olde secretarie hairbert."[68] Whereas the king jocularly saw himself as one of a "corporation" of "fooles, horses, & doggis," Cecil was "the little beagle that lies at home by the fire when all the good hounds are daily running in the fields."[69]

In a discourse that valorized the hunt, Cecil's contribution to the king's life was systematically belittled, although ultimately the king had to recognize that Cecil had taken over the reins of government. Once Cecil realized that not only did he have no access to the Bedchamber but for the majority of the time it would be physically far away, he set out to neutralize its powers as far as possible. He placed two of his own men, Sir James Hay and Sir Philip Herbert, within the Bedchamber. More importantly, within a month of James's entry into England, he set in motion a system whereby all grants had to be countersigned by a committee of six Privy Councillors before they were submitted to the king for signature.[70] Although favor and patronage still seeped out through the "hunting crew," Cecil was able to tighten his hold on government. As James put it in August 1608, Britain was effectively ruled by Cecil: "Ye sitte at youre ease and directis all; the newis from all the pairtis of the uorlde comes to you in youre chamber, the King's owin resolutions dependis upon youre posting dispatches, and quhen ye list ye can (sitting on youre bedde-sydes) uith one call or quhisling in youre fist make him to poste nicte and daye till he come to youre presence."[71] James characteristically recasts Cecil's administrative control through a hunting metaphor: he only has to call or to whistle in his fist. But as James acknowledges, "My littill beagill; Ye and youre fellowis thaire are so proude nou that ye have gottin the gyding againe of a Feminine Courte in the olde fashon, as I know not hou to deale uith you."[72] Power is now posited once again, in the style of Elizabeth's "Feminine Courte in the olde fashion," via intimate access. But it is access to Cecil's chamber, where he sits "at your ease," "on youre bedde-sydes." Although the king's entourage is revived, it is another bedchamber that has the true power. As the Venetian ambassador astutely noted in 1607, "one may truly say that he is Sovereign in name and in appearance rather than in substance and effect."[73] While the king is out hunting, his beloved little hound stays by the fire: government by beagle.

NOTES

I am grateful to James Daybell for his comments on an earlier draft of this chapter.

1. See Frederick George Marcham, "James I of England and the Little Beagle Letters," in *Persecution and Liberty: Essays in Honor of George Lincoln Burr* (New York: The Century Co., 1931), 311–34. During the period under discussion (roughly 1603–11), Sir Robert Cecil became successively viscount Cranborne and earl of Salisbury; for ease of reference here he is always "Cecil."

2. Of these, thirty-two are in the Salisbury manuscripts at Hatfield House (here-

after Salisbury MSS), and two others were printed in *The Progresses, Processions, and Magnificent Festivities of King James the First, His Royal Consort, Family, and Court,* ed. John Nichols, 4 vols. (London: J. B. Nichols, 1828), 2:203–4, 264–65. See Marcham, "James I," 312.

3. James to Cecil, various dates. Salisbury MSS 134/49, 48, 79, 66; cited in Marcham, "James I," 320.

4. James to Cecil, March 1605, Salisbury MSS 134/66.

5. Cecil to Lake, October 24, 1605. Public Record Office, State Papers (hereafter PRO SP) 14/15/105; *Calendar of State Papers, Domestic Series, of the Reign of James I* (hereafter *CSPD*), *1603–1610,* ed. Mary Anne Everett Green (London: Longman, 1857), 237.

6. Worcester to Cecil, July 22, 1609, Windsor, and July 24, 1609, Farnham. *Progresses,* 2:261–62.

7. Cecil to Lake, April 16, 1607. PRO SP 14/27/9; *CSPD, 1603–1610,* 355.

8. Marcham, "James I," 333.

9. This tradition is heavily indebted to the work of David Starkey. See the essays by Starkey, D. A. L. Morgan, John Murphy, Pam Wright, Neil Cuddy, and Kevin Sharpe in *The English Court: From the Wars of the Roses to the Civil War* (London: Longman, 1977).

10. David Starkey, "Representation through Intimacy: A Study in the Symbolism of Monarchy and Court Office in Early-Modern England," in *Symbols and Sentiments: Cross-Cultural Studies in Symbolism,* ed. Ion Lewis (London: Academic Press, 1977), 187–224, quotation on p. 220.

11. Starkey et al., *The English Court.*

12. See Neil Cuddy, "The Revival of the Entourage: The Bedchamber of James I, 1603–1625," in Starkey et al., *The English Court,* 173–225.

13. Ibid., 173, 183, 183–85, 188–91.

14. Gervase Holles, *Memorials of the Holles Family, 1493–1656* (London: Camden Society [3d series, vol. 55], 1937), 94.

15. "A grievance put up in the Parliament House by Sir John Holles," in Historical Manuscripts Commission, *Report on the Manuscripts of his Grace The Duke of Portland, K.G., preserved at Welbeck Abbey,* vol. 9 (London: HMSO, 1923), 113, cited in Cuddy, "Revival," 205.

16. Nottingham University Library, Portland MS PwV92, art. 17 (f. 7v), cited in Cuddy, "Revival," 192.

17. Cuddy, "Revival," 192. Very early in James's reign, he appears to have made an exception for Cecil. The French ambassador reported in May 1603 that the secretary "begins to grow great with the king, staying alone with him shut up in the *cabinet* for three or four hours together." Beaumont to Villeroy, May 17, 1603, PRO SP 31/3/35, cited in Cuddy, "Revival," 193. However, by *cabinet* Beaumont certainly means James's closet, a space beyond the Bedchamber.

18. Cuddy, "Revival," 197. Cuddy is paraphrasing Penry Williams on the Elizabethan polity: "Under Elizabeth—and probably before that under her sister as well—ministers had no need to place their creatures in the royal bedchamber. Burghley enjoyed closer relations with his Queen than anyone else. That is not to

say that royal favourites were unimportant, but that the Household officers had no special advantages of contact with the Queen, and that Council, Household and monarch revolved within the same orbit." Penry Williams, "Court and Polity under Elizabeth I," *Bulletin of the John Rylands University Library of Manchester* 65 (1983): 259–86, quotation on p. 264.

19. Thomas Wilson to Sir Thomas Parry, June 22, 1603, Greenwich. *Progresses,* 1: 188.

20. Giovanni Carlo Scaramelli to the Doge and Senate of Venice, September 4, 1603, Sunbury. *Calendar of State Papers and Manuscripts, relating to English affairs, existing in the archives and collections of Venice, and in other libraries of Northern Italy* (hereafter *CSPV*), vol. X, *1603–1607,* ed. Horatio F. Brown (London: HMSO, 1900), 90.

21. [James VI], *Basilikon Doron Devided into three bookes* (Edinburgh: Robert Waldegrave, 1599), T4v, Vr.

22. *The Journal of Nicholas Assheton of Downham, in the County of Lancaster, esq. for part of the year 1617, and part of the year following,* ed. F. R. Raines (Manchester: Chetham Society, 1848), 40 (entry for August 12, 1617).

23. Dudley Carleton to John Chamberlain, September 21, 1604, Syon. PRO SP 14/9/42; *CSPD, 1603–1610,* 151.

24. Scaramelli to the Doge and Senate of Venice, September 4, 1603, Sunbury. *CSPV, 1603–1607,* 90.

25. Cuddy, "Revival," 193.

26. Nicolo Molin, "Report on England" (1607). *CSPV, 1603–1607,* 501–24, quotation on p. 513.

27. James to Cecil, n.d. Salisbury MSS 134/48.

28. Molin to the Doge and Senate of Venice, February 10, 1605, London. *CSPV, 1603–1607,* 218–20, quotation on p. 218.

29. Worcester to Shrewsbury, December 4, 1604, Royston. *Illustrations of British History, Biography, and Manners,* ed. Edmund Lodge, 2d ed., 3 vols. (London: John Chidley, 1838), 3:110–11, quotation on p. 110.

30. Henry Howard, earl of Northampton to Lake, March 5, 1605. PRO SP 14/13/13; *CSPD, 1603–1610,* 203. On this occasion James did sign the grant; see Grant to Sir Henry Leigh, March 11, 1605, Greenwich. PRO SP 14/13/22; *CSPD, 1603–1610,* 204.

31. Cecil to Sir John Harington, 1603. John Harington, *Nugae Angiquæ: being a miscellaneous collection of original papers,* ed. Henry Harington, 2 vols. (London: Vernor and Hood, and Cuthell & Martin, 1804), 1:344–46, quotation on p. 345.

32. Lake to Cecil, October 21, 1608, Newmarket. PRO SP 14/37/23; *CSPD, 1603–1610,* 462.

33. Molin to the Doge and Senate of Venice, February 10, 1605, London. *CSPV, 1603–1607,* 218–20, quotation on pp. 218–19.

34. Zorzi Giustianian to Doge and Senate of Venice, May 31, 1606, London. *CSPV, 1603–1607,* 353–54, quotation on p. 353.

35. "Since that time neither that king nor any of his successors have visited the town." Thomas Martin, *The History of the Town of Thetford, in the Counties of Norfolk and Suffolk* (London: J. Nichols, 1779), 57.

36. Samuel Calvert to Sir Ralph Winwood, April 6, 1605, London. *Memorials of Affairs of State in the Reigns of Q. Elizabeth and K. James I. Collected (chiefly) from the original papers of the right honourable Sir Ralph Winwood*, ed. Edmund Sawyer, 3 vols. (London: T. Ward, 1725), 2:57–58, quotation on p. 57.

37. Morin to the Doge and Senate of Venice, November 9, 1605, London. *CSPV, 1603–1607*, 285–86, quotation on p. 285.

38. Godfrey Goodman, *The Fall of Man, or the Corruption of Nature, proved by the light of our naturall Reason* (London: Richard Lee, 1616), L2r–v.

39. Matthew [Hutton], Archbishop of York to Cecil, December 18, 1604, Bishop Throp. British Library [hereafter BL] Harley MS 677 ff. 45r–46r, quotation on f. 45v.

40. Worcester to Cecil, February 24, 1604/5, Royston. Historical Manuscripts Commission, *Calendar of the Manuscripts of the Most Honourable the Marquess of Salisbury . . . Preserved at Hatfield House, Hertfordshire* [hereafter HMCS], vol. 17, ed. M. S. Giuseppi (London: HMSO, 1938), 70.

41. Cecil to York [Hutton], n.d., n.p. BL Harley MS 677 ff. 46r–48r, quotation on ff. 47v–48r.

42. James to Cecil, n.d. Salisbury MSS 134/48.

43. James, "A carteill or challenge to a trinite of knaves," n.d. Salisbury MSS 134/66.

44. James to Cecil, March 1605. Salisbury MSS 134/71. James to Cecil, 1610. Salisbury MSS 134/145.

45. Edward [Hyde], Earl of Clarendon, *The History of the Rebellion and Civil Wars in England begun in the year 1641*, ed. W. Dunn Macray, 6 vols. (Oxford: Clarendon Press, 1888), 1:74.

46. Ibid., 1:74.

47. Roger Lockyer, *Buckingham: The Life and Political Career of George Villiers, First Duke of Buckingham, 1592–1628* (London: Longman, 1981), 12.

48. Buckingham to James, n.d. BL Harley MS 6987 f. 214, printed in David M. Bergeron, *King James and Letters of Homoerotic Desire* (Iowa City: University of Iowa Press, 1999), 179. Whereas Buckingham often used the "slave and dog" valediction, James usually used a language of family with his last favorite. See Bergeron, *Royal Family, Royal Lovers: King James of England and Scotland* (Columbia: University of Missouri Press, 1991).

49. Edward Topsell, *The Historie of Foure-footed Beastes* (London: W. Jaggard, 1607), N5r.

50. Giovanni Carlo Scaramelli, May 1603. *CSPV, 1603–1607*, 42, quoted in Mark S. R. Jenner, "The Great Dog Massacre," in *Fear in Early Modern Society*, ed. William G. Naphy and Penny Roberts (Manchester: Manchester University Press, 1997), 44–61, quotation on p. 48.

51. Corporation of London Record Office [hereafter CLRO], JCCC 18, fo. 136, quoted in Jenner, "Great Dog Massacre," 48.

52. CLRO, JCCC 23 fo. 13v, quoted in Jenner, "Great Dog Massacre," 48.

53. Jenner, "Great Dog Massacre," 55, citing CLRO JCCC 22 f. 402v.

54. Chamberlain to Carleton, August 1, 1613, Ware Park. *The Letters of John Cham-*

berlain, ed. Norman Egbert McClure, 2 vols. (Philadelphia: American Philosophical Society, 1939), 1:468–73, quotation on p. 469. I am grateful to James Daybell for this reference.

55. Chamberlain to Carleton, November 25, 1613, London. Ibid., 1:487–89, quotation on p. 487.

56. Chamberlain to Carleton, August 4, 1621, London. Ibid., 2: 395. Originally "a kind of hound which hunts by scent," *brach* was in early modern English use "always feminine, and extended to any kind of hound; a bitch-hound." *OED,* s.v. "brach."

57. Erica Fudge, *Perceiving Animals: Humans and Beasts in Early Modern English Culture* (2000. Reprint. Urbana: University of Illinois Press, 2002), 21.

58. Lake to Cecil, March 16, 1604/5, Royston. HMCS 17: 99–100, discussed in A. L. Rowse, *Shakespeare's Southampton: Patron of Virginia* (London: Macmillan, 1965), 188. As Rowse says, "So much for Jacobean humour."

59. G[ervase] M[arkham], *Countrey Contentments, in two bookes* (London: R. Jackson, 1615), B2v.

60. Topsell, *Historie,* O5r.

61. Thelma Gray, *The Beagle,* 4th ed. (London: Popular Dogs, 1980), 15.

62. Francis Quarles, *The Historie of Samson in his Works* (1717), 406, as cited in *OED,* s.v. "beagle"; Edward Halle, *The Union of the two noble and illustrate famelies of Lancastre & Yorke beeyng long in continual discension for the croune of this noble realme* (London: Richard Grafton, 1548), Cc.ij.r.

63. Topsell, *Historie,* O5r.

64. Thomas Naogeorgus [i.e., Thomas Kirchmeyer], *The Popish Kingdome, or reigne of Antichrist,* trans. Barnaby Googe (London: Richard Watkins, 1570), G.j.r.

65. Sir Walter Raleigh, *Maxims of State* (London: W. Shears, 1650), C9v, C11r.

66. Markham, *Countrey Contentments,* B4r, B4v.

67. Ibid., C3r–v.

68. James to Cecil, n.d. Salisbury MSS 134/71.

69. James to Cecil, n.d. Salisbury MSS 134/66, cited in Marcham, "James I," 320.

70. Cuddy, "Revival," 197, 199.

71. James to Cecil, August 5, 1608, Bletsoe. *Progresses,* 2:203–4, quotation on p. 204.

72. Ibid., 203.

73. Molin, "Report on England," *CSPV, 1603–1607,* 501–24, quotation on p. 510.

7

Reading, Writing, and Riding Horses in Early Modern England: James Shirley's *Hyde Park* (1632) and Gervase Markham's *Cavelarice* (1607)

Elspeth Graham

Thinking about animals—animal-human relationships, animals and culture—draws me back again and again to John Berger's "Why Look at Animals?," which begins with his claim that the "19th century, in western Europe and North America, saw the beginning of a process . . . by which every tradition which has previously mediated between man and nature was broken. Before this rupture, animals constituted the first circle of what surrounded man. . . . They were with man at the centre of his world."[1] At about the same time as Berger was writing about changed human relations with animals resulting from emergent and developing capitalism and consequent psychic, imaginative, and ideological losses, the economic historian Joan Thirsk (on whom I'm equally dependent in my initial thinking about early modern animals) remarked more specifically on the surprising lack of attention historians had given to a particular animal, the horse, in a particular period, the sixteenth and seventeenth centuries. She wrote, "Horses were as indispensable to men as is the car, the lorry, and tractor today, and their companionship in toil, travel and recreation brought much comfort." Directing attention to "the dramatic expansion of economic activity in the early modern period," she observed, "it is remarkable how little interest historians have shown in the way that horses were made available to meet . . . insistent and fastidious demands."[2] Although Thirsk's and Berger's projects have quite distinct political and intellectual impulses and implications, I want to work somewhere in the space between them. Taking Berger's perception of the centrality of animals in the preindustrial human world along with Thirsk's more particularized sense of the place of horses in the fabric of life of the early modern period, I want to consider ways in which we may read two or three early-seventeenth-century texts from very different genres to identify the elusive presence and meaning of animals for early modern humans.

Recent and important work on human-animal relations in the period has shown ways in which such relations raised questions about the boundaries of the human, both marking and destabilizing ideas about the distinctiveness and special status of humans in the world.[3] My own starting point is that not only do animals have relational identities in the period but that, as Berger suggests, their very centrality makes them simultaneously visible and invisible, distinct and indistinct. Animals and humans, I argue, are experienced and understood as participants in and objects of a whole series of overlapping discourses that are not specifically predicated on notions of human-animal difference. I want to consider how humans and animals are inscribed in any number of economic, medical, political, and aesthetic writings in a much less defined way. Because I am interested in the unseparated presence of animals and humans in early-seventeenth-century writings, I focus on horses precisely because of the crucial place they occupy in enactment of political initiatives, in the economic developments and the cultural shifts of the period. They are central to human culture and history. However, I am also interested in horses in a more abstract way because of their status as domestic animals. All domestic animals might be seen to occupy a threshold region between the wild and the tame, nature and cultivation, the purely human and the purely animal.[4] As powerful, working domestic animals, horses retain something of their animality, their distance from the human. But like all other domestic animals, they also have, as Yi-Fu Tuan's suggestive writings imply, entered into culture.[5] Horses provide a very particularized sort of test for ways of reading animals.

Because knowledge and experience of horses are part of the everyday texture of life in early modern England, horse terms are naturally and inevitably part of an unconsciously and consciously metaphoric vocabulary. For us, looking back, it is clear that one way of reading references to and representations of horses is as encodings of assumptions about human gender, race, and power, which serve as a shorthand form of reference to precise historical issues, cultural assumptions, and social relations.[6] However, my own approach is less concerned with unveiling references than with considering the inseparability in the early modern period of what today may seem distinct or parallel meanings. The texts I focus on exemplify issues of interdiscursivity and the simultaneous visibility and invisibility of horses in differing ways. James Shirley's comedy of manners, *Hyde Park,* traces the amorous adventures of his group of characters: Lacy and Mistress Bonavent (formerly married to a merchant missing at sea); her friend Mistress Carol and her suitors, Fairfield, Rider, and Venture; the rake Bonvile; Trier; and Julietta. The climax of the play occurs during a day at the races in London's Hyde Park. This dramatic text explicitly uses horse racing as a thematic analog to the romantic concerns of its characters and thus concisely exploits commonplace ideas about horses in a visible, even spectacular manner to comment on social and cultural changes. Exploration of the material history of the actual Hyde Park that is the topical focus of the play complicates and perhaps deepens these meanings, however. Extending beyond the text, the history of the park itself allows for a retrieval of more expansive but less visible or immediately apparent meanings. Horses, and the land with which they are associated, become the bearers of a long cultural history that underpins the representation of a particularized cultural moment in the play. Human and animal discourses converge to reveal a layering of historical moments and meanings that are behind and beyond Shirley's text but also contribute to its meanings.

Gervase Markham's *Cavelarice* and *Markham's Maister Peece,* on the other hand, function quite differently as texts. Far from being aesthetically or dramatically structured, they take the form of encyclopedic and practical expositions on every aspect of horse care, breeding, and riding. Horses and the instrumental relationship of humans to horses are at the forefront of Markham's texts. Yet these texts, like *Hyde Park,* call on surrounding discourses and material histories to produce a series of meanings in which the literary and the historical, the biographical and the textual overlap. The boundaries between horse and human history and being are blurred.

FOR SPORT: JAMES SHIRLEY'S *HYDE PARK*

James Shirley's *Hyde Park,* first licensed by The Master of the Revels and performed in 1632 by Queen Henrietta's Men, for whom Shirley was the contracted playwright, contains obvious allusions to horse-related activities throughout.[7] In Act I, Scene 2 of the comedy, for instance, the feisty Mistress Carol tells her friend, the presumed widow Mistress Bonavent, that she herself usually maintains her independence from her suitors, only sometimes, when she has "nothing else to do," encouraging them "for sport."[8] Her "for sport" announces one of the puns that structures the action of the play and around which several of its meanings cluster. *Sport,* as the *Oxford English Dictionary* definition testifies, carries an explicit variety of related meanings in the seventeenth century: pleasant pastime or diversion, amorous dalliance, pastime related to hunting wild animals, and participation in outdoor games or exercise. The play's focus and concerns are thus summarized: its topographic reference to and partial setting in Hyde Park, its amorous maneuverings, its depiction of gentry games and manners, its incorporation of a horse race into the plot and its themes, and its structural suggestion of the seriousness of leisure.

Throughout *Hyde Park* there is similarly an easy, perhaps pleasurably predictable play on "riding" as both equitation and sex. Not only are all of Mistress Carol's suitors named after aspects of horse-racing activity—Fairfield
(location, such as Hyde Park itself), Venture (chance, risk, and, by implication, gambling), and the obvious Rider—but there is sometimes more
pointed linking of sexual activity, class, and horse racing. Trier, in order to
test (as his name implies) the sexual integrity of his desired Julietta, encourages the rakish aristocrat Lord Bonvile in his attempts to seduce Julietta by informing him that she is a whore. In the context of setting up this
trial, Trier remarks to Venture, who has asked about Bonvile's identity, that
Bonvile is a "sprig of the nobility" and that

> 'tis no shame for men
> Of his high birth to love a wench; his honour
> May privilege more sins: next to a woman,
> He loves a running horse.[9]

Here, such reference to the dissolute pleasures of the aristocracy counter-
points the differently inflected enthusiasms for horse racing and marriage
games that become evident in the central scenes of the play when all the
characters, men and women, virtuous and dishonorable, become excited
by the races in the park and the thrills of betting:

> Julietta: Shall we venture nothing o' the horses?
>   What odds against my lord!
> Mistress Carol: Silk stockings.
> Julietta: To a pair of perfumed gloves? I take it.
> Mistress Carol: Done!
> Mistress Bonavent: And I as much.
> Julietta: Done, with you both![10]

And the resolution of *Hyde Park*'s overall plot hinges on a coming together
of the play's three love and courtship strands with the topical and topographic focus of the play: the horse race in Hyde Park. As Albert Wertheim
points out, "In both the horse and foot races watched so avidly by all the
characters in Hyde Park, a 'dark horse' candidate wins."[11] If courtship is
likened to a race in the play—a race with its strategies, its risks and possibilities of accident, and its dependence on a blend of skill and chance, nature, breeding, and control—the outcomes of both the actual horse race
and the love plots suggest that the odds are misleading: those with long
odds, the outsiders, may win after all.

This is most strikingly evident in the dramatically conventional but real-
istically improbable plot strand concerning Mistress Bonavent. She has sup-

posed herself widowed since her merchant husband was lost at sea seven years ago and, in accordance with her husband's wishes, has not contemplated remarriage for that period. On the very day that her promise expires and she is to marry Master Lacy, Bonavent reappears in London. The audience learns in Act I that he had been "taken by a Turkish pirate, and detained many years a prisoner in an island," escaping when "a worthy merchant . . . redeemed and furnished" him; Mistress Bonavent discovers his reappearance when he reveals himself to her at the end of the day in Hyde Park, but the other characters are kept in the dark until the final act. Bonavent's disguise allows him, in a structural variation on the trials of Julietta by Trier, to test his wife's behavior and to compete for her against her new husband, the smug Lacy. Competition, trial, and the triumph of the dark horse, the outsider (who in this case is an old favorite) is at the center of this and each of the love plots.

The excursion by all the characters to Hyde Park for the day at the races (human and horse) and the play's highlighting of the importance of Hyde Park and the activities associated with it through its title may be seen to point to more than the structural and thematic importance of racing, contest, sport, and play, however. As a topographic comedy *Hyde Park* is one of a series of plays, usually seen to originate with Ben Jonson's *Bartholomew Fair* and continuing into the Restoration, in which analysis of social interactions, manners, and cultural clusters intersects with an understanding of place as integral to the dynamics of change as well as being a signifier of it.[12] The broader significance of the historical and synchronic meanings of the actual Hyde Park are inscribed as an underlayer to the play's immediate significances. If landscape, and especially urban landscape, can be read as "a symbolic work in its own right, [as] a social production of space," where meaning is always public,[13] the inherited and changing meanings of Hyde Park are suffused through the meanings of *Hyde Park.* Hyde Park does not just serve as a backdrop to the action; the inclusion of horse racing does not merely allow for a strand of conventional verbal jokes or a plot structure. Rather, space and the activities that occur in it, which create it as place, are active signifiers in the play.

If we look at the history of the actual land that becomes Hyde Park we find a series of transitions between the monarchy, aristocracy, and wider populace and between humans, a natural environment, and animals written into it. Eleventh-century records describe the land as "the manor of Eia," given to the Norman noble Geoffrey de Mandeville for his part in the Battle of Hastings. De Mandeville subsequently gave the land to the Benedictine monastery of St. Peter in Westminster (later Westminster Abbey), but it was repossessed in 1536 by Henry VIII, who wanted "to have the games of hare, partridge, pheasant and heron preserved in and about the honour of his Palace of Westminster for his own disport and pleasure."[14] This sequestration of the Manor of Hyde and its enclosure gave Henry VIII an extensive tract of land westward from the Palace of Westminster to Hampstead Heath as a game park, where along with other game, deer were bred and hunted.[15] From this point, until the 1640s, there were traditionally two keepers of the park, one of whom was a keeper in name only. In 1612 Sir Henry Rich, a favorite of James I who later became Earl of Holland, was granted the sinecure title of Keeper of Hyde Park (it is to the Earl of Holland that Shirley's play is dedicated). And during Holland's keepership Hyde Park began to be opened to the public for the summer. Shirley's play may have been written to celebrate the first public opening.[16]

This brief history of the land demonstrates its change in nature and use: from an originally forested area, to highly cultivated agricultural land used for subsistence and profit by the monks of Westminster, to a legally protected royal game park, to a crown-owned but partially public leisure location. At each stage there is a reconfiguration of human-nature-animal relationships that is simultaneously anterior to, implicated in, and representative of purely human relationships and ideological formations. The transition from church agricultural land to royal game park, especially, marks an assertion of monarchical power, a shift in crown-church relations and in foreign and domestic policies. But the meanings of the park also emerge from a more specific history of hunting.

Hunting, first and foremost, is a reminder of the rootedness of power in possession of land. The right to hunt derives from ownership of or access to the land on which it takes place and in which game could be bred and managed. Therefore, one way in which issues of land-based power manifested themselves was in conflicts over the right to hunt and methods of hunting. So the increasing tendency of the aristocracy in the period to enclose chases and forests, converting them into game parks, and their related use of the law to protect their hunting rights is resisted by other rural classes who both flouted the law through persistent unlawful hunting, or poaching, and who used hunting practices that symbolized their resistance. (Practices such as the use of snare traps, which strangled animals to death, by hanging, may have represented "retribution against the king's deer, since the hunting dogs which game-keepers confiscated from poachers were often killed in this manner.")[17] Likewise, for the aristocracy hunting (which usually implied the hunting of deer on horseback) also had multiple symbolic functions: it served as training for warfare or as a replacement activity for war in periods of peace (as John Aubrey noted, hunting activity was at its peak in the peaceful years of the early seventeenth century), it provided an induction into the codes of honor of the English aristocracy and gentry, and it was an area in which the aspirational could attempt to acquire the cultural capital necessary for their assimilation into a socially elevated world.[18]

Henry VIII's establishment of Hyde Park as a game park taps into these meanings. By bringing the place of hunting into direct proximity to the major physical location of political power, he conflates actual and symbolic sources of power. The absolute identification of the monarch with the land that is later iconically represented in, for example, the Ditchley portrait of Elizabeth I, is prefigured here. But actual changes in the forms of hunting made and promulgated by Henry VIII equally contribute to shifting meanings. In the 1530s a combination of policy and the personal physical limitations of the aging monarch led to new practices. In the hunts in the Thames valley, deer might be driven past the stationary king and court to be killed with crossbows, or they might be coursed with greyhounds in deforested, open land. A transformation in the symbolic content of the hunt thus occurs. Both hunted animals and those used in the hunt, whether horses or dogs, have staged parts. The hunt no longer constitutes an exercise in developing physical prowess, in engaging human participants directly in a confrontation with (semi) wild animals. Rather, it becomes a theatrical event in which specially bred animals (sometimes imported from more distant breeding parks) are ritually supplied to be killed in an attenuated contest. Likewise, any animals used on the side of the human are supplied in such numbers, and are substituted so frequently as they become exhausted, that they become tools of the hunt rather than partners in a test of physical skill and endurance. The mimetic function that already informed royal and aristocratic hunting as a substitute activity for war is enhanced as hunting becomes further detached from its origins as human-nature contest, a contest of physicalities. Practices that are informed by the idea that understanding of the wild coexists with and is implicated in a violent relationship with it are replaced by practices dependent on a more synthesized relationship between humans and nature, where animals come closer to being commodities to be used in symbolic acts displaying power. In extension of such a tendency, hunting comes also to be used explicitly as a symbolic form of social and political control, conveying warnings to those in rebellion against the king between 1536 and 1541, or later in Elizabeth's reign.[19] It is precisely the proximity of the new hunting parks to London that allow them to have this theatrical function.

Horse racing develops out of this movement toward the spectacularization of hunting and blood sports. Henry VIII's establishment of the first royal stud at Hampton Court, James I's establishment of Newmarket first as a center for hunting, his subsequent purchase of an Arab horse named The Markham in 1617, the running of the first recorded race at Newmarket in 1622 between the horses of Lord Salisbury and the Marquis of Buckingham for a prize of £100, and the founding of Newmarket race course in 1636 all mark stages toward the full establishment of horse racing as an aristocratic and royal sport by Charles II. Racing extracts elements of hunting—speed, contest—and detaches them from their originating form. It is also bound up with an obsession with animal breeding for purpose that develops, partly at least, in response to an increasing, economically generated need for horses' diverse purposes.

Behind the performance of Shirley's *Hyde Park* in the 1630s and its revival in 1668 lies an implied history of relations to land, space, animals, and the wild. And emanating from the public opening of Hyde Park itself in the 1630s is a further series of topographic meanings. There is a gestural democratization, an opening up of crown and aristocratic privilege to the people of London. But more complex meanings also emerge from this opening up of space. Racing as an aristocratic sport is transformed into a leisure activity for a wider social audience. This making public (for limited periods of time, at least) of privileged space and activity further adds to the spectacularization of the natural already written into the park's history. Racing itself becomes a spectator sport allowing participation only at a secondary level, through betting, as *Hyde Park* shows. Circulation of money becomes separated from land-based financial activity, perhaps highlighting a new economics. This occurs alongside a direct further commodification of notions of the natural or the rural. In both the actual park and in Shirley's representation of it, the pleasures of buying milk fresh from red cows were available, for instance. Hyde Park functions, in this respect, as a seventeenth-century theme park.

Democratization of space and the animal-related activities associated with it are bound up with a proliferation of layers of spectacularization. And Shirley's dramatization of a day at the races adds another layer of theatricalization. The fact that the very gentry classes whose manners and interests are examined in the play also were a significant part of the Caroline audience compounds this effect. Writing about *Hyde Park* in the 1980s, Martin Butler suggested that the play's park is "a green world in urban London, is both country and town, nature and art. It is a cultivated nature, expressing the dual character (of town, and country) of the gentry who frequent it and who are cultivating themselves."[20] The park thus becomes for Butler a central symbol of a transforming culture and the particular cultural moment of the 1630s, where places of leisure—park and theater—become places of encounter between social classes. In particular, the space of the park is where the values of natural gentility, as opposed to game-playing nobility, are affirmed. *Hyde Park* becomes a Caroline version of Elizabethan pastoral, a space where values are explored, true selves are found. The moral journey of Mistress Carol, for example, from "supreme gamester" to advocate of "natural" privilege, of "property" as self-ownership or self-possession and dignity, is permitted in the space of the park and in relation to the horse race. Her self-discovery, bound up with the valuing of the natural, proclaims a triumph of gentry values and presents London as a place no longer in predatory relation to the country but a melting pot of social difference. A fusion of manners and nature emerges as crucial to the value system of an emergent class.

More recent work on London and writing in the early modern period has been interested in reconfigurations of urban spatial order, focusing particularly on the heterogeneous regions surrounding London, housing what was excluded from the city proper, in Steven Mullaney's words, "the anomalous, the unclean, the polluted, and the sacred" (including "gaming houses, taverns, bear-baiting arenas, marketplaces, and brothels . . . monasteries, lazar-houses, and scaffolds of execution").[21] Read in light of such work and in the context of the history of Hyde Park itself, Shirley's play perhaps carries less clear-cut, or more provisional, meanings than Butler suggests. The space of the park is not, after all, a green space in London but a space on the margins of the city inscribed with a history of negotiations of, resistances to, and assertions of power. The park, the race track, and the theater are all liminal places where social alliances and conflicts are acted out. The park, in particular, is not simply a natural space but a space in which human-nature-animal relationships have been refigured through the preceding hundred years, yielding complex contemporary meanings. Although I do not want to imply that the precise detail of the history of Hyde Park was present in the minds of *Hyde Park*'s first audiences, a broad sense of change in the meanings of land and an awareness of the implications of what we now perceive as spectacularization would have been clearly available to an early-seventeenth-century audience.[22] In such a context, it becomes hard to read the play as a straightforward assertion of values of authenticity. Since Butler's work on early modern theater, it has not been fashionable to see a clear-cut split between court and country opening up in the 1630s and developing into a cause of civil war in the 1640s.[23] But the 1630s remains a decade characterized by its transitional nature, where there is a great deal of cultural fluidity. If, at that moment, the values of an emergent class can be celebrated in a play such as *Hyde Park,* the history and nature of the space that gives reference to Shirley's play also contains within it signs of the tensions that will come to surround those values. Participation in the borrowed spectacular pleasures of the aristocracy may be only a temporary solution to the cultural dilemmas faced by the gentry and middling classes.

In 1668, after thirty-odd years in which cultural and political conflict had taken the extreme forms of civil war, the spectacular execution of Charles I, the establishment of Cromwell's Protectorate, and the Restoration of the monarchy, *Hyde Park* was revived. Pepys records for July 11, "After dinner, to the King's playhouse to see an old play of Shirly's called Hide parke, the first day acted—where horses are brought upon the stage, but is but a very moderate play."[24] In the context of the Restoration, different strands of *Hyde Park* become unraveled. The spectacularity of horse racing itself (a sport much developed in the 1660s) and the coincidence of forms of theatricality—racing and drama—implicit in the 1630s productions become explicit in the extraordinary spectacle of bringing actual horses onstage. A further act is performed in the series of spectacularizations of horse sports. But the negotiations of courtly and gentry values, the particular play of manners and virtue possible in the 1630s, are lost to Pepys as a Restoration man. What remains of interest fifty years after the play was written is the spectacle of horses; what has gone is the human drama.

FOR WEALTH: GERVASE MARKHAM

If *Hyde Park* draws implicitly on an underlying configuration of ideas about land and animals, the writings of Gervase Markham deal lengthily and explicitly with them. Indeed, his biography exemplifies directly the class negotiations and economic shifts that form a more generalized subtext to *Hyde Park*.[25] Markham (?1568–1637) was the third son of an impoverished gentry family. His father had been prominent as a soldier, courtier, and politician, but the family fortunes declined during Gervase Markham's lifetime (by 1618 the last of the Markham estates had been sold), although court connections were retained. After military experience in the Low Countries, Gervase Markham, like many younger sons, allied himself with the Earl of Essex until Essex's downfall in 1601 ended Markham's hopes of advancement at the Elizabethan court. He then married, also in 1601, and he and his wife became husbandman and woman for nine years. This does not seem to have been sufficiently profitable as an occupation, but the practical experience derived from it, in combination with his early education, which had produced in him the knowledges and skills of a gentleman or aristocrat (fluency in classical and European languages; the ability to write poetry and plays; and high proficiency in horse riding, including the aristocratic skills of the manège), led into another enterprise: his production of vast numbers of husbandry, animal (especially horse) management, military, and hunting manuals.

In the discursive maneuvers and contradictions of these skills, and in the history of production and sale of the manuals, it is possible to see clearly the marks of cultural, social, and economic shifts of the period: movements between the values and habits of thinking of an aristocratic culture and those associated with a new entrepreneurialism, between aestheticism and pragmatism, between internationalism and a new insistence on English national identity. Markham converted the varied work of his life into works on the management of life. In the person and writings of Gervase Markham there is an extraordinary discursive and material confluence where the boundaries between texts themselves, between texts and life, and between land-based production, animal management, and authorial activity are constantly blurred.

A tendency of the few modern attempts to describe or analyze the life and writing of Gervase Markham is to try either (as in the case of biographical accounts) to catalog his writings or (in the case of critical and historical analysis) to select a category of his writings, usually his husbandry manuals, for interpretive assessment. Although selection of a category of writings, in this case his horse manuals, is necessary to my own interests here, it is also worth remarking on the limited nature of such approaches in relation to Markham. It is precisely the unrestrained, the repetitive, the authorially erratic nature of his production that is significant. Famously, in 1617, the Stationers' Company required him to sign a statement: "Memorandum, that I Gervase Markham of London, gent., do promise hereafter never to write any more book or books to be printed on the diseases or cures of any cattle, as horse, ox, cow, sheep, swine, goats etc."[26] This unique sanction by the Stationers' Company responds to a flooding of the market by Markham's books (at least five on animal diseases and one forthcoming) and the seeming unfixedness of the identity of his books. Markham apparently republished unsold copies of books under new titles and repeatedly recycled the same material in the form of new books.

Such a manic productivity and obliviousness to any notion of the discreteness of individual publications on Markham's part and the unprecedented nature of the Stationers' Company's reaction brings to the foreground changing notions of authorship, of book as commodity, and, particularly, of originality as a sign of authorship in a new print marketplace. (Originality was not a necessary ingredient of authorial authority in the period. The incorporation of others' material and ideas often legitimated the knowledge offered; translation or imitation was not necessarily seen as a lesser form than original writing or invention, although the protocols of authorship, ownership, and publication were complex.)[27] Markham's own relationship with a print culture bears the mark of his flamboyant self-distancing from an aristocratic culture that still considered print vulgar, his immersion in a process that democratized both the content of published writing and the range of writers. His writing grasps the essence of the new culture: it can teach the fundamentals of profit making (a popular collected edition of his works was unequivocally titled *A Way to Get Wealth*) while making money. Yet the very extravagance of his exploitation of the entrepreneurial potential of popular print books comes almost parodically to mimic the reproductivity of the print process itself and to call for its limitation. Wendy Wall convincingly argues that the action of the Stationers' Company forced Markham "to argue for his works' novelty and distinction" by emphasizing their difference from the French husbandry manuals he used as a basis for his own, thus establishing "a principle of authenticity that comes to name textual and national difference."[28] Markham thus becomes a key figure implicated in the development of a concept of Englishness and in the related development of print capitalism.

What interests me is less his role in contributing to the development of a national identity, although insistence on Englishness is an obvious and significant part of his writings, and more the transitional and fluid nature of his texts. Taking his writings on horse management as a snapshot of a historical moment, it is possible to see a curious mishmash of a new entrepreneurialism and older habits of thought, of new ideas of originality and older ideas based on an assumption of a circulation and repetition of knowledges, a blend of a new scientificism and older, traditional ideas about animals deriving from both a popular knowledge and a classical tradition. Markham's writing on horses bears the same marks of change as his husbandry manuals, but it also shares forms of thinking that informed his "literary" writings: his translations of an eclectic series of texts and his collaborative dramatic writings such as *The Dumb Knight* (1608), based on a novel by Bandello. Markham's uses of translation and reformulation of existing texts both recirculate aspects of a culture based on immersion in a European commonality of knowledge and taste and, through the very dynamics of the print market and the act of making texts available in English, present them as new and distinct from their European heritage. In addition to these features common perhaps to all of Markham's writings, his horse manuals also particularly insist on the authority of experience and are suffused with his knowledgeable passion for horses and horsemanship.

The 1694 edition of *Markham's Maister Peece* (first edition 1610) was directly reproduced from editions in his lifetime. A glance at the two pages following the title page, containing an illustration and a rhyming key, provide an overview of his concerns and demonstrate the paradigm of horse understanding he propagated in Britain: "The Figure 1. A compleat Horseman shows, / That Rides, Keeps, Cures, and all perfections knows" (figure 7.1). The complete horseman, then, is someone with exhaustive knowledge of all aspects of riding and horse management. He is actively involved in horse care, not simply reliant on others for management. Horse care is a skill and a form of work that is necessary to all stations of life, from yeomen to aristocrats (and the various woodcut illustrations show forms of clothing that imply a range of social positions). But the illustration to Number 1 shows a rider, dressed as a gentleman or aristocrat, in the classical riding position and a horse trained in the high arts of equitation. The horse, in the tradition of many equestrian portraits of the aristocracy in the seventeenth century, has the tucked-in head position characteristic of the classical school and is performing a levade. This is "the first of the airs above ground" and the basis for the even more skilled courvette or curvet, in which the horse rears its forelegs at an angle of either thirty or forty-five degrees to a height of eight feet and then leaps forward several times while keeping its forelegs in the air. High equine skill and artistry is thus presented as the epitome of horsemanship.

In this Markham, or his publisher, places his work firmly in the tradition of the horse masters of sixteenth-century Italy, who had promoted horsemanship as a courtly and aristocratic art. The development of classical equitation and the use of the manège in sixteenth-century Italy derive in typical Renaissance fashion from a return to classical Greek writers, most notably Xenophon, mixed with direct influence from Byzantine forms of horse skills on horsemen in Naples from the twelfth to the fifteenth century. Particularly influential was the horsemaster Frederico Grisone, who established a horse school in Naples in 1532 and whose *Gli Ordini di Cavalcare* was published in eight editions between 1550 and 1600. Grisone was working with native Italian horses, which were heavily built, and in order to produce the responsiveness needed for the movements and "airs" of classical equitation—themselves aestheticized and refined versions of heavier movements that had been traditionally needed in war—he used what now seem extraordinarily cruel forms of training and bitting (the initial use of spiked cavessons). There was much emphasis on breaking resistance. This changes somewhat in the mid-sixteenth century, when, during the period of Spanish rule over Naples, much lighter Andalusian horses, the result of cross-breeding between Arab stallions and native Spanish mares, began to be used. The origins of classical horsemanship, then, bring into play a mix of factors: the intense move toward an aestheticization of all forms of court culture, issues of power and dynasty, power politics between the East and Europe, and artistic rivalries and exchanges between East and West, antiquity and modernity.

The illustrations to Markham's frontispiece, crude as they are, reveal, as a subtext, all of this. But also revealed is a distancing from the Italian School and from Grisone in particular, which becomes increasingly explicit in the texts themselves. The final illustration and explanatory rhyme that follows

Figure 7.1. From Gervase Markham, *Markham's Maister Peece* (1694 edition). Reproduced by permission of The British Library, classmark CUP 407 P 10.

it in the text—"The 10. shews Fury in untamed things / The only fountain whence Diseases springs"—presents the other extreme of things: horses in a wild state, kicking out at each other. This state of wildness is presented as the antithesis of art; it is violent, destructive, and the source of all "diseases." It is horse knowledge, art, and management that correct this unsatisfactory natural state of affairs.

Bracketed between these extreme states are examples of specific forms of horse tending: medical, dietary, and conformational, changing the physical appearance of horse (no. 5 shows how to create a star on a horse's forehead, considered a favorable marking). In these, the elevation of the high art is blended with allusion to something much more practical, experimental, experiential, and socially inclusive. It is this mix of the scholarly and experiential, the practical and the learned, the homely and the elevated, that characterizes Markham's work, distinguishes it from his Italian predecessors, and makes Markham a significant figure not only in the history of English horse management but also in the wider history of economic, social, and cultural changes in early modern Britain.

In Markham's *Cavelarice* the political, cultural, and ideological—as well as practical—underpinnings of Markham's thinking on horses are more fully fleshed out. The title page again summarizes his concerns. Joined with the Italianate title, *Cavelarice,* is the subtitle of his book: *The English Horseman: Containing all the Art of Horsemanship.* The tension implied between debt to Italian models and a nationalist desire to promote Britain and Englishness runs through the whole text. The first of the eight books of *Cavelarice* is dedicated to "The most High and most mightie Prince, Henry eldest Sonne of our Soveraigne Lord the King" on the grounds that Prince Henry has promoted horse arts. Markham describes his own work as an enterprise designed to prevent the return to obscurity of these recovered arts patronized by the Prince, just as the works of Xenophon, Russius, and Grisone have preserved horse learning. Having thus invoked these models, Markham is eager to assert the merits of English horsemanship: "However the world shall boast either Spaine, France or Italie, yet it shall then be knowne that they have not brought foorth so good horsemen as have beene bred and are now living in this Empire of Great Brittaine." This nationalist pride extends from native-bred horsemen to native-bred horses. In Chapter 2 of Book 1, Markham commences with a diatribe against some previous writers on horses. He suggests, "For me to enter into as frivolous and idle a discourse of the kindes of Horses and their coulers, as Conradus Gesner hath, filling leaves with names scarce heard of, at least never experienced in any of our climates," would make him merely "a second Trumpet of other mens falshoods." Rather, he intends only to describe "the kinds and generations of such Horses as I have approved and knowne within mine owne experience." Through a sort of double movement, a series of reverse back-handed compliments to both men and horses that describe the faults of each in order to praise them (the frivolousness and excessive modesty of English people, the heaviness of English horses), Markham goes on to describe the overall superiority of true-bred English horses. It is only the absence of de-scriptions of English horses from European descriptions that has led to false assumptions "that the English horse is a great strong Jade, deepe ribbed, side-bellied, with strong legges, and good hoofes, yet fitter for the cart [than] either the Saddle or any worthy imployment," he claims.[29] It is Markham's method as much as his promotion of Englishness that is of interest here. As throughout his writings, his insistence is on the primacy of knowledge gained through experience. This is elevated above book learning, at the same time as his references to horse authorities legitimate his writing through its range of learned reference.

Throughout *Cavelarice*, in his encyclopedic detailing of all aspects of horse management Markham goes on to produce a text in which writing and ex-perience, anecdote or fabulation and fact are in tension and in which the virtues of types and breeds of horses are saturated with a political and his-torical viewpoint whereby domestic and international relations are incor-porated in the horse and where the actual land of Britain is bred into the va-riety of native equine qualities. In "The first Booke" of *Cavelarice* on horse breeding, we find disparaging reference to the "wilde bringing up, and . . . rude manner of handling" typical of Irish human-horse relations, which "doth in [Markham's] conceite ingender . . . fearefulnesse in the Beast, which those ruder people know not how to amend." Worse, that characteristic lazi-ness and sloppiness, already stereotypically associated with the Irish, simi-larly afflict Irish horses in their way of going: "This Horse though he trot very wel, yet he naturallie desireth to amble."[30] On the other hand, Arab horses (with which Markham had been involved, selling the Arab, named after him, to James I) provoke not only praise but fine discriminations such as those between the "Turkie horse," although "not those horses which have beene bred in the Turks first dominions as in the upper parts of Scithia, Tartaria," and the "Barbarie."[31] A whole history of military, religious, and cultural trans-actions between East and West and an involvement in the burgeoning sport of horse racing underlie the detailed description of various Arab horses. In the same way, he expresses horror at the methods of horse breeding reput-edly used by the traditional enemies of England, the Spanish:

> In Spaine I have heard the Spaniards say, they let their Colts runne with their Mares, till they cover their Dammes: & indeed I have seene very yong

Horses in some of their Iland races; but I utterly dislike such breeding, for it is vild and unnaturall: for as Plinie reports, a Horse being hoodwinkt whilest he covred a Mare, after perceiving it was his owne Damme, ranne up to the rocks, and brake his owne necke: and also that a Mare in the territorie of Realte, kild her keeper for the like; which reports albe they carry not the fairest livries of truth, yet are precedents . . . and this in mine own experience I have both found and know, that if a man will continue his breede altogether in one straine, without any alteration or strangenesse, shall in the ende, find his studd to decay and loose both stature, strength and comeliness, which doth intimate to me, that there is great dislike in such kinde of breeding.[32]

Here again, the discursive shifts are characteristic and telling. Reference to experience authenticates by presenting Markham himself in different roles: first as sophisticated traveler, witness to the actuality of Spanish practices, and then as English horse breeder and husbandman whose opinions derive from homegrown experience. The horses described are Spanish by nature but also by misfortune of their breeding by Spanish men who impose unnatural, incestuous practices on them. The supremacy of the horses' natural apprehension of sexual probity is then revealed through the fabulous reference to the authority of Pliny, which is both used for legitimation and denied because the nonfactual nature of the story carries less weight than the truth of experience. Moral and practical, animal and human, fictional and experiential apprehensions of rightness jostle curiously.

Such a passage not only reveals the wealth of competing cultural determinants of Markham's writing and the nature of horses but also suggests something of Markham's overall attitude to horses. Among all the wanderings of Markham's thought, what emerges as consistent is his assumption that horses have a form of dual nature: they are beings in their own right, but they exist only as they are bred (for an ever-multiplying number of uses). The importance of benevolence toward horses, likewise, is a semispoken tenet of all that Markham writes. Cruelty finds many forms but manifests itself not as a moral fault but in practical ways. Cruel or erroneous practices lead to the production of horses that are not useful or manageable (as in the instance of Irish horses).

Horses emerge as beasts that are both natural and products of the human. They share human natures (his horse remedies replicate the assumptions and practices of contemporary human medicine, mixing understanding derived from humoral and newer anatomical understandings with an independent strand of traditional horse-lore) but have their own distinct natures. Above all, written into the bodies of horses is the actual land on which they are bred and on which they live.

The opening of *Cavelarice* makes sensitive, even apologetic reference to the political importance of horse breeding. Because it is "Princes, Potentates, and men of best place and estimation" who are "owners of the earth" and thus have the resources—land and money—to breed horses, his book is initially addressed to them. In addition, it is their responsibility to populate the land with good and useful horses to increase the wealth of the country. What follows is a discussion of geographic differences and the bearing that different forms of terrain have on the characteristics of the horses. Horses need adequate space, and ideally land should be "a ground neither exceeding ranke, nor extreame barreine, but of an indifferent mixture" to ensure an appropriate level of richness of grazing.[33] A direct link is made between environment and the conformation of horses: "Grounds that be rancke, marrish, cold & wet, are most vilde to breede upon, for the food being unwholsom, the layre unnatural, and the treading uncertainne; the foales that are bred thereon, are heavie, slowe, fat headed, great bellyed, round leggd, and weake joynetd, chieflie in the pasterne." Conversely, good ground produces qualities in foals that will later be useful.[34] There is a mix of the practical and experiential, the scientific and an understanding derived from humoral thought, in which there is an analogous relationship between animal and land, or rather a transference of the qualities of the land to the animal that is in part causal, in part metaphoric.[35] Markham returns from his discussion of ideal breeding land to the problems of the yeoman or husbandman whose resources are more limited in relation both to land and to availability of breeding stock. In such a move Markham takes care to address an audience of tenant farmers and may be seen to align himself, as Andrew McRae argues in relation to his husbandry manuals, with a new generation of improvers and writers in the agricultural sphere who address an audience beyond that of landowners.[36] As McRae suggests, Markham participates in and contributes to a changing socioeconomic order in which market forces and a new corresponding social stratification replace the older static system of land ownership and farming. The newer order, rather than embodying the older sense of profit as personal gain in the form of pleasure or gratification, consists of "'thrift-coveting farmer[s]', ambitious and innovative figure[s], who carr[y] the potential to 'improve' both [their] own fortunes and those of the commonwealth."[37]

But what I see as significant in Gervase Markham's horse treatises is not simply their implication in a new "thrift" economy nor the role Markham plays in the movement toward notions of authorship and developing a national identity. To be sure, all of these are important aspects of Markham's life and production. But what seems striking to me is the highly conflictual and contradictory nature of Markham's writings. Written into his texts is a history of national and international engagements and changes. His horse management manuals are driven by the familiar entrepreneurial impulse, the emphasis on usefulness, on breeding for purpose and therefore for profit. But in them there is also a sense of the absolute intertwining of horse and human history. Horses become texts to be produced and read. Human events and culture are incorporated into the actual being of horses through changes in breeding and management. Horses are also texts that can be read to reveal human history. Furthermore, the breeding and management of horses contribute to the development of a new economic structure and a new national identity.

Gervase Markham's horse manuals and James Shirley's *Hyde Park* may both be read in the light of Berger's history with which I began. The very different texts reveal traces of ways in which horses, even as domestic animals, become distanced from the human: by spectacularization and by objectification through the proliferation of management treatises. Yet both Markham's and Shirley's texts also reveal the full presence of horses in the early modern world. *Hyde Park* as an aesthetic, performative text may seem to use horse racing simply as a structural trope yet is also dependent on the history of land and associated animal sports, which exists as a subtext to the play and whose meanings seep into the play. Similarly, the meanings associated with land and animals that the play's topography call into circulation around it frame our understanding of the play as a product of a specific cultural moment. Markham's horse manuals appear practical and derivative, but they also may be read to reveal the interdiscursive mingling of the textual and corporeal, the human and the animal, the material and the verbal. Encapsulated into the history of these pragmatic texts is a moment in the development of literary form and function. Markham's writings are implicated in the establishment of the modern notions of authorship and in the series of generic separations that occur in the period between fact and fiction, the practical and the imaginative. These literary developments, in turn, bear on ways in which human-animal relationships come to change: animals as "messengers or promises," in Berger's words, come to be separated from animals who are functionally exploited.

NOTES

1. John Berger, "Why Look at Animals?," in *About Looking* (New York: Vintage Books, 1991), 3–4.
2. Joan Thirsk, "Horses in Early Modern England: For Service, for Pleasure, for Power," in Joan Thirsk, *The Rural Economy of England: Collected Essays* (London: Hambledon Press, 1984), 375.

3. See Erica Fudge, *Perceiving Animals: Humans and Beasts in Early Modern English Culture* (2000. Reprint. Urbana: University of Illinois Press, 2002).

4. See "The Fair, the Pig, Authorship," in Peter Stallybrass and Allon White, *The Politics and Poetics of Transgression* (London: Methuen, 1986). They include the anthropologist Edmund Leach's table of homologous relations: kinship relations, topographic relations, and human-animal relations (46). Horses have a somewhat anomalous place in a grid such as this. They occupy a space somewhere between "pet" and "livestock," yet more than either of these categories perhaps, they continue also to signify distance from the human, or wildness.

5. Yi-Fu Tuan, *Passing Strange and Wonderful: Aesthetic, Nature, and Culture* (New York: Kodansha International, 1995).

6. In an interview by Harriet Swain, "Prejudice and Pride in Noble Pedigrees," *The Times Higher Education Supplement,* 25 June 1999, Lisa Jardine comments that Henry VIII's famous reference to Anne of Cleves as "a great Flanders mare" is a specific comment on her suitability for breeding. Similarly, Peter F. Heaney, in "Petruchio's Horse: Equine and Household Management in the *Taming of the Shrew,*" *Early Modern Literary Studies* 4:1 (1988): 1–12, equates equine management terms with parallel domestic management ones.

7. See Simon Trussler, *James Shirley, "Hyde Park:" A Programme/Text with Commentary* (London: Methuen, 1987), for the stage history of the play.

8. James Shirley, *Hyde Park,* in *James Shirley,* ed. Edmund Gosse (London: T. Fisher Unwin, 1904), I.2.195.

9. Ibid., I.1.184.

10. Ibid., IV.3.236–37.

11. Albert Wertheim, "Games and Courtship in James Shirley's *Hyde Park,*" *Anglia* Band 90 (1972): 72. On the plot *of Hyde Park,* see also Richard Levin, "The Triple Plot of *Hyde Park,*" in *Modern Language Review* 62 (1967): 17–27.

12. Seventeenth-century topographic comedies also include Thomas Heywood, *The Fair Maid of the Exchange* (1607), and Richard Brome, *Covent Garden Weeded* (1632) and *The Sparagus Garden* (1635). See Richard H. Perkinson, "Topographical Comedy in the Seventeenth Century," *English Literary History* 3 (1936): 270–90, for a survey of topographic comedies in the period. For a further discussion of the vogue for topographic plays in Caroline London see Theodore Miles, "Place-Realism in a Group of Caroline Plays," *The Review of English Studies* 18 (1942): 428–40.

13. Steven Mullaney, *The Place of the Stage: License, Play and Power in Renaissance England* (1988. Reprint. Ann Arbor: University of Michigan Press, 1995), 10.

14. Quoted in Hazel Thurston, *Royal Parks for the People: London's Ten* (London: David & Charles, 1974), 17.

15. See Trussler, *James Shirley,* xviii.

16. See Ibid., xviii, and Julie Sanders, *Caroline Drama: The Plays of Massinger, Ford, Shirley and Brome* (Plymouth: Northcote House, 1999), 45.

17. Roger B. Manning, *Hunters and Poachers: A Social and Cultural History of Unlawful Hunting in England, 1485–1640* (Oxford: Clarendon Press, 1993), 25.

18. Manning refers to John Aubrey, *Aubrey's Natural History of Wiltshire,* ibid., 5.

19. See ibid., 199, 48–49.

20. Martin Butler, *Theatre and Crisis, 1632–1642* (Cambridge: Cambridge University Press, 1984), 179.

21. Mullaney, *Place of the Stage*, 22.

22. In the writings of "Puritans" such as Stubbes, or later Prynne, there is a clear link between different forms of spectacle such as theater and animal sports. It is perhaps not accidental that opponents to activities such as bear-baiting or cock fighting were also those who placed a theological value on the integrity of selfhood and who were suspicious of all forms of "playing" or theatricality.

23. See P. W. Thomas, "Two Cultures? Court and Country under Charles I," in *The Origins of the English Civil War*, ed. Conrad Russell (Basingstoke: Macmillan, 1973), for the influential argument that there was increasing division between courtly and gentry cultures in the 1630s. Butler's *Theatre and Crisis* is partly a rebuttal of Thomas's argument. Butler argues that there is not a simple cultural division between antitheatrical Puritans and courtly theatricality.

24. *The Diary of Samuel Pepys*, transcribed and ed. Robert Latham and William Matthews (Berkeley: University of California Press, 1995), IX, 260.

25. For a biographical summary see the *Dictionary of National Biography*, ed. Sir Leslie Stephen and Sir Sidney Lee (London: Oxford University Press, 1917), XII, 1051–53. See also Gervase Markham, *The English Housewife*, ed. Michael R. Best (Montreal: McGill-Queen's University Press, 1986), xi–xv.

26. *A Transcript of the Registers of the Company of Stationers of London, 1554–1640*, ed. Edward Arber (London: W. Aldis Wright, 1978), entry for July 24, 1617.

27. The first copyright laws date from the early eighteenth century. On copyright law and its implications see Joseph Loewenstein, "The Script in the Marketplace," *Representations* 12 (1985): 101–14. For issues of imitation and copia in relation to humanist education in England, see Richard Halpern, *The Poetics of Primitive Accumulation: English Renaissance Culture and the Genealogy of Capital* (Ithaca, N.Y.: Cornell University Press, 1991), especially chapter 1. On the impact of print culture generally see Marshall McLuhan's seminal *The Gutenberg Galaxy: The Making of Typographic Man* (Toronto: Toronto University Press, 1962) and Lucien Febvre and Henri-Jean Martin, *The Coming of the Book: The Impact of Printing, 1450–1800* (1958), trans. David Gerard (London: Verso, 1990).

28. Wendy Wall, "Renaissance National Husbandry: Gervase Markham and the Publication of England," *Sixteenth Century Journal* 27:3 (1996): 767–85, especially 780–81. Wall draws on Benedict Anderson's notion of imagined communities and his argument that a vernacular print culture creates "fields of exchange and communication" that become the "embryo of a nationally imagined community" (781). See Benedict Anderson, *Imagined Communities: Reflections on the Origin and Spread of Nationalism* (1983. Reprint. New York: Verso, 1992).

29. Markham, *Cavelarice*, 8, 9.

30. Ibid., 17.

31. Ibid., 11.

32. Ibid., 25–26.

33. Ibid., 2.

34. Ibid., 3, 5.

35. A tradition of describing horses in such terms continues today, of course. Distinctions are made between cold-, warm-, and hot-blooded horses that derive from early notions of breeding and the different qualities of native and nonnative horses.

36. Andrew McRae, "Husbandry Manuals and the Language of Agrarian Improvement," in *Culture and Cultivation in Early Modern England: Writing and the Land,* ed. Michael Leslie and Timothy Raylor (Leicester: Leicester University Press, 1992), 47.

37. Ibid., 37.

8

"Can ye not tell a man from a marmoset?":
Apes and Others on the Early Modern Stage

James Knowles

In the "Induction" to Marston's *Antonio and Mellida* (1600) the boy actors debate their upcoming roles in a scene suffused with anxiety about identity, sexuality, and, ultimately, the effects of playing. The boy playing Antonio (who later dresses as an Amazon) suggestively describes his cross-dressed role as "an hermaphrodite, two parts in one," but the part of Galeatzo, Duke of Florence, is reserved for most comment. This role is described as "a right part for Proteus or Gew; ho, blind Gew would ha' done't rarely, rarely."[1] Proteus provides an obvious figure for the transformative skills both required and threatened by the early modern stage, but "blind Gew" presents a puzzle. According to some critics "blind Gew" was a "blind performing baboon" alluded to in plays and in Jonson's *Epigrams* as a comparison for Mime to "out-zany" as he may also "out-dance the babion."[2] Yet the editions of these texts evidence some uncertainty as to Gew's identity. For some he is an ape, for W. R. Gair "an actor specializing in ape-like mannerisms," and for Ian Donaldson "a showman."[3] Interestingly, Gew appears as an ape in Nungezer's *Dictionary of Actors and Other Persons Associated with the Public Representation of Plays in England before 1642*, where he is the only animal among the human cast.[4]

This uncertainty does not simply testify to scholarly confusion but rather encapsulates the variety of apes and ape imitators on the early modern stage. More crucially, Gew's uncertain identity evidences the confusions that apes and their connection to humans engendered in the thinking of the period, confusions exacerbated by the mimetic (apish) activity of acting. Widespread testimony shows apes that danced and performed gestures obscene or political (the ape who "come[s] over the chain for the King of England, and back again for the Prince, and sit[s] still on his arse for the Pope and the King of Spain"), and at least one company of performing apes was licensed in 1606.[5] Masques seem to have been a particular venue for "ape" dances, and Bacon associates baboons with masques in his *Essays*.[6] Importantly, there seem to have been two classes of ape-performers on the early modern stage—trained apes and boys or men dressed as apes—and at least one adult actor, Thomas Greene, appears to have specialized in aping the apes. If apes themselves present a disturbing series of images that question the nature of human identity, adult ape-actors intensify these anxieties.

This chapter argues that apes had a particular—and disconcerting—place on the early modern stage. Centrally, the ape raised questions about the boundaries of the human and animal, a highly uncertain and contested limen. There existed a real fear that men (and, more likely, women or boys) might easily continue the postlapsarian trajectory of decay and metamorphose toward the animal. This fear raises the second dimension to the interaction of early modern stage and the simian as acting was often (even ubiquitously) described as "aping" or "apish." Often this "aping" trope is simply read as metaphorical, but in light of the unstable human/ape divide in early modern thought, the anxiety in "aping" may lie in the possibility that by playing the ape—or just playing—actors (boys in particular) risked becoming apelike or, even, apes. Overlaid by a further category confusion in which ape and apelike were not clearly distinguished, the issue of animal acting highlights the fragility of human status. For Protestant writers, in particular, animal-human cross-dressing reveals the dangerous "animality of humanity."[7]

The ape has a peculiarly potent place in early modern culture. The representation of apes encompasses a long, complex, and varied history of allegorical and symbolic representations in a wide range of forms. Apes were becoming more familiar, not simply as exotica in the specialized wonder-zones of the menagerie or theater but as domestic pets. Keith Thomas even claims that by the sixteenth century pet monkeys were a "normal feature" of urban middle-class households.[8] Thomas's suggestion bears out Daston and Park's argument that the early modern period saw a gradual disappearance of the marginal exotic and the emergence of the exotic within and also parallels the complexity of reaction they trace around the early modern monstrosity. Reactions to the monstrous, they argue, ranged across "horror, pleasure, and repugnance," and each emotion embodied a different, often overlapping mode of interpretation.[9] The situation of the monkey is intensified precisely because of its presence in the domestic sphere, its radical similarity to humanity, and, indeed, its entirely uncertain ontology, which means it remains unclear whether apes are men in the making or unmaking.

BABOONIZING: PLAYING THE EARLY
MODERN MONKEY

Babouinner, to baboonize it, to play the monkey; to use apish or
foolish tricks, or knavish pranks.
—R. Cotgrave, *A dictionarie of the French and English tongues*
(London, 1611), sig. H2v

Although editorial activity has identified specific ape-performers, few studies have considered the role, uses, and cultural significance of animals on the
early modern stage. While apes have received more attention than most other
animals (except perhaps for dogs or bears), the only study devoted to apes
treats their significance as almost entirely determined by "ape typology and
ape lore," and the "revolutionary" possibility that man is nothing but an ape
is discarded.[10] In fact, the early modern discourses around apes—and animals more generally—were far more various and complex, encompassing
Christian ideals of stewardship, through anthropomorphism, to more complex views that included an advocacy of animals as possessing sentient souls.[11]

Donna Haraway's characterization of modern Western primatology as
"simian Orientalism" usefully reminds us that, as with Western constructions of the foreign "other," our representations of apes are always about
defining the human.[12] As Kim Hall suggests, although much early modern
discourse around race and species differences was concerned to separate and
distinguish, it reveals "fear of underlying similitude."[13] This underlying
species similitude reminds us of the human need for animals to prove our
humanity.[14] Indeed, even as the early modern period experienced an ongoing redefinition of human relations with the apish other fueled by geographic expansion, developments in comparative anatomy, and the emergence of comparative anthropology, more traditional images of apes from
emblem books, bestiaries, and popular culture also still flourished.[15]

This hybrid, even overdetermined understanding is accentuated by early
modern awareness of the hybridity of mankind. As the top of the created
order, man existed above the animals yet connected enough to them so that
when he lapsed, his bestial nature was revealed. For earlier humanists such
as Pico della Mirandola, mankind's biform nature sounded with possibilities as Protean man might transform himself into a god, yet for later writers such as Bacon, imbued with Calvinism and the growing awareness of
the implications of the new empirical sciences, such hybridity was less op-
timistic. Bacon argued instead, "There is no nature which can be regarded
as simple; everyone seeming to participate and be compounded of two.
Man has something of the brute; the brute has something of the vegetable;

the vegetable something of the inanimate body; and so all things are truly biformed and made up of a higher species and a lower."[16] Although the possibility of upward transformation is present, it is the likelihood of decay and descent that echoes in the passage.

The most widely available discussion of the animal in the period, "Of the Ape" (in Topsell's *Historie of Foure-footed Beastes* [1607]), not only includes monkeys, marmosets, and baboons and distinguishes between African and Indian apes but also considers the "Satyre," the "Sphinx" and several other hybrid monsters, such as the "Norwegian monster." Topsell combines travel narratives (such as the Tartary apes sold as men), classical sources (the Pithecusan apes from Virgil), the anatomical dissections of Vesalius, and an account of Egyptian baboon worship. "Of the Ape" is characterized by the problematic separation of apes and humans, encompassing tales of the Tartary merchants who passed off depiliated apes as men and the tale of the French ape who was so adept that "any man would think he understood humane conditions: he stoode upright like a man, and sate downe like a Man, he discerned men and women assunder." In a discussion of the status of pigmies (human or animal?) Topsell argues that they must be apes as "they have no perfect use of reason, no modesty, honesty or justice of government . . . and above all they cannot be Men as they have no religion."[17] Indeed, his primary definition of their apishness relies on the fact that they imitate men, which shows them to be apes.

Although it might be thought that the advent of empiricism and science would undermine the survival of mythic interpretations and popular knowledge, as John Bulwer shows the implications of the new discoveries were more ambiguous: "For these strange Histories of Monstrous Nations which in Pliny and other Ancient Authors I have heretofore counted vain, do now require and deserve some credit: since in these times there is a new Nature revealed, new miracles, a new World, full of strange varieties and sincere novelties."[18] The evocation of "new miracles" and "sincere novelties" illustrates how geographic discovery, scientific experiment, and the older interpretations of the book of nature coexisted and cross-fertilized. Indeed, Bulwer's "sincere novelties" strikingly recall the ballad hucksters and broadsheet sellers, and in the conjoined worlds of popular print and theatrical entertainments, the monstrous remained a very real—and very profitable—category for Renaissance culture, and tales of sex with apes coexisted with learned dissections. Thus a *Discours Prodigeux et veritable, d'une fille de chamber* (Paris, ca. 1600) depicted the ape-child born to a servant-girl on its title page, and Drummond of Hawthornden recounted how a Scot had sex with an ape "not of any evil intention, but only to create a Monster," which he planned to show around the country and so earn his living.[19] Yet such instances contrast with Montaigne's celebration of monsters—in a passage that echoes Augustine—as an expression of natural fecundity, divine creativity, and "the infinitie of form contained therein." For Montaigne, "wee call that against nature, which commeth against custome. There is nothing, whatsoever it bee, that is not according to her. Let therefore this universall and naturall reason, chase from us the error, and expelle the astonishment, which noveltie breedeth, and strangeness causeth in us."[20] Montaigne's appeal to "universall and naturall reason" treats astonishment itself almost as a postlapsarian state in which our vulgar errors have proliferated because of our expulsion from the rational and divine order.

Some of the appearances of actual apes on the early modern stage—exemplified by Gertrude's appearance with the monkey in *Eastward Ho*—may allude to the fragile distinctions between animal and human. It is the human ape-actors who provide the most profound challenge to early modern ideas of humanity.[21] If Renaissance humankind was deeply concerned with the "animal within" and the possibility that humans might slip into animal form, the connection between acting and apish imitation exacerbates these uncertainties. In fact, the two broad discursive traditions by which monkeys and men and their interrelations are understood bring out two slightly different responses to the animal-human border. On one hand, the literary trope of the ape and apish imitation foregrounds the idea of metaphor and its own metaphoricity, actually accentuating the human-animal difference.[22] On the other hand, early modern natural science and even developing observational sciences suggest that the boundary is dangerously permeable.

The trope of the "poet-ape" or "poet-critic" who is degraded through servile poetic imitation just as the ape is debased through imitation of men, has a long history in Renaissance polemic. In poetic theory these attacks, which draw on the fabular history of the imitative monkey, often combine elements drawn from the wide vocabulary of simian symbolism, which ranges from treating the monkey as a symbol of natural imitation to its opposite, where the ape emblematizes debased and false copying. False poetic innovation is thus often associated with the gallants, slavishly mimicking foreign fashions, and their debasement of culture is symbolized by the lack of judgment, itself a sign of lack of control much like the unbridled appetites of the ape.

This collocation of ideas is pursued most extensively in Marston's *Scourge of Villainie,* which presents the world as a monarchy of monkeys who write, judge, copy foreign fashions, and debase culture, even smearing their excrement across the landscape. The satire rails,

Come down ye Apes, or I will strip ye quite,
Baring your bald tayles to the peoples sight.
Yee Mimick slaves, what are you percht so high?
Downe Jacke an Apes from they fain'd roialtie.
What furred with beard, cas'd in Satin sute
Judiciall Jacke? How hast thou got repute
Of a sound censure? O ideot times,
When gawdy Monkeyes mowe ore sprightly rimes!
O world of fooles, when all mens judgement's set
And rests upon some mumping Marmoset.

This passage compiles all the contemporary images of monkeys, from their status as "Mimick slaves" to their lewdness; later he condemns the "imitators of lewd beastliness" and comments, "Even Apes and beasts blush with native shame" at the antics not of apes but of men. In the image of the blushing beasts' "native shame" Marston neatly reverses the assumption of human civilization producing shame as a critique of a society that does not even manage natural animal responses.[23]

The men-monkeys of the satires and polemicists remain similes, however, themselves punning in a manner that enshrines difference. Simia may be similar to man, but they are not actually human. Even the image of an apish society suggests a comparison that, although it may imply the possibility of "downward" bestial translation, still retains the clear suggestion of its own metaphoricity. Moreover, the comparison is designed to encourage increased differentiation, through civility and rationality (or "judgement," as Marston calls it). Apes, as Topsell argued, were "ridiculous, by reason of an indecent likeness and imitation of man," which made them monstrous precisely because they looked too like men, but in the domain of the figurative ape we recognize its figurativeness precisely because only humans write poetry.[24] The image of the ape-poet or critic, paradoxically, in reminding us that humans are behaving like apes, reinforces—or at least restates—the boundaries between human and ape.

Acting raises a different problem. Whereas the ape/poet metaphor works to distinguish ape and man, when the process involved is acting, then in imitating other men, mimicking their facial expressions, gestures, and behavior, the human actor not only is imitating the ape but in the performance of imitation is behaving exactly like the monkey. Performance disconcertingly raises the possibility that aping, as an action, especially when staged, is actually and simply being an ape, as imitation of men's actions is the very thing that defines the ape.

This possibility of man becoming ape is broached in Chapman's *Sir Giles Goosecap* (1606?) when Bullokar, the "French page" of "a French affected traveller," is accosted by two English pages, Will and Jack.

> Jack: O' my word, Will, 'tis the great baboon that was to be seen in Southwark!
> Will: Is this he? God's my life, what beasts were we that we would not see him all this while! Never trust me if he look somewhat like a man. See how prettily he hold the torch in one of his forefeet! Where's his keeper, trow? Is he broke loose?
> Jack: Hast ever an apple about thee, Will? We'll take him up.—Sure, we shall get a monstrous deal of money with him.

The pages offer Bullokar an apple, but he has overheard them and speaks:

> Will: God's me, he speaks, Jack! O, pray pardon us, sir.
> Bullokar: Out, ye moped monkeys! Can ye not know a man from a marmoset in these Frenchified days of ours?

Bullokar then proceeds to cudgel them for their cheek.[25]

The incident is fascinating because of its ambivalence. Most commentators assume that Jack and Will deliberately insult Bullokar by *pretending* he is an ape, yet the dialogue offers a wider and more disconcerting series of possibilities.

Jack's opening question "What's that?" may be a comic objectification of the overdressed ("Frenchified") Bullokar, and the knowing allusiveness of the rest of the dialogue ("what beasts were we" and the "monstrous deal of money") bear out the comic irony. Yet other elements of the dialogue suggest the possibility that they genuinely, rather than teasingly, assume him to be an ape. This ambiguity suggests the ease with which men may become apes, and by the end of the interchange they have indeed become "beasts" named as "moped monkeys" themselves, either for their joke or for their bestial failure at rational discrimination: "Can ye not know a man from a marmoset?"

In the context of a page-boy scene in a comedy the possibility of human-ape translation is figured as comic, but in *The World's Folly* (1615) the ramifications are more serious. This sermon-like diatribe on the evils of the time condemns stage-playing ("more have recourse to Playing houses, then to praying houses") and especially the Fortune Theatre as the "Common-Sewer of Obscaenities" that consists in "barbarously diverting Nature, and defacing Gods owne image, by metamorphosing humane shape into bestiall forme." This barbarous metamorphosis is not, as might usually be the case, the gender cross-dressing player but rather the species cross-dresser "Greene's baboon."[26] This is Thomas Greene, the ape-imitating man, who reverses all contemporary assumptions about apes imitating men and hence becomes a symbol of the barbarous subversion of nature. Barbarians stand closer to the beasts as they reject the "humane" values of civilization.

I.H.'s opprobrium directed toward the adult actor playing the monkey predates Prynne's more famous attack in *Histriomastix* by twenty years. Prynne extends biblical injunctions against images arguing that the separation of the species is a rational consequence of biblical law: "That God who prohibits, the making or likenesse of any beast, or fish, or fowle, or creeping thing, whether male or female . . . must certainly condemne the putting on of such bruitish Vizards, the changing of the glory, the shape of reasonable men, into the likenesse of unreasonable beasts and creatures, to act a beastial part in a lascivious Enterlude."[27] Both anti-theatricalists see the crucial moment of transformation in "defacement" (I.H.) and the assumption of an animal mask or "bruitish Vizard" (Prynne), perhaps recalling man's supposed corporeal resemblance to God or possibly the injunction that we should look upward. Both suggest that this transformation brings about the loss of human rationality, and Prynne's phrase "changing the shape of reasonable man" seems to imply that the act of wearing the vizard also translates the rest of the body ("shape"). It is this moment of assuming a costume that leads to the loss of rationality and even the loss of species identity as the disguised animal-human performs "a beastial part in a lascivious Enterlude."

Prynne's phrase "beastial part" implies both the actor's role as an animal and the animal body, suggesting that the actor has become what he has performed. Species cross-dressing leads to cross-species transformation and the loss of human identity. To some extent this is implicit in Cotgrave's fascinating use of the verb "baboonize" in his French *Dictionarie* (1611). Although the definition suggests that playing the monkey and being the monkey can be separated, Cotgrave's initial coinage "to baboonize" implies that it is possible in playing the monkey to become the monkey. The ambiguity perhaps lies in whether the human-monkey is a monkey or is simply treated as a monkey. It appears that it is not easy to answer "Can ye not tell a man from a marmoset?"

"TO ROLL WITH PLEASURE IN A SENSUAL STY": THE CAROLINE MASQUE AND ANIMAL-HUMAN HYBRIDITY

> Put off the vizard that Poets maske in, . . . These are the Cuppes of *Circes,* that turne reasonable Creatures into Brute Beastes.
> —Stephen Gosson, *The School of Abuse* (London, 1579), A2v

Prynne's image of the vizarded actor performing "a beastial part in a lascivious Enterlude" points toward the main theatrical form in which masks of all kinds, including animal masks, were used: the masque. Bacon also linked baboons and masques in his *Essays,* and the evidence of masque texts bears out this association. In some instances, such as the *Recit du ballet des singes* (1612), live apes apparently danced a dramatization of the well-known Brueghel print of the peddler robbed by monkeys, but in most cases the apes appear to have been played by actors.[28] These were either men, as in the He and She Baboon from Beaumont's *Masque of the Inner Temple* (1613), or children, as in Chapman's *Memorable Masque* (1613), where the "mock-masque of baboons, attired like fantastical travellers" was performed by "a dozen little boys."[29] In fact, the extant design of an ape costume for Townshend's *Tempe Restored* provides us with the only direct visual and documentary evidence for the ape-actors' appearance and technique, the instructions requiring "heary scincotes" and the "hedes viszards"[30] (figure 8.1).

As the earlier Jacobean examples suggest, many of these uses of the ape are associated with the antimasque and with Renaissance notions of the grotesque, and "baboonery" was even used as a term to describe grotesque ornamentation.[31] Jacobean masque designs include several animal-headed masquers (perhaps associated with the *Essex House Masque* [1621]), a bird-headed masquer (*Vision of Delight* [1617]) and the contents of the cooking pot in *Neptune's Triumph* (1624). In general, the uses of the animal as grotesque helped reinforce the boundary between human and animal, and masque form, with its movement from antimasque to masque, was an ideal vehicle for demonstrating the primacy of the civil, human, and royal over the barbarian, satirical, and bestial.

Yet in the later Caroline masques in particular, apes belong with the hybrid, liminal, and fantastical forms that proliferated in the antimasques, especially dwarves and, less frequently, giants. The presence of these liminal creatures suggests that the Caroline masque synthesized not only the emblematic and mythic traditions about apes but also the newer geographic and scientific discourses that cross-fertilized in early modern writings. This is hardly surprising in an elite form that was itself highly scientific and drew on mechanics, optics, and the novel system of perspectival drawing and the spatial politics of classicism to demonstrate the power of the monarchy. The technological theater of the Caroline masque parallels the scientific program at Laudian Oxford that combined Copernicanism and royalist hierarchy.[32]

The complex use of apes, hybrids, and liminal forms can be seen in Townshend's *Tempe Restored,* the central—and rather neglected—text in a crucial period in the politics of the Caroline culture, the 1632–33 season. In many

Figure 8.1. Inigo Jones, "An Ape," for *Tempe Restored* (1632). Devonshire Collection, Chatsworth. Reproduced by permission of the Duke of Devonshire and the Chatsworth Settlement Trustees. Photograph: Photographic Survey, Courtauld Institute of Art.

ways *Tempe Restored* is Henrietta Maria's *Masque of Queens*. It represents a defining moment in the Caroline reformation of the masque and in the politics of representation of the performing queen, and the masque consciously revisits many of the same issues around female performance and even recycles some of the witchcraft myths used in Jonson's 1609 text. Written and designed by Inigo Jones and Aurelian Townshend, *Tempe* establishes the new Caroline aesthetic ("these shows are nothing else but pictures with light and motion") against the Jonsonian insistence on the priority of the word. In this case, visual display is tied to intellectual apprehension through the platonic framework whereby the contemplation of corporeal beauty "may draw us to the contemplation of the Beauty of the soul."[33] As we shall see, however, this emphasis on the visual over the verbal does not simply belong to the ongoing debate over the nature and function of the masque but answers specific issues raised by the queen's stage performances. Moreover, the Jonesian proclamation of "pictures with light and motion" encompasses the difficulty of the "engining" by which the great cloud with fifty inhabitants descended ("the greatest that hath been seen here in our time") as technological innovation serves royal theurgy.[34] The "apparitions" are not the false illusions of witchcraft but rather move the viewer toward a higher rationality.

Tempe Restored is also significant in that it contains a performance by the first female actresses on the English stage; by Madam Coniack, a French singer apparently associated with Henrietta Maria's chapel, and one Mrs. Shepherd.[35] Crucially, the appearance of Madam Coniack as Circe responds to the critique of the queen's theatrical performances that had emerged in the 1630s to mount a defense against those who regarded female actors as "whorishly impudent."[36] The figure of Circe deliberately refutes the antitheatrical polemicists, turning their own rhetoric and tropes against them and using the image of Circe's bestially transformed victims to counter images of the theater audience—and especially its female performers—as "playing the beastial part in a lascivious Enterlude."

A "Description of the Scene" prefaces the text. The proscenium arch—for which no designs survive—frames the masque-picture with personifications of Invention and Knowledge in the upper frame on either side of the compartment that read "Tempe Restauratum."[37] These figures provide a way of viewing the masque, and Invention and Knowledge carry attributes associating them with Mercury (wings) and enlightenment (book and torch). They both ignore the distractions of the "children holding ugly masks" or "riding on tame beasts," "blowing wreathen trumps," and "hardening darts in lamps" that surround them. Invention and Knowledge also stand above the false values represented by the two half-human, half-satyr figures of Envy (female) and Curious Ignorance (male), who stand in niches in the side borders. These personifications are also provided with animal symbols in the form of a forked tongue and snaky locks (Envy) and a wreath of poppy crowned by a frog and a bat flying above (Curious Ignorance). In contrast to the balance of male and female offered by Invention and Mercury, these figures are conspicuously hybrid, and such hybridity associates them with the mixed nature of Circe and her cup with its concoction of herbs.[38] Even the opening stage picture presents a triumph over the grotesque and the hybrid.

Circe's appearance in *Tempe* introduces the key Renaissance myth of hybridity and animal transformation, turning it to defend female agency and refute ideas of female monstrosity and animality. As a performance it was an extraordinarily adversarial and daring gesture, especially in the casting of a French female singer-actress as the symbol of dangerous femininity, performance, and even Catholicism. Two elements of the myth in particular address the issue of female actors: her voice and her prophetic powers. Against Circe's voice the audience is offered the vision of the all-powerful queen's silence, which outstrips the bewitching voice of Circe and even the Highest Sphere: "The music that ye hear is dull / But that ye see is sweet indeed." The queen's own harmony exudes an "air" that appeals to the "Intelligences" to create "a Cupid, that is never blind" and draw the "senses all one way." Royal silence or "presence" is seen to outstrip even Orpheus and certainly the powers of Circe, not merely taming or creating beasts but creating a higher order of men devoted to the "fair and good, inseparably conjoined." Indeed, the high point of the masque lies in the descent of Henrietta Maria in her triumphal chariot, surrounded by her attendants, on the "great cloud."[39] Regal silence is not disempowerment but rather a choice that stresses the queen's ultimately superior power above the mundane issues of body and voice.[40]

The actual casting of the masque may have furthered the exploration of Circe as monstrous woman. Madam Coniack, who played Circe, was the subject of a poem by Thomas Randolph that dwelt on the contrast between her "incomparably sweet" voice and her apparently "deformed," even diabolic appearance: "I thought her one of those that fell / With *Lucifers* Apostate traine / Yet did her Angels voice retaine."[41] Randolph's poem raises many of the tropes around female performance found in *Tempe,* as the singer is seen as a perverted Orpheus enticing the birds with song only to frighten them with her looks, "Which for a good Priapus goes / And well may serve to scarre the crowes." The implication of monstrous hermaphrodism is emphasized as Randolph describes her as "monster strange" but cannot define her "pedigree": "What but a panther could beget / A beast so foule, a breath so sweet?"

He wonders whether she might be "of *Syren's* issue" as she may "be fish the upper part" and, developing from the siren image, comments, "The tongue, a part which us'd to be / Worst in thy Sexe, is best in thee." This last couplet focuses directly on the issue that contemporaries raised to depict women actors as rebellious and monstrous: the voice. Indeed, Randolph's poem suggests that Madam Coniack may have been cast precisely because as a French Catholic actress-singer she symbolized all that the anti-theatricalists feared. The casting of specific individuals to dance appropriate roles accentuated the interest of masque watching and performance for members of the coterie audience, but in this case the information was also published in the livret, making the casting almost directly a public gesture of defiance. Randolph's poem, too, survives in multiple copies suggestive of the degree of interest that Madam Coniack excited.[42]

Although Circe's voice was her main weapon, according to Homer once she had been stripped of her powers by the moly, she displayed different vocal powers, assuming a prophetic role to warn Odysseus of Scylla and Charybdis, themselves symbols of female monstrosity.[43] This potentially beneficial female voice emerges at the end of *Tempe Restored* when Pallas and Circe come together under Jove's direction and—in the alliance between the contrasting forces of the female singer as Circe and the male singer as Pallas—undermines any simplistic depiction of female monstrosity. Indeed, both figures are conspicuously powerful yet also willing to submit to Jovian command. As the paired male and female figures on the proscenium frame suggest, this platonic androgyny was often deployed by Henrietta Maria and Charles as an image of the marriage and their jointly held powers. Here, Pallas becomes a symbol of acceptable political androgyny rather than the monstrous hermaphrodism imagined by her critics and also depicted as false values on the proscenium frame. Significantly, it is Circe who becomes the voice of the mistaken critics of female power, a gesture that neatly turns the anti-theatricalists' imagery upon themselves.

The central feature of the Circe myth is animal-human transformation, and *Tempe* recasts this metamorphic fiction to embody the new neoplatonic mode of the court. Importantly, Townshend's masque allows the possibility of downward transformation, but these transformations are deployed within an idealized model of restoration by consent. Circe "voluntarily" resigns her scepter just as the Fugitive Favourite insists that "Promethean fire" impels him to reject even the bravest animal form, the lion, and aspire to humanity "governed by reason, and not ruled by sense." The masque also establishes a complex hierarchy of animals, humans, and hybrids, at its clearest in the antimasques that consisted of "Indians and Barbarians (who naturally are bestial) and others which are voluntaries, and but half-transformed into beasts." Among these figures are hare and hounds, lions, apes and an ass dressed "like a pedant teaching them prick-song," and hogs. The allegory explains that these "beasts in part transformed . . . contrary to their natures make her [Circe's] sport," representing "that sensual desire makes men lose their virtue and valour, turning parasites and slaves to their brutish affections."[44]

The animal-headed antimasquers represent literally hybrid forms, but the text places a particular emphasis on their agency in their hybridity, differentiating the "naturally . . . bestial" and the "voluntaries." Unlike the animal-headed antimasquers of *A Masque Presented at Ludlow* who have been transformed yet "so perfect is their misery / Not once perceive their foul disfigurement / But boast themselves more comely than before," the animalized humans in *Tempe Restored* are conscious and have accepted their "easy" position.[45] As the Fugitive Favourite states, "It is consent that makes a perfect slave."[46] This emphasis on will, the "Promethean fire," and on the importance of "reason" over "sense" contributes to an element in the masque that stresses the rational dimensions of neoplatonism. In the allegory, indeed, great play is made of the power of the "true lovers of science and virtue" to lead men away from vice. Thus, it is interesting that the antimasque's figures of the apes are being taught a "prick-song" by the ass, suggesting how hybrid forms through an act of will can transform themselves, in this case toward the brutish "prick-song," the antitype of the noncorporeal desire espoused in the text.

Tempe's antimasques dramatize the absolute antithesis of Circean sovereignty and Henrietta Maria's regime. The antimasque is not so much a chaotic or grotesque foil to the main masque as a complete anti-order as the enthroned Circe watches what Sophie Tomlinson aptly describes as an "imperial tableau": "Let me my subjects view!"[47] This false vision of sovereignty momentarily usurps the spectatorial politics of the Caroline masque as the audience watches Circe watching her own masque, providing an uncomfortable parallel to the actual situation in the masquing room. The center of Circe's false masque of animals, Indians, and barbarians is the strange hybrid figure of the "Pagoda"[48] (figure 8.2).

This "Idoll" consists of a human body, with black wings, pointed gold shoes, elongated fingernails, and a quasi-oriental headdress above an animal—possibly ape—face. This monstrous figure embodies the false worship promoted by Circean sovereignty and the debasement of the human into the bestial that her rule creates against the proper worship promoted in Divine Beauty's "regal rites." This improper bodily worship is echoed in Circe's own want of "physic" to cure her distempered heart as she, like her subjects, is "confined" by her bodily desires. In contrast, Henrietta Maria's

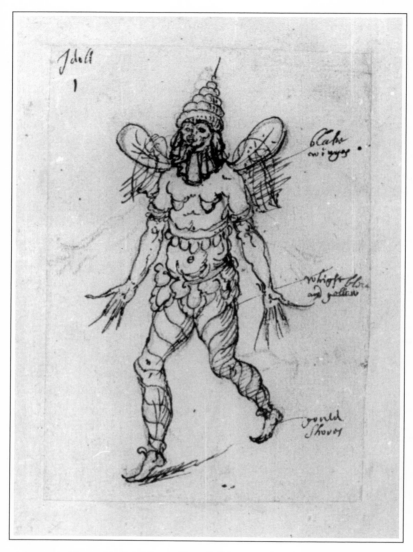

Figure 8.2. Inigo Jones, "Pagoda," for *Tempe Restored* (1632).
Devonshire Collection, Chatsworth. Reproduced by permission of
the Duke of Devonshire and the Chatsworth Settlement Trustees.
Photograph: Photographic Survey, Courtauld Institute of Art.

descent and the power of the stellar Influences by implication liberate from the body, offering "music to all eyes" rather than the corporeal captivity of Circe's masque.[49]

Although Townshend's masque is largely shaped by the religiously inflected neoplatonism of Henrietta Maria's circle, rationality rather than mystery is also stressed, just as the Circean masque provides an image of a false corporeal idol. Thus, Circe's submission to Pallas is allegorized as showing how the "rational and highest part of the soul" can control the "irascible and concupiscible parts." Townshend's emphasis on the "voluntaries" also stresses human agency and will, informed by "Promethean" desire, in actively moving toward either virtue or vice. From a political viewpoint this places the onus on the subject to choose to love the monarch, to aspire toward the best rather than accept the "easy" way. More controversially, the text omits much of the myth as used in the earlier ballet, especially the deployment of the apotropaic herb moly against Circe's charms. This omission of moly, often used as a symbol of divine assistance (as in the Sandys commentary on Ovid also published in 1632), shifts the focus of the masque away from divine intervention, or rather it replaces it with Henrietta Maria's spectacular descent. Tellingly, it is the king's presence that converts the Fugitive Favourite along with his aspiration toward divine beauty, but, crucially, Townshend's hybrids must choose their direction of translation. The contrast with Milton's beast-masquers is instructive, for they are animals without reason and unable to recognize their own bestiality, perhaps itself part of a critique of the courtly beast-masquers who falsely consider themselves rational animals.

The emphasis on choice and rationality suggests that the masque represents another inflection of platonism.[50] This less overtly mystical version draws on a discourse of reason and science to explain the power of virtue and the preeminence of the monarch. Charles and Henrietta as constellations are less expressions of mystical power than the universal reason that orders the world and to which mankind has lost access since the Fall. To choose reason and to aspire toward virtue is to escape from the enchantments of the degenerate body, "making man only a mind using the body and affections as instruments . . . to bring . . . all the happiness which can be enjoyed here below." The king as Heroic Virtue is not so much a mystical force as ultimate rationality "who therein transcends as far common men as they are above the beasts, he truly being the prototype to all the kingdoms."[51]

The central image of Circe's masque, of the "naturally bestial" Indians worshipping their hybrid false idol, may have had much wider resonances in the context of the continuing criticisms of Henrietta Maria, her Catholicism, and her theatrical performances, some of which became scandalously public in 1632–33. Although it has often been suggested that Walter Montague's *The Shepherd's Paradise* prompted Prynne's attacks on Henrietta Maria's stage performances, the chronology of composition for *Histriomastix* suggests that Townshend's masque, performed and printed shortly before Prynne's publication, may have acted as the catalyst for his critique.[52] Significantly, Prynne's attack connected acting, the perceived falsity of Catholicism, and ideas of the animal, and although it was not explicit in its references to Henrietta Maria, it was widely perceived by contemporaries as an attack on the queen, especially in the famous index entry that cited women actors as "notorious whores."[53]

Prynne denigrated both actors and Catholics, yoking them together so that "most of our present English *Actors* . . . [are] professed *Papists*," and "all our Roman Catholiques . . . are much devoted to . . . Theatricall Spectacles." For Prynne, Catholic ceremonials had transformed "the sacred solemnity of our Saviours Incarnation into a Pagan Saturnal, or Bacchanalian feast" and the "gestures, crouchings and noddings" echo the false gestures of the theater. The main thrust of this attack is on the lack of spirituality and the worldly fleshiness of Catholicism, which can be traced in the "voluptuous" celebration of Christmas, and the excessive use of gestures that draw attention to the priestly body confirms Prynne's hypothesis.[54] The attack continues through the idea that all acting is a dangerous and hypocritical counterfeit that "infuseth falshood into every part of soule and body," especially as it reproduces the "apparent vanity, follie, and fantastique lightnesse which appeares in those ridiculous antique, mimicall, foolish gestures . . . motions of the eyes, head, feete, hands, and whole intire body which Players use." Although Prynne is concerned primarily with gestures that produce laughter, his attack on acting per se and excessive gesture derives from his argument that these distort the human form: they are "absurd irrationall, unchristian, if not inhumane gestures and actions, more fit for skittish goates then men." In fact, they are symptoms of "vanity, folly, or frenzy," especially when humans perform: "Yea a reasonable man [plays] the horses, Beares, Apes, Lyons &c, or a male the womans part."[55] Prynne's linked concerns about Catholicism and acting—as forms that are essentially false, bodily, and, in their excessive emphasis on the body, irrational—depend on an awareness of the fragility of the human state and the ease of transformation. Indeed, the figure of Circe often was used in anti-Catholic polemic to suggest the seductive, mundane, and fleshly qualities of Catholicism and its power to translate men into beasts.[56] For example, John Gee trumpeted against the "palpable fiction and diabollicall fascination" of "this foraine Idoll" whose "enchanted Chalice of heathenish Drugges and Lamian superstition hath the power of Circes and Medeas cup, to metamorphize men into Bayards and Asses."[57]

In describing Prynne's *Histriomastix* as the antitheatrical tract "most underwritten with ideas of monstrous androgyny," Laura Levine persuasively argues for the centrality of a concern about sexual ethics, sodomy, and hermaphrodism.[58] Although Levine's account traces the centrality of gender cross-dressing in Prynne's writing, she curiously underplays the weight given to species cross-dressing. If gender cross-dressing adulterates and effeminates (a greater concern than female to male transvestism), then species cross-dressing threatens "the glory, the shape of reasonable men, into the likeness of unreasonable beasts and creatures." Circe, of course, embodies the potential power of women, and especially women actors, to do precisely this, to transform men into beasts through "diabollicall fascination."[59] Townshend uses this image as the embodiment of false sovereignty, and the range of female figures, including Pallas and Divine Beauty, present a more nuanced account of female power. Indeed, Circe's voluntary submission to the more rational forces of Pallas, the sighted Cupid, and Jupiter replaces Prynne's simple equation of female performance and power with foreignness and monstrosity.

Although Prynne's attack draws on a long-established antitheatrical polemic, the parallels between the grounds of his attack and the language of Townshend's recently performed masque are striking. Rather than accepting the hierarchy that Townshend and Jones establish between good and bad uses of the body and recognizing the possibility of upward transformation, Prynne's rhetoric suggests that acting dehumanizes and animalizes. Moreover, his understanding of acting rejects the neoplatonic idea that the imperfect forms below can aspire to reperfection through contemplation of the prototype because the very idea of performance is rooted in the body and its tendency toward the bestial. At the heart of the difference lies a debate over what constitutes the human. For Townshend man and his body can be translated and transformed, ruled by reason, away from bestiality and toward universal reason, whereas for Prynne the very idea of transformation through the body is anathema; transformation comes through the soul.

This central role of the body and its physical sign, such as the voice, in *Tempe Restored* marks a rejection of earlier critiques of female actors as dangerously bodily and provoking their spectators to lust and sin. Recently, it has been argued that Belessa's songs in *The Shepherd's Paradise* refute Prynne's critique of the impudency of female actors by stressing "blushing" pudency, but in Townshend's masque, the whole notion of corporeality is metamorphosed, a true Circean power to counter the false Circe.[60]

Henrietta Maria's performing body is reconfigured as "symmetry, colour, and certain unexpressable graces" that "may draw us to the contemplation of the Beauty of the soul" just as the enchantress's voice is replaced by that of Pallas, redefining voice not as siren song but as reason. Moreover, the gaze that in the hands of antitheatrical polemicists translates the spectators into lust-filled beasts is also changed as the Highest Sphere sings "I cannot blame ye if ye gaze." This is a new, almost divine gaze:

> How rich is earth, and poor the skies,
> Deprived of heavenly Beauty's eyes,
>   Whose image men adore.
>
> . . . .
>
> And since more th'object than the sight
> Makes each spectator blest,
> How are we ravished with delight,
>   That see the best.[61]

Most importantly, just as the antimasque rejects the barbarian and the animal and proposes a world of hybrids that can choose to improve or degenerate, the masque creates a series of "pictures with light and motion" that refute the anti-theatricalists' view of the disordered female body and the corporeal gaze. Circe, who could almost stand as a symbol for the antitheatricalists themselves (a figurative cross-dressing that would not have pleased Prynne), is not simply rejected but like everyone else translated and brought to recognize the force of royal love.

ORANGES ARE THE ONLY FRUIT: VAN DYCK'S QUEEN HENRIETTA MARIA WITH JEFFREY HUDSON AND AN APE, PUG THE MONKEY

The interplay between *Tempe Restored, Histriomastix,* and Randolph's poem on Madam Coniack and even some publicly staged plays shows how Henrietta Maria's performances garnered force as a cultural issue and, once Prynne had been arrested in 1633, became a public political scandal. It is in this context that Van Dyck painted his portrait, gifted to Thomas Wentworth in 1633, of Henrietta Maria in a blue hunting dress (figure 8.3). The image that this portrait projects stands as a refutation of the Prynne imagery of the monstrously hybrid women actors who transform themselves and others. It exudes stability and calm and, most of all, symbolizes her female and royal power not through words and acting but through "pictures with light and motion."

The portrait is calculated to stress Henrietta Maria's dominance. She

Figure 8.3. Antoine Van Dyck, *Queen Henrietta Maria with Sir Jeffrey Hudson* (1633). Samuel H. Kress Collection, Photograph © 2002 Board of Trustees, National Gallery of Art, Washington.

stands on a dais against a background of classical balustrade and drapery, flanked by an orange tree on the left and the crown on her right.[62] The picture is clearly a political and religious allegory, as the orange has associations with love, constancy, chastity, and generosity and was linked to the Virgin Mary, much as the whole gardenlike setting may recall the *hortus conclusus* of Marian iconography. The association with hunting asserts her chastity as a modern Diana, and the picture may also allude to Van Somer's portrait of Anna of Denmark in hunting gear, also dressed as Diana and accompanied by the owl of Minerva. The viewpoint of the picture, painted from slightly below, with the queen also raised on a step, accentuates the sense in which she towers over the viewer as much as she outstrips her dwarf, Jeffrey Hudson.[63] Indeed, the presence of Jeffrey Hudson adds several inches to the Queen's actual height.[64]

Hudson's presence suggests the way in which Henrietta Maria literally and metaphorically towers over the homunculus, an image that prefigures the frontispiece of *Leviathan,* with its body politic filled with miniature men. Indeed, in at least one contemporary tract it was argued that Hudson was "a most perfect abridgement of nature" and that dwarves were particularly suitable servants for the monarch. Dwarves are "accounted *emblematically* necessary, to denote those who desire to approach neere Princes ought not to be ambitious of any Greatnesse, but [ought] to acknowledge all their courtlustre is but a beame of the Royall Sunne their Master."[65] Hudson was a regular performer in royal masques, especially those mounted by the queen, and his presence accentuates the masquelike quality of the picture.

Interestingly, the almost central figure of the painting is the monkey, Pug, who sits on Hudson's shoulder. Most studies of the painting argue that the iconography derives from the chained monkeys of the emblematic tradition as a symbol of the queen's control over her passions. Yet in light of the dialogue between the masques and Prynne's work, it also seems possible that the image of the controlled monkey, dominated by the queen, is a rejection of Prynne's depiction of Catholicism and acting as false forms of imitation. As in Townshend's masque, the suggestion is that the queen is beyond the kinds of transformation risked by ordinary humans and that she embodies universal reason and order, and, unscathed in her acting by the bestial, she towers over man and animal. Because women were often regarded as more passionate and closer to the animal within, the studied control of the portrait asserts the queen's rejection of the anti-theatricalist readings of her body as disordered and bestial. Thus, the queen's gesture, touching the monkey, not only demonstrates her control over the passions but also implies ownership and even parallels Adam's act of naming the beasts.[66] This incident often was used as a symbol of man's dominion, and here Henrietta Maria claims the male privilege as part of her regal power without becoming the monstrous hybrid female of Prynne's tract.

The control over the animals and the control over the passions discerned in animals and then extrapolated to humans was seen as the basis of the exercise of power. Van Dyck's picture echoes his own *Charles Ier à la Chasse,* where the horse's submissive, bowed head replicates the animal homage depicted in nativity scenes.[67] Here, Henrietta Maria does not simply control her own passions; this gesture claims her political right to rule. The monkey perched on the dwarf's shoulder emphasizes her distance from the mundane, and the gazes of the two creatures mark their correct position in the natural hierarchy. The dwarf looks up to the queen, aspiring toward her (super)human status, whereas the monkey looks down toward the mundane and the bestial. This may be the ordinary order, but the optical distortions of the picture allow Henrietta Maria to stand outside the quotidian scale. Instead, Henrietta Maria, almost a giant, gazes out serenely and asserts her dominion, which interpolates the viewer below even the apes and dwarves of her court.

NOTES

The quotation in the second subheading (see p. 145) is from John Milton, *A Masque Presented at Ludlow Castle,* in *The Complete Shorter Poems,* ed. John Carey (Harlow, U.K.: Longman, 1968), line 77.

1. John Marston, *Antonio and Mellida,* in *The Selected Plays of John Marston,* ed. M. P. Jackson and M. Neill (Cambridge: Cambridge University Press, 1986), "Induction," lines 79–80 and 157–59.

2. Ben Jonson, "To Mime," *Epigrams,* 129, lines 12 and 16 in *Ben Jonson,* ed. Ian Donaldson (Oxford: Oxford University Press, 1985), 275.

3. See *Antonio and Mellida,* ed. G. K. Hunter (Lincoln, Nebr.: Regents Plays, 1965), 9, and *Antonio and Mellida,* ed. W. R. Gair (Manchester: Manchester University Press, 1991), 68.

4. E. Nungezer, *Dictionary of Actors and Other Persons Associated with the Public Representation of Plays in England Before 1642* (New Haven, Conn.: Cornell University Press, 1929). On Gew, see also W. J. Strunk, "An Elizabethan Showman's Ape," *Modern Language Notes* 32 (1917): 215–21.

5. Ben Jonson, *Bartholomew Fair,* "Induction," lines 15–16 in *Ben Jonson: Four Comedies,* ed. H. Ostovich (Harlow, U.K.: Longman, 1997).

6. Francis Bacon, "Of Masques and Triumphs," in *Francis Bacon,* ed. Brian Vickers (Oxford: Oxford University Press, 1996), 417.

7. Erica Fudge, *Perceiving Animals: Humans and Beasts in Early Modern English Culture* (2000. Reprint. Urbana: University of Illinois Press, 2002), 89.

8. Keith Thomas, *Man and the Natural World: Changing Attitudes in England, 1500–1800* (Harmondsworth, U.K.: Penguin, 1984), 123.

9. Lorraine Daston and Katherine Park, *Wonders and the Order of Nature, 1150–1750* (New York: Zone Books, 1998), 176.

10. Anat Feinberg, "'Like Demie Gods the Apes Began to Move': The Ape in the English Theatrical Tradition, 1580–1660," *Cahiers Elisabéthains* 35 (1989): 1–13, especially 1.

11. Nathaniel Wolloch, "Dead Animals and the Beast-Machine: Seventeenth-Century Netherlandish Paintings of Dead Animals, as Anti-Cartesian Statements," *Art History* 22 (1999): 705–27, especially 706.

12. Donna Haraway, *Primate Visions: Gender, Race and Nature in the World of Modern Science* (London: Verso, 1992), 10.

13. Kim F. Hall, "'Troubling Doubles': Apes, Africans, and Blackface in *Mr Moore's Revels*," in *Race, Ethnicity, and Power in the Renaissance*, ed. J. G. MacDonald (Cranbury, N.J.: Associated University Press, 1997), 120–44 and 139.

14. See Fudge, *Perceiving Animals*, 4 and chapter 1 ("Screaming Monkeys"), especially 28 ("who is human and who is not is never clear").

15. See Susan Wiseman, "Monstrous Perfectibility: Ape-Human Transformations in Hobbes, Bulwer, Tyson," in *At the Borders of the Human: Beasts, Bodies and Natural Philosophy in the Early Modern Period*, ed. Erica Fudge, Ruth Gilbert, and S. J. Wiseman (Basingstoke, U.K.: Macmillan, 1999), 215–38.

16. Bacon, *Of the Wisdom of the Ancients*, cited in Erica Fudge, "Calling Creatures by Their True Names: Bacon, the New Science and the Beast in Man," in *At the Borders*, 97.

17. Edward Topsell, *The Historie of Foure-footed Beastes* (London, 1607), B1v–C3r, B5r, and B2r.

18. John Bulwer, *Anthropometamorphosis: Man Transform'd, or the Artificial Changeling* (London, 1653), 23.

19. Dudley Wilson, *Signs and Portents: Monstrous Births from the Middle Ages to the Enlightenment* (London: Routledge, 1993), 57, and W. Drummond, "A Letter on the True Nature of Poetry," in *Poems and Prose*, ed. R. H. MacDonald (Edinburgh: Scottish Academic Press, 1976), 192.

20. Montaigne, "Of a Monstrous Child," cited in Wilson, *Signs*, 77.

21. George Chapman, Ben Jonson, and John Marston, *Eastward Ho*, 1.2.45–46 and opening stage direction, in *The Roaring Girl and Other City Comedies*, ed. J. Knowles and G. Giddens (Oxford: Oxford University Press, 2001).

22. Wiseman, "Monstrous Perfectibility," 217.

23. John Marston, *The Scourge of Villainie*, Satire 9 ("Here's a toy to mocke an Ape indeede"), lines 11–20 and 87, in *The Poems of John Marston*, ed. A. Davenport (Liverpool: Liverpool University Press, 1961).

24. Topsell, *Historie*, B2v.

25. George Chapman, *Sir Giles Goosecap*, 1.1.11–20 and 32–35 in *The Plays of George Chapman: The Tragedies*, ed. A. Holaday, G. B. Evans, and T. L. Berger (Cambridge, U.K.: D. S. Brewer, 1997).

26. I. H., *The World's Folly* (London, 1615), B1v and B2r.

27. William Prynne, *Histriomastix* (London, 1633), 5X4r.

28. H. W. Janson, *Apes and Ape Lore in the Middle Ages and Renaissance* (London: Warburg Institute, 1952), 217, 234, and 90.

29. George Chapman, *The Memorable Masque,* lines 33–34, in *Court Masques,* ed. David Lindley (Oxford: Oxford University Press, 1995), and N. E. McClure, ed., *The Letters of John Chamberlain,* 2 vols. (Philadelphia: American Philosophical Society, 1939), 1:425.

30. Stephen Orgel and Roy Strong, *Inigo Jones and the Theatre of the Stuart Courts,* 2 vols. (Berkeley: University of California Press, 1971), 2:490 (pl. 228).

31. *OED,* s.v. "baboonery," 1.

32. Nicholas Tyacke, "Science and Religion at Oxford before the Civil War," in *Puritans and Revolutionaries,* ed. David Pennington and Keith Thomas (Oxford: Oxford University Press, 1978), 73–94.

33. Aurelian Townshend, *Tempe Restored,* in *Court Masques,* lines 43 and 336–38. All references are to this edition.

34. Ibid., line 192.

35. R. Booth, "The First Female Professional Singers: Madam Coniack," *Notes and Queries* 242 (1997): 533.

36. Prynne, *Histriomastix,* 6R4r, cited by S. E. Tomlinson, "Too Theatrical? Female Subjectivity in Caroline Interregnum Drama," *Women's Writing* 6 (1999): 71 and note 22.

37. Townshend, *Tempe,* lines 23–43 ("The Description of the Scene").

38. Ibid., line 299. For the importance of Circe, see Gareth Roberts, "The Descendants of Circe: Witches and Renaissance Fictions," in *Witchcraft in Early Modern Europe,* ed. Jonathan Barry, Marianne Hester, and Gareth Roberts (Cambridge: Cambridge University Press, 1996), 183–206, especially 204; and Marina Warner, "The Enchantments of Circe," *Raritan* 17 (1997): 1–23.

39. Townshend, *Tempe,* lines 218–19, 224, 216–17, 221–22, 223, and 175–204. Melinda Gough notes that this descent "constitutes the visible agent of victory" over Circe; see Gough, "Beauty Restored in *Tempe Restored:* Henrietta Maria and the Traditions of Women's Courtly Performances in France and England," forthcoming in *Modern Philology.*

40. David Lindley, "The Politics of Music in the Masque," in *The Politics of the Stuart Court Masque,* ed. D. Bevington and P. Holbrook (Cambridge: Cambridge University Press, 1998), 273–95.

41. *The Poems of Thomas Randolph,* ed. G. Thorn-Drury (London: Haslewood Books, 1929), 115–16.

42. Booth, "First Female," 533.

43. Warner, "Enchantments," 7.

44. Townshend, *Tempe,* lines 68, 70, 120–38, and 315–19.

45. Milton, *Masque Presented at Ludlow Castle,* lines 73–75.

46. Townshend, *Tempe,* line 83.

47. Sophie Tomlinson, "Theatrical Vibrancy on the Caroline Court Stage: *Tempe Restored* and *The Shepherd's Paradise,*" in *Women and Culture at the Courts of the Stuart Queens,* ed. C. McManus (Basingstoke, U.K.: Palgrave Macmillan, 2003).

48. Orgel and Strong, *Inigo Jones*, 2, 491 (pl. 226).

49. Townshend, *Tempe*, lines 151, 115, and 161.

50. See Julie Sanders, "Caroline Salon Culture and Female Agency: The Countess of Carlisle, Henrietta Maria, and Public Theatre," *Theatre Journal* 52 (2000): 449–64, especially 452–53.

51. Townshend, *Tempe*, lines 329–31 and 332–35.

52. According to the various depositions collected at the time of Prynne's trial, *Histriomastix* was begun in April to June 1631 and completed in mid- or late 1632, when it was printed, appearing in late 1632 despite its 1633 title page date (see W. W. Greg, *A Companion to Arber* (Oxford: Oxford University Press, 1967), 85). Prynne himself pointed out the absurdity of the claimed attack on Montague's play, stating he had planned to have the volume "published in the country above four weeks before her Majesty's pastorall, against which it could not possibly be intended" (S. R. Gardiner, *Documents relating to the Proceedings against William Prynne* (London: Camden Society, 1877), 52). Prynne may have been disingenuous, but if cross-dressing is the issue and not just the role of female actors, then *Artenice* (1626) actually involved female to male cross-dressing (see Orgel and Strong, *Inigo Jones*, 1, 384–85). It is possible that Prynne knew of the rehearsals, but if 1631 is the correct date for the commencement of *Histriomastix*, then other events, including the defense of female performance and the clear example of a French actress offered by *Tempe Restored*, are more likely occasions. See also Sophie Tomlinson, "She That Plays the King: Henrietta Maria and the Threat of the Actress in Caroline Culture," in *The Politics of Tragicomedy*, ed. Gordon McMullan and Jonathan Hope (London: Routledge, 1992), 195.

53. Prynne, *Histriomastix*, 6R4r (Index, s.v. "Women Actors"). Sir John Finch raised this issue in the Star Chamber examination of Prynne and posited a "generall aspertion on Hir Maiesties nation"; see Gardiner, *Documents*, 10.

54. Prynne, *Histriomastix*, T3v, C2v, 5E3r, 6Dr, and G4v.

55. Ibid., X4r and 5T4r.

56. See Roberts, "Descendants," 203.

57. John Gee, *The Foot out of the Snare* (London, 1624), F2r.

58. Laura Levine, *Men in Women's Clothing: Anti-theatricality and Effeminization, 1579–1642* (Cambridge: Cambridge University Press, 1994), 24.

59. Gee, *Foot*, F2r.

60. Tomlinson, "Too Theatrical?," 171 and note 22.

61. Townshend, *Tempe*, lines 336–37, 213, 227–29, and 241–44.

62. See *Van Dyck: Paintings*, ed. A. Wheelock, S. J. Barnes, and J. C. Held (Washington, D.C.: National Gallery, 1990), 262–65 for the iconography and provenance of this painting.

63. George Vertue noted that Henrietta Maria was painted taller than she actually was in real life through the use of a low vantage point; see *Van Dyck: Paintings*, 263.

64. *Van Dyck, 1599–1641*, ed. C. Brown and H. Vliege (London and Antwerp: Royal Academy Publications and Antwerpen Open, 1999), 246.

65. Microphilus, *The New Year's Gift* (London, 1636), F5r.

66. Peter Harrison, "Reading the Passions: The Fall, the Passions, and Dominion over Nature," in *The Soft Underbelly of Reason: The Passions in the Seventeenth Century,* ed. Stephen Gaukroger (London: Routledge, 1998), 40–78, especially 52–53 and 55.

67. R. M. Smuts, *Court Culture and the Origins of a Royalist Tradition* (Philadelphia: University of Pennsylvania Press), 236.

9

Pliny's Literate Elephant and the Idea of Animal Language in Renaissance Thought

Brian Cummings

In his catalog of "vulgar errors" committed by natural historians concerning the behavior of animals, Sir Thomas Browne entertained with special relish the odd tale of an elephant that had been taught to speak and write. It is a paradox he describes with simultaneous rough skepticism and whimsical delight: "That some Elephants have not only written whole sentences, as Aelian ocularly testifieth, but have also spoken, as Oppianus delivereth, and Christophorus a Costa particularly relateth, although it sound like that of Achilles horse in Homer, wee doe not conceive impossible." Browne constructs a number of arguments to show that these venerable anecdotes are not, contrary to intuition, outside the realm of possibility. Some of his reasoning he derives from the well-attested tradition of the wisdom of elephants, what he calls the "affinity of reason in this Animall."[1] Others he derives from the elephant's anatomy. Here he observes that among birds the beak and tongue size is critical to the performance of speech. The elephant's capacious mouth and its prodigious "lips and teeth" provide in a similar and even superior way a physical mechanism for the act of speaking.

In the process, Browne apparently dispels each of the principal inhibitions traditionally understood to disqualify animals from the exclusive human domain of language. These, deriving ultimately from Aristotle and repeated in a wide variety of formulations, were the ability to pronounce sounds in articulate form (usually understood to require both vowels and consonants) and the ability to use these sounds to signify conventional (and symbolic) meanings.[2] Language therefore was understood to involve both a physical and a mental test of qualification. These tests, Browne bluffly declares, the elephant passes with flying colors. In mentalist terms, the "proximity of reason" of the elephant to humanity he takes as axiomatic and almost unproblematic. As for the physical test, "whether the musculous and motive parts about the hollow mouthes of beasts, may not dispose the passing spirit into some articulate notes, seems a querie of no great doubt."[3]

Only a predisposition to disbelieve the story of the speaking elephant, Browne implies, stands in the way of its theoretical plausibility.

Nevertheless, Browne presents his case as one that is defiantly paradoxical, an affront to human reason in every sense. He knows his readers do not believe his argument and do not believe that he does either. He is making a case to show off the limits of his own powers of induction. However carefully he tries to persuade the reader of the other possibility, that an elephant could actually talk and mean its own meaning to be understood, Browne does not expect the persuasion to be anything other than for the sake of argument. As if to provide authority, Browne cites (with disingenuous seriousness) "the Serpent that spake unto Eve" and dogs and cats that talk to witches. Yet elsewhere in *Pseudodoxia Epidemica* Browne casually dismisses St. Basil's description of Adam and Eve talking to the beasts before the Fall as wantonly absurd.[4] Philosophically, Browne appears already to belong to the opinion of John Locke, with whom the last word on animal language seems to belong. A bird can be taught how to speak, but it will not understand what it is saying. Fascinated as he is by Prince Maurice's talking bird, Locke nonetheless excludes him absolutely from the linguistic community. The speaking parrot is a conjuror's trick or at best a creature of habit. The illusion is based entirely on imitation or ventriloquism. It tells us nothing about language because language is an expression of mind. It belongs to the science not of zoology but of epistemology and is a function of knowledge and ideas. To attribute language to an animal is to attribute first a structure of ideas, something that to Locke is absurd. When a parrot speaks, as when a child parrots the speech of an adult, what comes out is "nothing but so much insignificant Noise."[5]

Conventionally, the move toward Locke's finality on the question has been seen as the inevitable victory of the Cartesian model of the animal machine over less stringent tests for animal intelligence, and at the same time an inevitable victory for scientific observation over the fanciful natural history of the ancients. Browne, as one of the earliest readers of Descartes in England and the owner of a copy of the 1637 first edition of the *Discours de la méthode,* in this context is part of the wider reception of a new view of animals.[6] Yet there are reasons for caution over too brusque a historical division. The triumph of the exceptionalist claims of human intellect as resident in human language concurred with a gradual erosion of the assumption that animal speech was an anatomical impossibility. Closer observation of animal and human anatomy revealed more continuity than had been expected.[7] Keith Thomas has also argued that the seventeenth century in general saw a "narrowing gap" in perceptions of human and animal intelligence.[8]

At the same time, Descartes's very certainty on the issue encouraged some vigorous responses, from Gassendi initially and also notably from the royal physician at the court of Louis XIV, Cureau de la Chambre. Cureau lovingly and admiringly conveyed the ethnography of the world of animal sound and gesture, from the swan's song to the hum of the bee.[9] In the opposite direction, there is equal reason to be doubtful about any widespread credulousness in relation to animal language in the pre-Cartesian tradition. It has recently been emphasized that "early modern natural philosophers almost universally insisted that only humans were capable of language and speech" and that in doing so they also followed the almost universal opinion of their ancient masters.[10]

This puts into more acute focus the mysterious appeal of the story of the language of elephants. For this story is immediately more outlandish and unsettling than the familiar tales of performing apes and loquaciously trained magpies and parakeets. In his late retelling Browne self-consciously borrows from this sense of the uncanny. He knows his readers will not believe him, but they will half want to, and they will play along with his game. The first crucial point about the elephant writing in the sand is that it is a tale of the imagination and of the picaresque. It is immediately and irreducibly comic. This element of the comic plays havoc with the certainties of the *philosophe* and the empiricist, exposing their blank theories to the risk of bathos and platitude. In this, Browne is not making new skeptical play but is drawing on some of the oldest traditions in natural history. It is to some of these traces of ambiguity, both in classical writers and in early modern responses to them, that this chapter attends.

An elephant that speaks, or even writes, treads elegantly across the margins and between the lines of Renaissance zoology. However extraordinary it may now seem, it is a commonplace, derived from Greek and Roman writers such as Plutarch, Pliny, and Aelian and repeated from source to source without expression of surprise. This in itself requires explanation because the writers involved would have been perfectly familiar with the philosophical argument that language is one of the defining categories of the human. A case in point is the botanist and polymath Conrad Gesner, whose *Historia animalium* (published in 1551) became a standard text throughout Europe despite being placed on Paul V's Index of prohibited books in 1559 because of Gesner's Protestantism. Gesner's method, like all natural histories of the sixteenth century, is encyclopedic.[11] In his first book on the quadrupeds, Gesner reports comprehensively on the known occurrences of elephantine writing. The passage is translated almost word for word in the standard English treatment by Edward Topsell, who nonetheless, unlike the elephant, stumbles a little over his Greek characters in his transliteration into a Latinate alphabet:

> Mutianus which was thrice Consul, affirmed to *Pliny,* that he saw an Elephant which learned the *Greek* letters, and was able with his tongue to write these words, *Autos egoo Tadegrapsa laphura te kelt' anetheca;* that is, I wrote these things and dedicated the *Celtican* spoils: but in these actions of writing, the hand of the teacher must be also present to teach him how to frame the letters, and then, as *Ælianus* saith, they will write upon Tables, and follow the true proportion of the Characters expressed before their face, whereupon they look as attentively as any *Grammarian.*[12]

Gesner is silent on his view of the stories and records them simply as part of the documentary evidence that he has before him. Yet he does show an interest in the instrumental contingencies of the elephant's abilities. The elephant must be taught, by a teacher who is physically present, to train his tongue or trunk in the right direction. Then, after he has mastered the rudiments, he is ready to write from a crib, like any apprentice or child.

Gesner seems less interested in the implicit philosophical questions about an elephantine language or intelligence than he is in providing a verifiable account of the learning process involved by which the elephant acquires a physical skill or *techne.* Perhaps he also implies that this is an acquired technique: that it is not a natural skill, and that an elephant would or could not do such a thing without human training. It is possible that he does not think that this is an example of elephant language at all. He does not express any wonder, for instance, at the elephant launching straight into Greek, and epic Greek at that. His story may be another example of the elephant's well-known and much-admired capacity to learn new tricks, but no more than that. The elephant is trained to write the letters but has no conception of what lies behind them, no sense that they have a meaning, never mind what that meaning is. Therefore, this is an anecdote that even in a modern context might evince surprise but not a conviction of impossibility.

Gesner denies the elephant speech and gives him only insignificant noise. Indeed, he uses the nasal braying of the elephant as an explanation for its Latin name (although the etymology in reality probably works the other way round): "Their voice is called by the word *Barrire,* that is, to bray, and thereupon the Elephants themselves are called *Barri;* for his voice cometh out of his mouth and nostrils together, like as when a man speaketh breathing."[13] A somewhat different line of argument is drawn by the great Bolognese naturalist Ulisse Aldrovandi (1522–1605), whose *De Quadrupedibus Solidipedibus* is the early modern master text on mastodons and the major source for Browne's chapter "Of the Elephant." Aldrovandi repeats the stories from Pliny and Aelian of elephants writing but puts them in a broader linguistic context. Joannes Metellus, he says, records evidence of Indian elephants learning to understand not only local dialects but also foreign languages ("non modo vernaculam, sed etiam peregrinas linguas si doceantur").[14] Aldrovandi uses this instance to prove the elephant's remarkable capacity to follow complex orders. The *ingenium* of the elephant encourages it to seek out the company of humans, seeking in such company a reciprocal mental activity.

Although the capacity to follow human speech (especially complex commands) is an example of high intelligence, it does not yet involve elephant language. It belongs still to the realm of instruction and training. Further cases take Aldrovandi into new territory. Oppian in his travels saw elephants talking among themselves, he reports.[15] Worrying perhaps that he is straining his readers' beliefs, Aldrovandi adds a modern sighting. An anecdote from Cristoval Acosta's *Aromatum Historia* tells how an elephant was heard enunciating "Hoo, hoo," taken to be Malayalam (the language spoken in Kerala) for "I will, I will."[16] Acosta, Aldrovandi continues, has even seen Malayan elephants holding a conversation, showing every sign of linguistic intention and mutual comprehension.[17] Here Aldrovandi finally provides evidence of elephant speech in the full sense. The elephants not only follow human commands but talk back, using a local dialect that they have learned to understand and articulate. Furthermore, not only do they participate in speech in imitation of their human auditors, but they also converse among themselves for their own pleasure and purposes.

How are we to take Aldrovandi's incipient essay on animal language? It is not offered as part of any general theory. Rather, it is presented as relevant only to this individual species. Indeed, Aldrovandi can do no more than record individual cases among this one species, for in all likelihood he never saw an elephant himself. He relied on other naturalists and on travelers' tales from Africa and India. Elephants on the continent of medieval and Renaissance Europe were an exotic rarity.[18] Charlemagne was given an elephant by the caliph of Baghdad and kept him in a park in Germany for several years. Frederick II brought one home from the Holy Land and used it in his attack on Cremona in 1214. Another, later depicted in stone at Notre Dame in Paris, was carried back from the crusades by Louis IX and eventually sent to Henry III of England, who added it to his ample menagerie. Such extravagantly uncommon examples increased visibly after the Portuguese explorations in West Africa and coastal India. Nevertheless, the famous white elephant Hanno, presented to the Medici Pope Leo X in 1514, was the first seen in Rome since ancient times and was not followed by another for more than a century. Others were sent as gifts to the emperor in Vienna and the King of Spain in Madrid; one destined for Henri IV in France in 1591 found its way instead to Queen Elizabeth in London via Dieppe.[19] Although many of these beasts (and others) traveled part of their route through Italy, Aldrovandi is not known to have seen one. On the other hand, he may have seen and even handled a rhinoceros. In 1515, a rhinoceros was presented by the Sultan of Gujarat to Manuel I of Portugal, who arranged for it to fight with one of his elephants to prove Pliny the Elder's theory of a natural animosity between the two beasts. This rhinoceros (after putting the elephant to flight) was intended as a gift for the same pope, but it drowned when the ship sank en route. Nevertheless, the animal had a distinguished afterlife, forming the model for Albrecht Dürer's celebrated engraving of 1515.[20] Meanwhile, it is said, the carcass found its way (via the attentions of a taxidermist) into the Medicean collections in Florence. It may be the same specimen that Aldrovandi exhibited in his museum of natural history in Bologna later in the century.[21]

Hanno the elephant caused a sensation in Italy, and his wonderful history, whether known to Aldrovandi or not, resonates powerfully with the naturalist's account. The name, despite its redolence of ancient Carthage, probably derived from the word for elephant (*aana*) in Malayalam. The King of Cochin sent two elephants to Lisbon in December 1510, one as a gift to King Manuel of Portugal, along with two nairs (royal custodians) to teach them. By the time the beast arrived in Rome in a magnificent triumphal procession, as the prize gift of the Portuguese mission, he was highly trained. Hanno sent the papal court into raptures. Among a number of poetic panegyrics was Aurelio Sereno's "De elephante carmen." Thus began the persistent stories of the gift of Hanno for languages: "How great is the power of the Creator which shows to us today the beast, in which are contained so many virtues, that can live for three centuries, that progenitates one time in its life, that respects religion, that salutes our Holy Father, that understands human speech."[22]

The gestures of reverence made by the elephant in the papal presence were particularly noted. This tallied with ancient accounts (going back to Pliny) of the recognition paid by elephants to the royal person or other dignitaries: Topsell especially admired the elephant's capacity "to discern between Kings and common men."[23] More recent voyagers noted the same: Richard Hakluyt, who knew all about praising monarchs, approved the "quick sense and sharpness of wit" of the elephant on the basis of its capacity to "do due honour to a king."[24] In the case of Pope Leo's elephant, Pasquale Malaspina described how Hanno stretched himself on the ground and then straightened himself up "in reverence to the Pope and to his entourage."[25] The physical description of the elephant's gesture makes it an imitation of the human practice of genuflection. A house was made for the elephant at the end of the Borgo Sant'Angelo with a spacious courtyard where the pope, watched by crowds of the curious, could play with his pet. It was commonly observed how the elephant genuflected before his master, trumpeted to announce his presence, showered him with affection, and shared tears with him. His mahout encouraged him in tricks and games. In all of these antics, it was said, Hanno demonstrated a sensitive understanding of Portuguese and of Indian languages.[26]

The reverential obeisance of the elephant to the pope became the subject of much mockery among Protestants later in the century. Donne's first *Satyre* made playful reference to the comic reverence made by Elizabeth's elephant to the name of Philip II.[27] Anticlerical skepticism also extended to the elephant's gift of speech. The only reference to Hanno speaking, rather than responding to the speech of his mahout and his other keepers, comes in Ulrich von Hutten's second book of *Epistolae obscurorum virorum* of 1517. The letter, written in pastiche scholastic Latin, records with some pathos the death of Hanno in June of the previous year, the love of Leo X for his great beast, and his care and sadness during the elephant's last illness. "In sooth it was a marvellous brute, and it had a great abundance of long snout; and when it saw the Pope it would kneel to him, and cry in a terrible voice, 'Bar, bar, bar!' There is, I trow, not the like beast in the whole world."[28] Hutten's satire of the rotund Pope, his love of hunting, his extravagance, his buffoonery, and his sentimental attachment to his menagerie of exotic animals is never far away, even from this sympathetic anecdote of the mournful love of one enormous creature for another of different species. The ambiguity reaches into the brief recall of Hanno's speech. For what is articulated in the elephant's stentorian cry, "bar, bar, bar?" Is it a fanfare of welcome, a paean of praise, lending weight to his graceful genuflection? Or is it just the sound an elephant makes? Hutten's choice of vocabulary, put into the mouth of his ignorant monk Johann Kalb, is enigmatic. The *bar* is the note of the *barritus,* the noise (as Gesner and Topsell later argued) proper to the *barrus.*

Thirty years later, Rabelais in *Le Tiers Livre* (1546) describes the solitude of the philosopher shouted down by the bruit of beasts. Here, the cry of the elephant ("barrient les elephans") takes its place in the midst of a virtuoso list of the generic gutturalizations of any number of other species.[29] In typical encyclopedic style, Rabelais provides a glossary of seventy-one different onomatopoeic animal sounds. The "barring of elephants" is no more articulate in Rabelais's list than "grunting of swine, girning of boars, yelping of foxes, mewing of cats, cheeping of mice, squeaking of weasels, croaking of frogs, crowing of cocks, cackling of hens."[30] In a footnote, Rabelais refers to "an elephant, which out of reverence for the pope his master would barr and bend the knee." The ambiguity is opaque. Is the "barr" to be understood like the gesture, as an expression of elephantine meaning, however simple, or is it accompanying sound, the same sound it makes on all occasions, like a barking dog or a buzzing bee?

❦

The history of Hanno is in every respect an oddity. For more comprehensive evidence of elephant behavior, Aldrovandi and his fellow zoologists continued to rely on the abundant testimony of the ancients. Here, as always, the primary source was Pliny the Elder's *Naturalis historia.* The fortunes of Pliny's book are themselves an index of the progress of early modern natural science. This classic of medieval knowledge was one of the staple bestsellers of the early printed book trade, produced in edition after edition throughout Europe. In that sense it is a Renaissance book as much as an ancient book. Pliny was a more widely available source of knowledge on animals than either Gesner or Aldrovandi. In the case of the elephant, this was one of the few places where the beast could be seen (figure 9.1). Pliny's decline in the eighteenth century and beyond is just as spectacular. His book has long since been reduced to a curiosity, a repository of fake lore and old gossip. In this respect its previous aura of authority has been a principal pretext for modern derision. It stands as an epitome for old, bad science.

Perhaps few books of the ancient world are easier to misunderstand and to misread. For as Italo Calvino (a rare modern champion) writes, although the use of Pliny as a work of reference or repository of ancient opinion became universal in the Middle Ages, Pliny was also a writer of singular imagination and sympathy for the natural world: "We might perhaps distinguish a poetic-philosophical Pliny, with his feeling for the universe and his love of knowledge and mystery, from the Pliny who was a neurotic collector of data, an obsessive compiler who seems to think only of not wasting a single jotting in his mastodonic notebook."[31] Nothing could be further from the truth, as Calvino goes on to state, than the view that Pliny is indiscriminate in his treatment of his sources, that he is equally credulous about every foolish story that is handed down to him, or that he relies on secondhand knowledge at the expense of observation. He distinguishes critically between authorities, rejecting some as fanciful even when including them. Careful attention must be paid to the way in which he introduces a story, and not just to the fascination with which he recounts every detail as the story unfolds. Concealed in his apparently eclectic method is a complex epistemology, but it is not one based on the preconceptions of the postempiricist world. This epistemology is (in Calvino's words) "unstable and unpredictable" and involves both a sophisticated handling of textual authority and a prevailing skepticism about

108

C. PLINII
SECVNDI NATVRALIS
HISTORIAE LIBER
OCTAVVS.

De animalibus terrestribus, elephantorum commendatio, & de sensu eorum. CAP. I.

Figure 9.1. Portrait of an elephant (side and front view) from Pliny, *Naturalis historia* (Frankfurt, 1582). By permission of The British Library, classmark 453.g.6.

the certainties of any system of knowledge based on perception. For all Pliny's apparent literal-mindedness, his book is haunted by uncertainty and by the infinite mystery of the world of organic matter.

The elephant is given pride of place at the opening of Pliny's eighth book, dedicated to the description of land animals. The first sentence gives the key to Pliny's magnificent chapter on this most magnificent of beasts: "*Maximum est elephans proximumque humanis sensibus*" ("The elephant is the greatest of animals in size and the closest to man in sensibility").[32] What follows shows that this praise is not meant merely sentimentally. Pliny gives a portrait of the life of elephants in the round, with an ample sense of behavioral and physical characteristics that are peculiar to the species. Though hardly an exercise in animal psychology in the modern sense, it has something of the flavor of Konrad Lorenz's animal studies, a description written with respect and even love for a fellow being.[33]

Later writers went to Pliny on elephants to take the animal out of the circus or the peculiar habitat of the Papal Curia, and for that matter out of the freak show of travelers' tales, and place him back in his natural landscape. The elephant was a far more common sight among Europeans in antiquity than at any time until the twentieth century. Unknown before the eastern campaigns of Alexander the Great, by the Roman imperial period they were used as draught animals and in shows. Some were kept near the city in vivaria as state-owned herds; Juvenal refers to "Caesar's herd" in the late first century C.E. There was an official civil servant known as the *procurator ad elephantos*.[34] Most animals were imported from Africa or India, but Aelian reports that some were bred in captivity.[35] Pliny therefore could easily observe the life of elephants for himself, as individuals and in groups. In addition to such sightings in captivity, because of the wide reach of the empire he could also make use of a substantial literature concerning elephants in their indigenous homes in the jungle or on the plains. Although superficially similar in style to early modern descriptions such as Aldrovandi's, Pliny's therefore is quite different in character.

Pliny presents nothing less than the ethnography of the elephant. The declared proximity of the elephant and the human mind is not incidental, for Pliny imagines elephant life along lines similar to his descriptions of far-off human tribes in Book VII: "The rites and customs of elephant society are represented as those of a people with a culture different from ours, but nonetheless worthy of respect and understanding."[36] This both is and is not an anthropomorphic tendency. Pliny demonstrates not only that the animal is like the human but also that the human, too, is animal. The elephant lives in a complex community with subtle rules of organization. The elephant follows what he is commanded, remembers what he has been taught, and learns to carry out duties in a proper order. He responds to and gives back in return the higher emotions, he has a sense of honor and even of the Roman cult of glory, and he is capable of ascending to virtues that are rare in humankind, such as *probitas, prudentia,* and *aequitas.* These are the values of the Roman citizen, indeed of the top of the social scale.

This comes from a distinct culture of the animal. Modern accounts of the elephant readily admire an elephant's "memory," "intelligence," "loyalty," and "affection." But these ideas are distanced within implied quotation marks. "Intelligence" in such a context is understood in the diminished, etiolated sense reserved for the nonhuman. Pliny places these categories within a comprehensible ethical system. In fact, it is far from clear that he follows the Aristotelian first principle of denying the animal *ratio.*[37] It is not Pliny's style to debate such a question in the abstract. Instead he behaves as if it is not really an issue. Elephant behavior requires categories of intelligence and of moral explanation, whether or not Pliny understands the consequences of applying them in a nonhuman sphere.

The elephant's intelligence is shown to consist in more than the commonplace tales of its dexterity, of its ability to walk along ropes or even turn round and walk back again. The skill of elephants in circus acts is indeed extraordinary, but Pliny is struck by the elephant's sense of participation in the event, its talent for the ludic and the histrionic, and its enjoyment of theater and theatricality. Besides, the elephant shows not only a developed spatial awareness but also the capacity to imagine the sequence of its steps and routines in advance. Pliny's favorite anecdote of performing elephants is of one that kept getting its moves wrong, was punished for his mistakes, and so took to rehearsing his act in the middle of the night (*"eadem illa meditantem noctu repertum"*).[38]

The elephant is capable of a refined sense of self-consciousness, Pliny shows. It has a sense of bodily awareness and of the care of the self, taking the greatest care of the tusks, sparing the point of one to keep it sharp in case of emergency and using the other as a tool for daily life. The elephant knows its tusks are valuable and buries them in the ground if they fall off. In one peculiar episode, Pliny reports that a herd, knowing that their attackers were interested only in the tusks, put those with smallest tusks in front "so that it may be thought not worth while to fight them." As an ultimate sacrifice they broke their tusks in self-violence before admitting defeat, thus robbing their captors of the booty (*"praedaque se redimunt"*).[39]

Perhaps most important is the way Pliny demonstrates that elephants display a high form of socialization. The life of the community is natural to the elephant: *"Elephanti gregatim semper ingrediuntur."*[40] Moreover, the gregariousness of the elephant goes beyond living in a herd. It involves a social organization with duties and fellow feeling. The oldest member of the herd leads the column, the next oldest brings up the rear. By working together they protect the interests of all because all members of the herd are of value to all. In fording a river, the smallest goes first so that the depth of the river is not increased by the deep impression made by the tread of the larger animals.

The idea of fellow feeling is essential to ancient, particularly to Stoic, concepts of justice and social ethics. Stoic thought also conventionally denied to animals any such concepts.[41] Pliny's position on such matters is puzzling, perhaps reflecting his eclectic approach. A connection between a sense of mutuality and a concept of justice, found for instance in Cicero, seems to structure Pliny's moral assumptions.[42] Yet this is not something he denies to animals. Indeed, even though it runs against most ancient philosophical principles, Pliny attaches the elephant's elevated principles of communality to a refined emotional and ethical life of the mind. Elephant society encompasses a culture of shame and mutual respect. When the army of Antiochus was crossing a river, Ajax the chief elephant refused, having always previously led the line. His place was given to Patroclus, who happily took up the task and was rewarded with the customary marks of leadership: a silver harness, "an elephant's greatest delight." Poor Ajax in his disgrace starved himself to death rather than endure the humiliation. Following a similar ethical structure, the defeated elephant withdraws from the voice of its conqueror and offers him tribute of earth and foliage.

Elephants are guided by a powerful culture of sexual modesty. They mate in private ("*in abdito*") and confine their mating to a set week of the year (for five days and no more). In a startling moment of his narration, Pliny describes how the elephants observe rituals of purification after sex. On the sixth day they take a shower bath in the river and do not return to the herd until the sacred cleansing is performed ("*sexto perfunduntur amne, non ante reduces ad agmen*").[43] Adultery is unknown among them. The sensitive emotional life of the elephant is also confirmed by its relationship to humans. Pliny recounts, with obvious emotion of his own, a series of anecdotes showing the affection between the species. One elephant manifests clear signs of his delicacy and sensibility by falling in love with an Egyptian flower girl who was also the favorite of the grammatical scholar Aristophanes. Another elephant, smitten by love for Menander, a Syracusan soldier in Ptolemy's army, would pine and cease from eating when deprived of the sight of his beloved. Whereas Renaissance writers such as Topsell cheapened and eroticized these stories (referring to an elephant fondling the breasts of a girl with his trunk and another killing his rival in a bizarre interspecies love triangle), Pliny stresses the insight these love stories give into the mental life of the elephant.[44] He describes a nuanced emotional world in which the elephant signifies his attachments through facial looks, gifts, or "*blanditiaeque inconditae*" ("clumsy gestures of endearment"). Some of these Pliny interprets as love tokens. The elephant keeps branches given as prizes by the public and showers them in his lover's lap.

The emotional life of the elephant encompasses a sense of the past and even the future. One remembers a mahout from his youth many years later; another sorrowfully anticipates a parting. The elephants have regard for the preservation of life, protecting some sheep from a stampede by removing them from the path with their trunks. Even the emotion of fear Pliny understands not as a sign of animal instinct but of the elephant's intelligence in assessing danger, especially when threatened by humans. Elephants show courtesy toward humans when treated with honesty but can tell when humans are trying to deceive them, and they rally the herd to forestall an attack.

Is it possible to discern from Pliny's accumulated reportage a theory of animal rationality, if not explicitly then implicitly? Whereas the philosophical traditions he worked in all assumed that animals were incapable of reason, for Pliny such a doctrine is arbitrary and irrelevant. The elephant's life for Pliny is all of a piece and makes sense under its own terms. An elephant's behavior follows reasons (in the sense of rational principles), and the elephant shows that he understands these reasons in the way he exercises that behavior. In short, the elephant knows what he is doing. In a carefully limited sense, Pliny finds that elephant intelligence may fruitfully be compared with human intelligence, even with reason in its higher forms. One comparison he makes explicitly comes when he tells the story of King Bocchus attempting to enlist a herd of elephants in the punishment of thirty of their number who had disobeyed military orders. Despite every inducement, it proved impossible to make the elephants assist in acts of cruelty against another being. Pliny finds only one conclusion possible: that the elephants have some insight into the concept of justice ("*idem divinationem quandam iustitiae*").[45]

Pliny shared with the Roman world in general a feeling of unusual affinity toward the elephant, an incipient feeling of sharing the same (or at least a very similar) world of the mind and of the emotions. One of the few known episodes of revulsion against spectacles of cruelty against animals in ancient times appears in the anecdote (recorded by Pliny and others) of the Roman populace rising up in horror against Pompey's disgusting staged elephant battle.[46] Cicero surmised this was because the crowd in the amphitheater possessed a sense of *societas* with the elephants.[47] Pliny also shares the commonly held Roman belief that elephants were worshipers and protégés of the god Helios or Sol and extends this religious sensibility to reverence for the moon and other stars.[48] Authorities state, Pliny says, that at new moon in Mauretania elephants go to the river to perform a ritual of purification (*"ibique se purificantes sollemniter aqua circumspergi"*) after which they carry their young in their arms in procession.[49] Such instances seem to show Pliny at his most endearingly batty. Yet on the contrary, they underline his respect for the integrity of the elephant's world and, it is tempting to say, worldview. In this, Pliny goes far beyond Roman popular belief. To ascribe to the elephant a sense of justice, however tangentially, is for any Roman of learning a serious philosophical statement.

Where, finally, should we place Pliny's references to elephant language? These are scattered seemingly randomly through his chapter. Here in Pliny is the origin of the anecdote from Mutianus the consul of the literate or even literary elephant, inscribing in the sand (*"perscribere eius linguae verbis"*) his pride at the despoiling of the Celts. Pliny also states, in contradiction of modern views, that elephants are capable of recognizing their own names.[50] In the opening sentence of his chapter, corroborating his epigrammatic statement of the proximity of elephant to human intelligence, Pliny states unequivocally that the elephant understands the language of its local country (*"intellectus illis sermonis patrii"*). This involves understanding complex speech acts. Some elephants embark on a ship only when they are given a sacred promise by the mahout. At one point it also involves making their own meaning known, a case Richard Sorabji (with tongue half in cheek) calls "a graphic ascription of utterer's meaning" in the precise sense of modern philosophy of language.[51] When Pompey's elephants are cornered in the amphitheater, they entreat the crowd with "indescribable gestures" and attract their sympathy with a strange wailing noise of lamentation (*"quadam sese lamentatione conplorantes"*).[52] These comments, although made with an element of the whimsy that is part of Pliny's charm, are not expressed in a way that suggests they are at all outlandish or even out of the ordinary. They are circumscribed within the logic of Pliny's psychology of the pachyderm mind. The elephant whose actions are performed on such a sophisticated plane, who displays so many everyday signs of reason and sympathetic intelligence, is not acting against nature in following human language or even incipiently learning it for himself within carefully defined limits. The elephant is part of the moral world and lives within the outer borders of a linguistic community.

❦

It might be thought that ancient testimonies of speaking and writing animals imply a lack of discrimination in relation to their sources, a willing suspension of disbelief, or a lurch into the wilder reaches of hearsay. On the contrary, Aelian prefaces his account of elephants with a careful demonstration of his scientific credentials and his commitment to truth. He bases his study on what he himself has seen ("*egô dê eidon*") and on the corroborated observations of others. He has been selective in his use of evidence.

Pliny's approach to epistemology is best summed up by his remarks at the beginning of Book VII (the book devoted to the human race). This is the prelude to a passage generally regarded as the most dubious in the whole of Pliny, the section on monsters. Perhaps tellingly, Pliny says these creatures congregate most of all in India and Ethiopia. Possibly, he thinks of the elephant, too, as half fantastic, a creature of nature on the edge of the imagination. However, Pliny on monsters is susceptible to gross misunderstanding. He is no ingénu; indeed, he prefaces these stories by saying that there are some "*in quibus prodigiosa aliqua et incredibilia multis visum iri haud dubito*" ("among which I doubt not will appear portentous and incredible to many").[53] As if unawares, Pliny interpolates a miniature theory of knowledge: "What is not deemed miraculous when first it comes into knowledge? How many things are judged impossible before they actually occur? Indeed the power and majesty of the nature of the universe at every turn lacks credence if one's mind embraces parts of it only and not the whole." Pliny may not be the likeliest source of an essay on the nature of scientific revolutions or the relationship between truth and belief, but his remarks, especially in this of all contexts, deserve notice.

Here Pliny simultaneously justifies his own method of omnivorous compilation (the "neurotic collector of data") and casts doubt on the casual skepticism that so often passes for informed opinion. All science begins with make-believe, with an act of imagination that can surpass what is already known. Yet in the path of new understanding lies settled previous opinion. What would make me believe an elephant had spoken? Probably only the evidence of my own eyes, yet what would such evidence look like? Countless inhibitions would lie in the way of my accepting such evidence. Indeed, the belief that the elephant had spoken might itself be of such a character as to cast doubt on the categories on which the evidence itself was based. The question of animal language, even when pursued in the most rigorous zoological terms, is always a question of epistemology. For what is meant by language (and what is an animal)? It is in relation to the idea of other animals speaking that the definition of language is most fiercely contested. Very often the question is posed in terms of whether language (in this sense, or in all senses) is unique to humans. Here, the categories keep shifting. Is it articulation that makes language, or is it sounds as words? Is it convention, or words as symbols? Is it syntax, putting words into different orders, in the right place?

Or does language depend on a criterion of the beliefs or thoughts a speaker has? (Or is it the other way around?) Or is language language only when the speaker intends a meaning and also intends the intention to be recognized? Which of these can a parrot do, which can a raven, which can a chimpanzee? Can an elephant do any of them?[54]

The question of epistemology at issue is not animal language, after all, but human language, and the tests applied prove not whether animals speak animal language but whether animals speak human language; on the whole, it turns out that they do not. Yet no matter how narrowly the tests are conceived, one animal or other can be found that will question the test to the limit. So the category of exclusiveness in human language moves one step further. These slippages have characteristically drawn the attention of Derrida, who categorizes the many oddities involved in the category of human uniqueness and, for that matter, in the very words *human* and *animal* themselves.[55] If an octopus divided the world into the octopian and everything else, would that make sense? Yes, but only in the sense of what is subjectively different about the octopus's own experience, a problem with which I intend to conclude.

In his skepticism about the human, Derrida, ever the skeptic's skeptic, uncovers a whole history of past skepticism among both ancients and early moderns about animal thought and animal language, that is, not skepticism about animal language but skepticism about such skepticism. For the mark of the skeptic is not for me to doubt the beliefs of others (everyone does that) but to doubt my own beliefs. This is Pliny's empiricism: to write down all available opinions while expressing his own as rarely as possible. It is in this context that Pliny's elephant comes face to face with Montaigne's cat: "When I play with my cat, how do I know that she is not passing time with me rather than I with her?"[56] Montaigne jotted his famous epigram among the manuscript notes in his copy of the *Apologie de Raimond Sebond,* made in preparation for a last printed edition of his lifetime. He used his cat (*his* cat? Derrida is judiciously sharp about Montaigne's peculiar familiar pronoun, "ma chatte") to cast doubt on the human capacity to understand "the hidden, inward motivations of animate creatures." To provoke his readers' certainties still further, in this heavily worked passage, the 1595 posthumous edition then playfully switched species: "We entertain ourselves with mutual monkey-tricks [*singeries*]."[57]

What is it in the comparison of humans and beasts that leads us to convince ourselves of "la bestise" of the beast? Montaigne contents himself with the rhetorical question. At this point he embarks on the question of talking to the animals: "Why should it be a defect in the beasts not in us which stops all communication between us? We can only guess whose fault it is that we cannot understand each other: for we do not understand them any more than they understand us. They may reckon us to be brute beasts for the same reason that we reckon them to be so."[58] Does a dog know that I am speaking to you, or does it assume that my noise is insignificant? To put it another way, if a chimpanzee were to place cups of different colors in front of me, would I realize the intention to test my capacity for language? The questions are not entirely frivolous. The problem Montaigne raises is whether, if animals could talk, we would be able to know.

It is sometimes suggested that Montaigne's argument here is a moralist one, concerned only with showing the vanity and incapacity of human reasoning.[59] Montaigne has a more truly philosophical problem in mind. This is what explains the violence of Descartes's response, for Descartes's denial of animal language can hardly be understood outside its context in a specific refutation of Montaigne and his sympathizers.[60] This provokes Descartes into an utter renunciation of the topos of Pliny's elephant and its many equivalents: "And we ought not to confound speech with natural movements which betray passions and may be imitated by machines as well as be manifested by animals; nor must we think, as did some of the ancients, that brutes talk, although we do not understand their language."[61] For if animals could talk, Descartes asserts, we would be able to understand them. Their lack of speech is not caused by a defect in anatomy; magpies and parrots have the right organs to speak. The deaf and dumb are more deprived of the means to communicate than the animals, yet they make their minds known by signs and gestures. The only conclusion is that animals have no minds to make known. Even if they could be made to talk, just as would be the case with a machine made to talk, we would know it was not language because "they cannot speak as we do, that is, to give evidence that they think of what they say."[62]

The violence of this prohibition is evident from the conclusions that were soon drawn from it, that animals have no souls or, for that matter, feelings, that they cannot even feel pain. It is doubtful Descartes himself meant to go so far.[63] Sorabji surmises that Descartes went as far as he did only because of what Montaigne had said.[64] What was the threat contained in Montaigne's cat? It is that if the animal does speak and we do not understand her, our own speech is deprived of its innate power to make itself understood. Cutting out the animal's tongue is necessary because otherwise the animal's muteness deprives humans of the reassurance that we ourselves make sense. Descartes's prohibition is an attempt to shore up human rationality against the possibility of something worse than incomprehension or nonsense: to be condemned to solipsism, self-referentiality, talking to oneself, alone.

Montaigne's argument should not be confused with one of full solipsism, that all experience is private or that no meanings can be inferred from person to person. Indeed, Montaigne allows for some communication between the species: "We have some modest understanding of what they mean: they have the same of us, in about equal measure."[65] Animals fawn on us, threaten us, and entreat us, as we do them. Yet any communication must be incomplete, and crucially, human intelligence provides no more security of understanding nonhuman animals than the other way around. That is, if we fail to understand animal speech, it is not because those animals are deficient but because of the difference in species. Descartes's assertion, that we know that animals do not speak because we know that we cannot understand them, is left baffled by this. Indeed, such an assertion would also apply to the speech of foreigners, yet as Sextus Empiricus pointed out, just because we do not understand a foreign language, we do not presume that the person cannot speak.[66] This is one way of understanding the reflexivity of Montaigne's response, in implying that perhaps the animal has no reason to listen rather than cannot hear.

In this way, Montaigne's argument is less a conventional one of the vanity of human understanding than a much subtler one about what Thomas Nagel has called "the subjective character of experience." Montaigne recognizes that an animal has a subjective sense of its own experience, but he also recognizes that he cannot know at all precisely what that experience is. He cannot know, in Nagel's phrase, "what it is like to be a bat": "Even without the benefit of philosophical reflection, anyone who has spent some time in an enclosed space with an excited bat knows what it is to encounter a fundamentally *alien* form of life."[67] It is possible to make some inferences, and it is likely that the inferences would be better the closer the two species are. Montaigne remarks that an animal can make its feelings known to another species as well as its own and that humans also differentiate, by making different calls to different species. Yet the differences between species still mean that at some level the experience remains alien. To know what it would be like for me to be *like* a bat is an entirely different and less interesting question.

Pliny strains to listen to the elephants. He cannot make out what they are saying. He does not claim that the elephants speak, certainly not in the sense that humans speak. Yet in reporting what he does hear, he expands in several different ways both the question of what an elephant might be thinking and what language is. His elephants can understand human speech, and even in more than one language. This is something that was remarked of Hanno in Rome. Hanno understood Portuguese and Malayalam, not just what one mahout happened to want to get him to do. Pliny's elephants can also make their own feelings known, at least in desperate straits, not only in the sense that they cry out in pain but also that they do so in such a way as to persuade human onlookers that this is their meaning. Pliny's openness of imagination—in the matter of the elephant writing in the sand, as elsewhere—is in this sense philosophical, in its own way scientific. This is Pliny's legacy to the early modern understanding of animals. Yet it was a legacy not completely acknowledged or understood. Even though his text was reprinted so widely, some aspects of his imagination were lost in the translation. His elephant, an autonomous being with its own form of life, is made by Topsell and even Aldrovandi into a creature of half-fantastical curiosity. The question of elephant language is left in Browne as an awkward but diverting aside. Nonetheless, Pliny left in place a countertradition on the question of animal rationality that Montaigne and others could still draw on. For Pliny accepts that (in Nagel's words) "there are facts that do not consist in the truth of propositions expressible in human language."[68] Pliny is less interested in deciphering what the elephant is saying than in recognizing that the elephant is feeling things and thinking things, in ways that Pliny himself cannot properly understand. What the elephants are saying to each other is something best left to the elephants themselves.

NOTES

I would like to thank Rickie Dammann and Erica Fudge for conversations and various favors, and Terence Cave for commenting on a draft with his customary generosity and erudition.

1. Sir Thomas Browne, *Pseudodoxia Epidemica,* ed. Robin Robbins, 2 vols. (Oxford: Clarendon Press, 1981), 1:164.

2. Arguments concerning animal language are summarized in Richard Sorabji, *Animal Minds and Human Morals: The Origins of the Western Debate* (Ithaca, N.Y.: Cornell University Press, 1993), 80–86; early modern versions are described in R. W. Serjeantson, "The Passions and Animal Language, 1540–1700," *Journal of the History of Ideas* 62:3 (2001): 427–33; and in Terence Cave, *Pré-histoires II: langues étrangères et troubles économiques* (Geneva: Droz, 2001), 29–44.

3. Browne, *Pseudodoxia Epidemica,* 1:164.

4. Cited in Serjeantson, "Passions," 426.

5. John Locke, *An Essay Concerning Human Understanding,* ii.11, ed. Peter H. Nidditch, corrected edition (Oxford: Clarendon Press, 1979), 159–60, 333–34, and 408, see also 402. On speaking parrots, see Cave, *Pré-histoires II,* 29–44.

6. René Descartes, *Discours de la méthode. Pour bien conduire sa raison, & chercher la verité dans les sciences* (Leiden, 1637). Browne cites the work in *Pseudodoxia Epidemica.*

7. Serjeantson, "Passions," 442.

8. Keith Thomas, *Man and the Natural World: Changing Attitudes in England, 1500–1800* (Harmondsworth, U.K.: Penguin, 1985), 121–36.

9. Cureau de la Chambre, *Traité de la connaissance des animaux où tout ce qui a esté dit pour, & contre le raissonnement des bestes, est examiné* (Paris, 1648), Part IV, chapter 3. This was part of a controversy with Pierre Chanet, *De l'instinct et de la connaissance des animaux* (La Rochelle, 1646).

10. Serjeantson, "Passions," 442. Cave, *Pré-histoires II,* 40–42, demonstrates that earlier writers such as Du Bartas and Claude Duret, in *Thresor de l'histoire des langues de cest univers* (ca. 1607), assume the case against animal speech.

11. See M. St. Clare Byrne, *The Elizabethan Zoo* (London: Etchells and Macdonald, 1926), vi–vii.

12. Edward Topsell, *The History of Four-footed Beasts and Serpents,* 2 vols. (London, 1658 edition), 1:162, translated from Conrad Gesner, *Historia animalium,* 3 vols. (Basel, 1551), 1:421.

13. Translation from Topsell, *History,* 1:154.

14. Ulisse Aldrovandi, *De quadrupedibus solidipedibus* (Frankfurt, 1623), i.210. The edition cited is that used by Thomas Browne.

15. In fact, Oppian relates this only as hearsay. *Cynegetica,* Loeb edition, ed. A. W. Mair (London: Heinemann, 1958), ii.540–43.

16. Cristoval Acosta, *Aromatum et simplicium aliquot medicamentorum apud Indos nascentium historia* (Antwerp, 1582), 54.

17. Aldrovandi, *De quadrupedibus,* i.210.

18. See Donald F. Lach, "Asian Elephants in Renaissance Europe," *Journal of Asian History* 1 (1967): 133–76.

19. Silvio A. Bedini, *The Pope's Elephant* (Nashville, Tenn.: J. S. Sanders & Co., 1998), 30, 56, 223, and 222–23. Various sightings of London's very own elephant by John Donne, Sir John Davies, Ben Jonson, and others are lovingly ferreted out by H. J. C. Grierson in *The Poems of John Donne,* 2 vols. (Oxford: Oxford University Press, 1912), 2:100–101.

20. See Giulia Bartrum, *Albrecht Dürer and His Legacy: The Graphic Work of a Renaissance Artist* (London: British Museum, 2002), 285.

21. Bedini, *Pope's Elephant,* 132–33.

22. Aurelio Sereno, *Theatrum Capitolinum Magnifico Iuliano institutum per Aurelium Serenum Monopolitanum et de elephante camen eiusdem* (Rome, 1514), G1v. English translation in Bedini, *Pope's Elephant,* 60.

23. Topsell, *History,* 1:162.

24. Richard Hakluyt, "The Second Voyage to Guinea," in *Hakluyt's Voyages,* compiled by Richard Eden (London: J. M. Dent, 1992), 207. For a discussion of this passage in relation to the elephant as exotic other, see Kim F. Hall, *Things of Darkness: Economies of Race and Gender in Early Modern England* (Ithaca, N.Y.: Cornell University Press, 1995), 51–52.

25. Quoted in Bedini, *Pope's Elephant,* 62.

26. Ibid., 78.

27. John Donne, *Satyre,* 1:79–82, in *Poems.*

28. Ulrich von Hutten, *Epistolae obscurorum virorum,* ii.48 (25–28), ed. and trans. Francis Griffin Stokes (London: Chatto & Windus, 1909), 490.

29. François Rabelais, *Le Tiers Livre,* chapter xiii, ed. M. A. Screech, Textes Littéraires Français (Geneva: Librairie Droz, 1974), 103.

30. Thomas Urquhart's translation, *Gargantua and Pantagruel,* 2 vols. (London: J. M. Dent, 1929), 2:299. This is the first reference in *OED* to "barr" as the sound an elephant makes, although there is a 1594 reference to "bary" in the same sense.

31. Italo Calvino, "Man, the Sky, and the Elephant," originally the Introduction to the Einaudi Italian translation of Pliny (1982), reprinted in *The Literature Machine* (London: Vintage, 1997), 316.

32. Pliny, *Naturalis historia,* Loeb edition, 10 vols., vol. 3, ed. H. Rackham (London: Heinemann, 1967), viii.1. I have compared this edition with *Historia naturalis* (Heidelberg, 1582).

33. Konrad Lorenz, *King Solomon's Ring* (London: Methuen, 1952), chapters 8 and 11, nonetheless argues specifically that birds (such as ravens) do not use language in the human sense.

34. J. C. M. Toynbee, *Animals in Roman Life and Art* (London: Thames & Hudson, 1973), 32 and 46.

35. Aelian, *De natura animalium,* Loeb edition, 3 vols., vol. 1, ed. A. F. Schofield (London: Heinemann, 1958), ii.11.

36. Calvino, "Man," 328.

37. Aristotle, *Politics,* 1253a9–18. On the far-reaching consequences of this view, see Sorabji, *Animal Minds,* 8.

38. Pliny, *Naturalis historia,* viii.3.

39. Ibid., viii.4.

40. Ibid., viii.5.

41. On the Stoic concept of *oikeiôsis* and its relationship to the mental world of animals, see Sorabji, *Animal Minds,* 123–25.

42. Cicero, *De finibus,* Loeb edition, ed. H. Rackham (London: Heinemann, 1957), iii.62–68.

43. Pliny, *Naturalis historia,* viii.5. The sexual modesty of elephants, cited from Pliny, is approved in Renaissance sources such as Hakluyt.

44. Topsell, *History,* 1:163 and 164; Pliny, *Naturalis historia,* viii.5.

45. Pliny, *Naturalis historia,* viii.5. This phrase is repeated in many early modern accounts, such as Aldrovandi, *De quadrupedibus,* i.208, and Topsell, *History,* 1:163.

46. Toynbee, *Animals,* 22–23.

47. Cicero, *Epistolae ad familiares,* Loeb edition, 3 vols., ed. E. O. Winstedt (London: Heinemann, 1958), vii.1.3.

48. Toynbee, *Animals,* 53.

49. Pliny, *Naturalis historia,* viii.1.

50. Ibid., viii.3 and viii.5 (*"etiam cognominibus fuisse; etenim novere ea"*). On elephant names in modern zoology, with respect to the case of Hanno's name, see Bedini, *Pope's Elephant,* 80.

51. Sorabji, *Animal Minds,* 86. The phrase "utterer's meaning" comes from Paul Grice, meaning that "meaning" means "intending their intention (to mean) to be recognized." Such criteria have been applied, largely without success, in modern

experiments on chimpanzees; see Sue Savage-Rumbaugh et al., "Can a Chimpanzee Make a Statement?," *Journal of Experimental Psychology: General* 112 (1983): 457–92, with replies on 493–512.

52. Pliny, *Naturalis historia,* viii.7.

53. Ibid., vii.1.

54. All of these examples are paraphrased from Sorabji's elegant summary in *Animal Minds,* 80–86.

55. Jacques Derrida, "The Animal That Therefore I Am (More to Follow)," *Critical Inquiry* 28 (2002): 369–418.

56. Michel de Montaigne, *An Apology for Raymond Sebond,* trans. M. A. Screech (Harmondsworth, U.K.: Penguin, 1987), 17.

57. Ibid., 16–17 and 17n.

58. Ibid., 17.

59. Serjeantson, "Passions," 437, following George Boas, *The Happy Beast in French Thought of the Seventeenth Century* (Baltimore: Johns Hopkins University Press, 1933).

60. "I cannot share the opinion of Montaigne and others who attribute understanding or thought to animals." Descartes, "To the Marquess of Newcastle, 23 November, 1646," *The Philosophical Writings of Descartes: Volume III: The Correspondence,* trans. John Cottingham, Robert Stoothoff, Dugald Murdoch, and Anthony Kenny (Cambridge: Cambridge University Press, 1991), 302.

61. Descartes, *Philosophical Works,* trans. Elizabeth S. Haldane and G. R. T. Ross, 2 vols. (Cambridge: Cambridge University Press, 1979), 1:117.

62. Ibid.

63. John Cottingham, "'A Brute to the Brutes?' Descartes' Treatment of Animals," *Philosophy* 53 (1978): 551–59.

64. Sorabji, *Animal Minds,* 206.

65. Montaigne, *Apology,* 17.

66. Cited by Sorabji, *Animal Minds,* 83. In this context it should be remembered that some early modern explorers did indeed assume that native languages were mere babbling; Miranda assumes this of Caliban in *The Tempest,* I.2.

67. Thomas Nagel, "What Is It Like to Be a Bat?," in *Mortal Questions* (Cambridge: Cambridge University Press, 1979), 166 and 168, something my family encountered in Montepulciano last summer.

68. Ibid., 171.

10

Reading Vital Signs:
Animals and the Experimental Philosophy

Peter Harrison

> Thus, in animals, there is neither intelligence nor souls as ordinarily
> meant. They eat without pleasure, cry without pain, grow without
> knowing it; they desire nothing, fear nothing, know nothing; and
> if they act in a manner that demonstrates intelligence, it is because
> God, having made them in order to preserve them, made their bod-
> ies in such a way that they mechanically avoid what is capable of de-
> stroying them.
>
> —Nicolas Malebranche, *The Search after Truth,* trans. and ed.
> Thomas Lennon and Paul Olscamp (Cambridge: Cambridge
> University Press, 1997), VI.ii.7 (495f.)

Nicolas Malebranche's striking denial of animal sentience often is regarded
as an apposite illustration of the general principle that there is no claim so
foolish that some philosopher or other has not argued for it. The position
set out here by Malebranche is more commonly associated with René Descartes (1596–1650), author of the notorious "beast-machine" hypothesis.
That such a counterintuitive proposal regarding the mental lives of animals
emerged in the seventeenth century is usually taken as a sign that during
this period the fortunes of animals were at a particularly low ebb. This state
of affairs is plausibly attributed to these developments in philosophy and science linked to the "Scientific Revolution." Thus, although the beast-machine
hypothesis itself is acknowledged to have been controversial even in its
seventeenth-century setting, the denial of sentience to animals by these philosophers is considered to be symptomatic of a more general early modern
trend in which increasing numbers of animals found themselves subjected
to painful experiments, attached to dissecting tables, or confined within the
chambers of air pumps and in which the natural world itself became vic-
tim to the exploitative tendencies thought to characterize the worst features
of the Scientific Revolution and of modernity generally. Accordingly, analyses of more recent controversies over the moral status of animals and the
legitimacy of animal experimentation and exploitation often trace the historical origins of the issue to the seventeenth century.

One of the consequences of locating the origins of contemporary scientific attitudes to animals in the seventeenth century has been the problematic attempt to discern what the relevant historical actors thought about animals in categories familiar to our own time. Thus, much scholarly work has focused on elaborating early modern understandings of the "moral status of animals" or has discussed the "ethics of animal experimentation" in the seventeenth century.[1] At times, the historical protagonists have even been characterized as being either champions of animals' interests or as being "antianimal," which unhelpfully suggests some kind of polarization of opinion and again reflects a difference of viewpoint more characteristic of our own period.[2] In this chapter I suggest that these are anachronistic and inappropriate ways to approach this historical issue and that they have militated against a clear-sighted understanding of the thought and practices of the period as they relate to animals. Seeking to ascertain what seventeenth-century philosophers held the moral status of animals to be, for example, is simply to ask a question that no one in the early modern period would have asked. To pose the question in this fashion therefore inevitably gives rise to distorted answers. This is not to say that in the seventeenth century there were not attempts to express concern about nonhuman animals in a coherent way or that there were no voices calling attention to the suffering of animals in the name of experimental science. Yet there were then neither utilitarian calculations that might have weighed the pain suffered by animals against other considerations nor robust notions of rights and duties that might have been extended beyond the boundaries of the human world. In short, the kind of discourse that makes it possible to include animals in our current moral agendas simply did not exist then, and it is in vain that we attempt to interpret early modern thought on the mistaken assumption that it did.

A more appropriate focus for gaining insights into the "scientific" beliefs about and treatment of animals in the early modern period are broader issues of attitudes toward nature and changing ideas about the place of the human being in the natural world. These also have been the focus of scholarly attention, but even these broader analyses have been tainted with anachronistic interpretations. Therefore, the rise of the mechanical worldview and the Cartesian position in particular are of central importance and have plausibly been linked to the cavalier experimental treatment of animals. However, it was also the case, as I hope to demonstrate, that the mechanical worldview could enhance the status of some animals, although not necessarily in ways that would elevate what we would call their moral standing. It must also be said that the limited focus on the moral status of animals, and even more broad considerations of conceptions of nature and anthropocentrism, lead to an ignoring of the vital importance of the institutional setting for many relevant scientific practices. Therefore, a major factor in the early modern treatment of animals by natural philosophers was the emergence of specific social practices—"experiments"—that had their own performative logic, which, though informed by a conception of nature, nonetheless brought a certain standardization of the experimental treatment of animals regardless of the personal views held by the relevant actors. Only by including consideration of what we might call the ritual aspects of experimentation can we account for a surprising uniformity of experimental practice where animals were involved, despite significant differences in the personal attitudes of those involved. Finally, I suggest that general attitudes toward nature, along with the development of experimental methods and their application to the study of animals, can be regarded as exemplifying a new hermeneutical approach to the "book of nature" in which dissection and experimentation represent a new exegetical practice, one entrusted with the task of determining both the practical uses and transcendental meanings of living creatures.

THE METHODS OF RENAISSANCE NATURAL HISTORY

It is important to understand at the outset that the scientific approach to animals took place in the seventeenth century in one of two related disciplines: natural history and natural philosophy. The former was concerned more with description, classification, and, from the late seventeenth century, natural theology. Natural philosophy focused on explanation and increasingly mathematical accounts of physical reality. Both disciplines underwent significant transformations in the early modern period, hence the historiographic commonplace "the Scientific Revolution." This was a revolution premised on changing conceptions of the natural order.

One of the most conspicuous changes to take place in the study of nature during the Renaissance was the move away from books about nature to the "book of nature" itself. Over the course of the sixteenth and seventeenth centuries, natural history was gradually transformed from an essentially scholarly enterprise and the preserve of humanist philologists to an empirical activity. As the English physician William Harvey (1578–1657), best known for his discovery of the circulation of the blood, expressed it, "It was, however, dear Colleagues, no intention of mine, in listing and upturnings of names, works and views of anatomical authors and writers, to make display by this book of my memory, studies, much reading, and a large printed tome. In the first place, because I profess to learn and teach anatomy not from books but from dissections, not from the tenets of Philosophers but from the fabric of Nature."[3] This approach contrasted starkly with the traditional Renaissance natural histories that had essentially been encyclopedic digests of written sources on animals. Harvey's contemporary, the clergyman and naturalist Edward Topsell (1572–1625), proudly announced that his popular *Historie of Foure-footed Beastes* (1607) had been compiled from "Narrations out of Scriptures, Fathers, Phylosophers, Physicians, and Poets."[4] Most sources used in such natural histories had been written by such revered ancient writers as Aristotle and Pliny. Thus, for example, the standard text of Renaissance natural history, compiled by the humanist scholar Conrad Gesner (1516–65), drew its information from more than 250 Greek and Latin authors.[5] In contrast to the bookish activities of these encyclopedists, Harvey stated as his goal the discovery of the functioning of the organs of animals "through the use of my own eyes instead of through books and the writings of others."[6] It is hardly surprising, given this commitment, that Harvey should have been responsible for introducing the practice of vivisection into the University of Oxford.[7]

To a degree, more active experimental practices arose out of attempts to emulate the actual methods of the ancients rather than merely rehearsing their findings. The "new anatomy" of Andreas Vesalius (1514–64), set out in *De humani corporis fabrica* (1543), was informed by notions of Renaissance scholarship but managed to progress beyond mere recapitulation. By adopting the procedures set out in the new 1541 edition of the *Anatomical Procedures* of the ancient physician Galen (ca. 130–ca. 200)—the publication of which owed much to the linguistic skill of humanist scholars—Vesalius was able to emulate the methods of the Greek master.[8] Even so, Vesalius himself did not claim to have founded a new anatomy but merely to have restored a discipline practiced "of old in Alexandria."[9] William Harvey went even further, claiming that his discovery of the circulation of the blood had been made possible by experiments recommended by both Galen and Vesalius but apparently conducted by neither: "The experiment is spoken of by Vesalius, the celebrated anatomist; but neither Vesalius nor Galen says that he has tried the experiment, which, however, I did. Vesalius only prescribes it, and Galen advises it."[10] It is against this background that we are to understand Harvey's advocacy of consultation with the book of nature rather than the books of the ancients.

It must also be pointed out that the natural history of the early modern period not only turned away from texts about nature to nature itself but increasingly did so with a different end in mind. Traditional natural histories of the period tended to include material that we would consider literary, moral, and theological, as opposed to purely "scientific." As we have already seen, Edward Topsell's natural history of four-footed animals relied on, in addition to philosophers and physicians, the Bible, the church fathers, and poets. Moreover, his descriptions of animals typically included their "moral" characteristics, relevant tales from classical sources, symbolic associations, practical information about raising and caring for them, artistic representations, and practical and medicinal uses. As the seventeenth century progressed, literary references to animals were increasingly excluded from what was considered to be "proper" natural history. Nehemiah Grew (1641–1712), one of the pioneers of microscopy and plant physiology, wrote in a catalog of one of the collections of the Royal Society that "After the Descriptions; instead of medling with Mystick, Mythologick, or Hieroglyphick matter; or relating Stories of Men who were great Riders, or Women that were bold and feared not horses; as some others have done: I thought it much more proper, To remarque some of the Uses and Reasons of Things."[11] In his apologetic *History of the Royal Society* (1667) Thomas Sprat agreed that "while the Old [learning] could only bestow upon us some barren Terms and Notions, the New shall impart to us the uses of all the *Creatures.*"[12] This more limited emphasis on description and use often is an explicit commitment of naturalists of the late seventeenth century.[13]

The focus on the "uses" of animals was in one sense not particularly novel. What was innovative about the new natural histories was an increasing emphasis on the practical uses of animals and a different conception of how these uses were to be discovered. Before this time animals had been regarded as useful in a variety of ways—useful as moral exemplars, useful as symbols of theological truths, even useful for sermon illustrations. Wolfgang Franz, a professor of divinity at Wittenberg, informed readers of his *Animalium historia sacra* (1653) that his natural history would be of particular use to divines, who should find it to be "very useful in sermons."[14] By the end of the seventeenth century this kind of passive depiction of animals as moral exemplars or theological emblems was supplanted by a more active utilitarian approach. The narrowing of focus to the material exploitation of animals was in turn informed by changing conceptions of nature during this time and by links between natural history and the developing discipline of experimental natural philosophy. Even the more traditional moral and emblematic uses of animals that were retained in works of natural history were also thought to be made evident not from literary references but from the empirical methods of an experimental philosophy.

THE LOGIC OF THE EXPERIMENTAL PHILOSOPHY

For Aristotle and his medieval successors the study of nature began with everyday observations of nature in its normal course. One of the distinctive features of the approach of experimental philosophers in the seve? century was the claim that one could learn of the normal operation. ture by studying the world under unnatural or artificial constraints. To take a simple example, although a feather and lead weight are observed to fall at different rates in the normal course of events, under the experimental conditions of a vacuum they both fall with a uniform acceleration. The counterfactual conditions of experiments thus led to some of the most important advances in early modern knowledge of nature. Francis Bacon (1561–1626) explicitly stated that naturalists should concern themselves with three aspects of the natural order: nature observed in its normal course, nature "erring and varying," and nature "altered and wrought."[15] The first of these categories is straightforward and was in keeping with traditional Aristotelian natural history and natural philosophy. Under the second category, however, Bacon proposed to study unusual aspects of nature, as he himself expressed it, "all prodigies and monstrous births of nature; of everything in short that is in nature new, rare, and unusual."[16] The third category, elsewhere described as "experimental history," entailed the study of nature diverted from its normal course by experimentation. These last two categories incorporate into natural history the unnatural and artificial and thus represent a significant departure from the Aristotelian position. For Bacon and the Baconians, nature would fully reveal its operations only when put to the test and forced out of its "natural" state. The secrets of nature are revealed, Bacon insisted, only "when by art and the hand of man she is forced out of her natural state, and squeezed and moulded."[17]

Although the idea that Bacon exploited notions of judicial torture and interrogation for his natural philosophy has been greatly exaggerated, it remains true that Baconian methods called for an aggressive approach to the investigation of nature that was largely unprecedented.[18] This position was subsequently adopted by Fellows of the Royal Society who regarded themselves as putting into practice Baconian prescriptions for the study of nature. In the preface to his celebrated *Micrographia* (1665), Robert Hooke (1635–1703) thus declared that "the footsteps of Nature are to be trac'd, not only in her ordinary course, but when she seems to be put to her shifts, to make many doublings and turnings, and to use some kind of art in indeavouring to avoid our discovery."[19] The experimentalism of Robert Boyle (1627–91) was described by the mathematician John Wallis (1616–1703) in similar terms: "In the hunt for true philosophy . . . you pursue nature as if by iron and fire . . . you follow to the most hidden secret recesses, and penetrate as if to its visceral parts, that it is really a wonder if the prey does not give itself up to you. In any investigation you harass nature as if it is tied to a rack, harshly, or even cruelly I would say, by torture and more torture, that ultimately leads to all the secrets being confessed."[20] This kind of active experimentalism can be regarded as a new interpretive strategy for reading the book of nature. Galileo had famously suggested that mathematics was one key to reading God's "other book."[21] Dissection was posited as another. It is the natural philosopher, Boyle himself wrote, who "is able to read the stenography of God's omniscient hand." He continued, "And on the opened body of the same animal, a skilful anatomist will make reflections, as much more to the honour of its Creator, than an ordinary butcher can."[22] For Boyle, animal dissection was thus a key element of a complex hermeneutical process for rereading the natural world.[23]

Much of this changed attitude toward the natural world was the consequence of a renewed emphasis on the obscurity of nature's operations and on the impotence of human sensory faculties. These pessimistic views about the possibility of a complete knowledge of nature and its operations were informed in part by a reformed theology that stressed the cognitive consequences of the human fall from grace. The Fall typically was thought to have affected not only the moral rectitude of Adam, Eve, and their progeny but also their cognitive capacities. Since those sorry events in Eden investigators were less able to discern the visible signs on living things that told of their virtues. As one contemporary writer summed up the matter, "This intellect hath its darkness and ignorance, it is naturally blind, because of *Adam's* fall."[24]

Equally importantly, when Adam and Eve fell, the whole of the sublunary world fell with them. The great humanist scholar Juan Luis Vives (1492–1540) described this dual calamity in these terms: "Through sin man's intelligence became dull and obtuse, and his reason was obscured by darkness. Pride, jealousy, cruelty, all appetites and desires were set in turmoil and disorder; loyalty was broken; man lost his capacity to love: the body was plagued by diseases and the earth was damned, stink in the air, corruption in the waters, freezing winters and burning summers."[25] The divine curse on nature—"the ground is cursed because of you" (Genesis 3:17)—that accompanied the human Fall thus rendered nature's operations obscure, and nature ceased to serve the human race as its obedient vassal. More specifically, as a consequence of the fall of the natural order, the signatures that once had made the uses of the creatures so conspicuous were obscured. Physician Gideon Harvey (1640–1700) wrote that before the Fall, "there was no resistance or obscurity in any of the objects; because they, being all created for the service of man, had their natures (as it were) writ upon their breast, so that herein they were at the command of the understanding."[26] So it was that in addition to the deprecations of the human soul, the uses of living things once obvious to Adam were now lost through changes to the creatures themselves.

In his description of the Edenic state, Harvey observed that natural objects had their natures "writ upon their breast," thus alluding to the Renaissance doctrine of signatures, according to which animals and plants had their natures, and by implication their uses, marked on their external physiognomies. The Swiss physician Paracelsus (ca. 1493–1541) thus observed that "nothing is without external and visible signs which take the form of special marks." Adam had been the first interpreter of this "art of signs," a lost art, which now ought to be recovered.[27] The standard application of the doctrine of signature was medicine, or "physick." As one writer expressed it, "the outward *Signature* or impression which is on some Plants, shews their inward Virtue; and . . . from the resemblance which they have to the parts of a Man's Body we may gather their secret power, and know to what particular part they are appropriated."[28] Although there are numerous instances of signatures, the stock example used to illustrate the principle was the walnut, which "hath upon its Fruit the Signature of the Head and Brain." Walnuts were thus prescribed for headaches and various ills of the head. The vulgar names of plants often provide an indication of their particular signature, hence "liverwort," "lungwort," "kidney beans," and so on. The physician Richard Saunders (1613–75) referred to this interpretive practice as a "Botanical Physiognomy," a reading of the internal virtues of plants, whose "natures are known by the signatures thereof." This practice paralleled the reading of the internal virtues of humans and animals from their external appearances. Physiognomy, wrote Saunders, "teacheth the method of knowing the internal affections of natural bodies by the external signs thereof." Thus, "Physiognomical signs are certain notes, which manifest the internal affections of body and mind."[29] The educational reformer John Webster (1610–82), in his attack on the traditional Aristotelian curriculum at Oxford and Cambridge, praised "that laudable, excellent, and profitable science of *Physiognomy*," describing it as "that Science from which and by certain external signs, signatures and lineaments, doth explicate the internal nature and quality of natural bodies."[30]

Although in the seventeenth century there remained, in certain quarters at least, some enthusiasm for signatures and the prospect of the recovery of their use, on the whole during this period the doctrine suffered a major decline.[31] For some who accepted the doctrine, the ability to read signatures had been irrevocably lost with Adam; for almost all, the worldview on which the doctrine rested—of microcosm and macrocosm, of astrological influences and occult qualities, of webs of resemblances and similitudes—was becoming increasingly untenable. Francis Bacon thus distinguished "the true signatures and marks set upon the works of creation" from "empty dogmas."[32] But these "true" signatures were not simply to be read of the natural world but were to be laid bare only after much labor, intensive investigation, and, crucially, experimentation. So it was that for Bacon, and for later advocates of the experimental philosophy, Adam's "use" of the creatures, or his dominion over them, was to be restored to his progeny. For proponents of the new mechanical philosophy, however, this knowledge and dominion could be recovered only by alternative and more invasive means. Neither internal properties nor human uses could simply be read from surface signs. Knowledge of these now required the direct scrutiny of internal structural and physiological properties and hence the invasive procedures of dissection, vivisection, experimentation, and microscopic examination. In the words of Boyle, "for as (such is God's condescension to human weakness) most of the texts, to whose exposition physiology is necessary, may be explicated by the knowledge of the external, or at least more easily observed qualities of the creatures; so, that there are divers not to be fully understood without the assistance of more penetrating indagations of the abstrusities of nature, and the more unobvious properties of things, an intelligent and philosophical peruser will readily discern."[33] In short, exegesis of the book of nature called for the active investigation of what lay beneath surface appearances, and it was the experimental philosophy that provided the means by which this could be accomplished.

EXPERIMENTAL PHILOSOPHY AND THE USES OF ANIMALS

The work often credited with having inaugurated modern anatomy—Andreas Vesalius's *De humani corporis fabrica*—concludes with a chapter "On the Dissection of Living Animals." The practice of animal dissection, including live dissection, seems not to have been unusual in Renaissance Italy. William Harvey, who had spent five years at Padua studying anatomy, was heir to the Vesalian tradition and introduced the practice to Oxford in the 1640s, where he conducted vivisections on a number of different animals.[34] It must therefore be allowed that the revival of the practice seems initially to have been a consequence of attempting to follow the prescriptions of the ancients (although as Harvey himself indicated, the ancients did not always follow their own advice). This having been said, the new natural philosophy ensured the continuation and expansion of the practice.

The institutional practices inaugurated by Harvey at Oxford involving dissection, vivisection, and experimental embryology were perpetuated by a second generation of experimentalists including Robert Hooke, Robert Boyle, and Richard Lower.[35] Perhaps the most famous experiments involving animals in the seventeenth century concern those conducted with the air pump by Robert Boyle and Robert Hooke. The "pneumatic engine," a device capable of creating a vacuum, had been invented by Otto von Guericke in 1647 and subsequently came to play a major role in experiments on animals in the 1660s.[36] Robert Hooke fashioned a similar contraption for Boyle and went on to collaborate with him in its experimental applications, investigating the physical and physiological properties of air. From 1659 various animals were subjected to the ordeal of the air pump, being placed in a glass chamber from which the air was then evacuated.[37] This duo conducted additional but equally dramatic experiments on respiration without the aid of their famous prop. In the mid-1660s, Hooke conducted an acclaimed series of experiments demonstrating the link between vital functions of respiration and circulation. These involved the dissection of a dog in which the lungs were artificially ventilated with bellows while the beating of its heart was observed.[38] These trials were followed by attempts, usually unsuccessful, at blood transfusion.[39]

Across the Channel similar ventures were undertaken. Nicolas Fontaine famously recorded in his *Memoirs* how advocates of the beast-machine hypothesis nailed animals to boards and claimed that their cries were nothing but the noise of insensible machines.[40] But vivisection was by no means restricted to the Cartesians. At the *Académie Royale des Sciences,* Christiaan Huygens (1629–95) reproduced the air pump experiments of Hooke and Boyle, suffocating a variety of small animals.[41] In Paris, trials in blood transfusion were also carried out after the manner of those being conducted by Fellows of the Royal Society. These were eventually extended to human subjects, and "willing" madmen were hastily sought in an attempt to gain priority over the English in what was regarded as a pioneering operation of real significance. In June 1667, Jean Denis successfully transfused seven ounces of lamb's blood into a human subject, apparently leaving him none the worse; indeed, Denis claimed that the procedure had brought positive therapeutic effects.[42] In Holland, too, vivisection seems to have been standard practice in both private and public investigations of physiology. At the University of Leiden, Jan Swammerdam (1637–80) and Nicolaus Steno (1638–86) conducted a series of experiments on pregnant bitches to investigate the respiration of the embryo.[43]

In all of this, the focus of experimental attention on the vital functions of living things—respiration and circulation—is highly significant. The study of the very basis of life itself seemed to call for living specimens, but only in a particular conception of life, specifically a materialist, mechanical one. This is the importance of the Cartesian contribution, for it was Descartes who first saw most clearly that if the vital forces were purely mechanical ones, they could be the objects of the empirical investigation. Life for the Cartesians did not require an immaterial soul, or as the Aristotelians described it, a "substantial form." If matter and motion were responsible for the vital functions of living things, as most of the "mechanical philosophers" came to believe, then the very principles of life itself could be investigated by the senses in ways previously thought impossible. The materials and processes thought to give rise to the animation of living things, in this new conception, were available for sensory inspection, if one was committed to the search. Again, the study of inanimate bodies simply could not provide the kind of information sought. Although Descartes's notorious denial of sentience to nonhuman animals was perhaps the logical conclusion of such a position, commitment to this extreme position proved to be largely irrelevant to the ideology that informed the practice of live dissection.[44]

Thus, the only significant difference between the Cartesians and other advocates of a mechanical worldview was that the former could perform their experiments with a less troubled conscience. As for the rest, it is clear that despite the universality of vivisection and the suffering it visited on its hapless subjects, many of those involved were moved by the plight of the creatures involved. Although the respiration experiments conducted by Hooke with the bellows met with great acclaim, he was reluctant to reprise them. In a letter to Boyle he confided, "I shall hardly be induced to make further trials of this kind, because of the torture of the creature."[45] Eventually he was persuaded by continued pressure from Fellows of the Royal Society to repeat the experiment, and in 1667, with the assistance of the zealous Richard Lower, he repeated the procedure before the full Royal Society.[46] John Evelyn (1620–1706), then a leading figure in the Royal Society, was present at the occasion and remarked in his diary, after his description of the experiment, that it was "of more cruelty than pleased me."[47] Hooke seemed to be of the same opinion, for he never repeated it, although he persevered with less traumatic experiments. Steno, who had conducted the embryological investigations with Swammerdam, had also entertained reservations about his involvement, desiring to be convinced that the Cartesians were right about animal insensitivity: "I wish they could convince me as thoroughly as they are themselves of the fact that animals have no souls!!" Cartesian convictions would at least assuage the guilt he felt when causing creatures "prolonged pain."[48] Even Robert Boyle noted the suffering of some of the animals that he subjected to experimentation, and on one occasion he ended an experiment on live kittens prematurely, thinking it "severe" to subject the survivors to more torment.[49] Yet Boyle's sentimentality seemed not to have dampened his enthusiasm for dissection. In this regard he was fairly typical. Most vivisectors did not hold animals to be insensible, nor were they unsympathetic to the suffering of their subjects, yet they seemed to have overriding reasons for persevering with these unsavory experimental practices.

It must be allowed that the sensitivities of some investigators seem, as in the case of Hooke and some others, to have eventually precipitated a withdrawal from the program of vivisection. Yet rarely did arguments put forward by such people amount to a reasoned objection to vivisection on the basis of what we would call the moral status of the experimental subjects. Hooke himself declared that "when we endeavour to pry into her [nature's] secrets by breaking open the doors upon her, and dissecting and mangling creatures whil'st there is life yet within them, we find her indeed at work, but put into such disorder by the violence offer'd." Yet this is strangely at odds with his own claim in the Preface of *Micrographia* that nature was to be scrutinized "not only in her ordinary course, but when she seems to be put to her shifts, to make many doublings and turnings." In any case, in this context Hooke is concerned less with vivisection than with pointing out the signal virtues of the microscopic investigation of insects. It was his goal "to shew of how great benefit the use of a *Microscope* may be for the discovery of Nature's course in the operations perform'd in Animal bodies, by which we have the opportunity of observing her through these delicate and pellucid teguments of the bodies of insects acting according to her usual course and way."[50] Moreover, Hooke's reservations seem not to have been based on the inconvenience caused to the experimental subjects but rather whether the scientific outcome would be compromised.

The French anatomist Jean Riolan II (1580–1657) was another experienced vivisector who eventually became disenchanted with the whole business. Again, however, his stated objections were couched in scientific rather than moral terms. Riolan pointed out that the significant structural differences between animals and humans counted against the application to human anatomy of knowledge gained through the inspection of animal bodies.[51] In responding to Riolan, William Harvey observed, "Nature, however, is the best and most faithful interpreter of her own secrets; and what she presents either more briefly or obscurely in one department, she explains more fully and clearly in another."[52] Harvey thus suggested not unreasonably that there was a good case for comparative anatomy and physiology. In his response to the criticisms of Riolan, Harvey also pointed to another line of criticism: "There are some, too, who say that I have shown a vainglorious love of vivisections, and who scoff at and deride the introduction of frogs and serpents, flies, and other of the lower animals upon the scene, as a piece of puerile levity, not even refraining from opprobrious epithets."[53] Here again the objection had less to do with the suffering visited on experimental subjects than with the fact that these activities were undignified or unnecessary. The educational reformer Samuel Hartlib (ca. 1600–1662), for example, declared animal experimentation to be impious, undignified, and unnecessary. "To mangle tyrannise etc over the Creatures for to trie exp[e]riments or to bee imploid in so filthily about them as to weigh pisse etc as Verul[amus] p[re]-scribes is a meer drudgery curiosity and Impiety, and no necessity for it."[54] Although on the face of it such objections seem to be specifically directed against the cruelty of vivisection, in fact these sentiments were consistent with a general pattern of criticism of the new experimental philosophy, according to which the whole program was a useless exercise of pointless curiosity, that it involved undignified activities and objects unworthy of interest, that it produced knowledge that was unedifying and useless, and that it was conducted by people who were blinded by their own pride.[55] Samuel Butler (1612–80) made specific reference to the air pump in his satirical representation of the scientific pedagogue, who

> Is Puft up with his own conceipt, and Swels
> With Pride and vanity and Nothing else,
> Like Bladders in the Late Pneumatique Engine,
> Blown up with nothing but their owne Extension.[56]

Jonathan Swift's merciless lampoon of the experimental activities of the Royal Society in *Gulliver's Travels* provides another insight into this general line of criticism.[57] It is also significant in this connection that opponents of the Cartesian beast-machine hypothesis tended to ridicule it for its prima facie implausibility rather than mount ethically motivated criticism on the basis that it might promote an indifference to animal suffering.

The continuation of a practice widely regarded as distasteful can be attributed to some extent to the fact that arguments against it did not really give voice to the personal sensitivities of those involved. Hooke, Riolan, and Steno were hardly likely to sympathize with a general line of criticism that counted against experimental philosophy in general. But more than this, there were strong epistemological and ideological arguments for the necessity of this kind of knowledge, reinforced by an institutionalized practice that legitimated it.[58] On the latter point, Simon Schaffer and Steven Shapin argue persuasively that public experimentation became an important and authoritative enterprise from about the middle of the seventeenth century. As a "disciplined space" the laboratory could thus stake its claim as a unique site for the public creation of authentic knowledge.[59] Integral to the emergence of this authoritative space were impressive mechanical devices, a public audience that could verify results, and skilled operators to conduct the experiments. Thus, in the latter half of the seventeenth century there emerged experimental procedures that were larger than the people involved. In such developments can be observed the origins of notions of scientific method and objectivity that transcend the interests and sensitivities of the people involved. The puzzling yet common phenomenon of the reluctant vivisector can be accounted for in part by the evolution of procedures, methods, and public spaces that together delineated the sphere of authentic knowledge. The personal sensibilities of the experimenter thus became increasingly marginal in the social processes of knowledge production. In these developments lay the origins of modern conceptions of "scientific authority" disconcertingly exposed in the notorious experiments of Stanley Milgram.[60]

However, such factors alone are insufficient to account for the emergence and persistence of the relevant experimental practices. Also required were epistemological and broader ideological motivations involving the "uses" of animals. Chief among these was dual claim that anatomical and microscopic investigation of animal bodies provided new and unimpeachable evidence of the wisdom of the Deity and that hitherto hidden mysteries of nature were for the first time revealed. William Harvey, for example, observed that "the examination of the bodies of animals has always been my delight: and I have thought that we might thence not only obtain an insight into the lighter mysteries of nature, but there perceive a kind of image or reflex of the omnipotent creator himself. And though much has already been made out by the learned men of former times, I have still thought that much more remained behind, hidden by the dusky night of nature, uninterrogated."[61] Robert Boyle expressed a similar view about animal experimentation. Animals were made for man, and "he alone of the visible world is able to enjoy, use, and relish many of the other creatures, and to discern the omniscience, almightiness, and goodness of the author in them." The anatomist enjoys an advantage, he observed, "that he may in the bodies of brutes make divers instructional experiments, that he dares not venture on in those of men."[62] One would think, he observes elsewhere, "that the conversing with dead and stinking carcasses (that are not only hideous objects in themselves, but made more ghastly by putting us in mind, that ourselves must be such) should be not only a very melancholy, but a very hated employment." Yet, Boyle remarks, "I have often spent hours much less delightfully, not only in courts, but even in libraries, than in tracing in those forsaken mansions, the inimitable workmanship of the omniscient Architect . . . now I would confess, I could with more delight look upon a skillful dissection, than the famous clock at *Strassburgh.*"[63] Microscopic investigation also brought to light new arguments for the ingenuity of the Deity. Anglican divine and Fellow of the Royal Society Joseph Glanvill (1636–80) revived the vocabulary of "divine signatures," but in a quite different sense. Signatures were now simply the evidence of design newly manifested in microscopic creatures: "The most despicable and disregarded pieces of decayed nature, are so curiously wrought, and adorned with such eminent *Signatures of Divine wisdome,* as speake *it* their Author, and that after a curse brought upon a disorder'd Universe."[64] It is design that now points to the wisdom of God. This is a generic signature that has retained its legibility after the Fall and is made more obvious through the application of magnifying instruments.

Such sentiments were so widespread that by the end of the seventeenth century they were commonplace. William Wotton (1666–1726), in the context of his famous controversy with Sir William Temple concerning the relative merits of ancient and modern knowledge, cited as evidence of the advanced state of moderns improvements in knowledge of "the Anatomy of Brutes, Birds, Fishes and Insects," which he insisted was "much more perfect than it could possibly be in former Ages." Moreover, these anatomical discoveries had been made possible by dissections: "As Dr. Tyson has given of the Rattle-Snake; or Dr. Moulin, of the Elephant: Such dissections of Fishes as Dr. Tyson's of the Porpesse, and Steno's of a Shark's Head: Such of Insects as Malpighius's of a Silk-Worm: Swammerdam's of the Ephemeron; Dr. Lister's of Snails, and Testaceous Animals; Mr. Waller's of the Flying Gloeworm; and the same Mr. Tyson's of Long and Round Body Worms."[65] For Wotton these activities served a dual function, promoting knowledge of human anatomy and providing evidence of the wisdom and ingenuity of the Deity. Advancement of knowledge in human anatomy, Wotton insisted, rested on a foundation of animal experimentation: "There is hardly one eminent Modern Discovery in Anatomy, which was not first found in Brutes, and afterward examined in Humane Bodies. Many of them could never have been known without the help of Live-Dissections; and the rest required abundance of Trials upon great Numbers of different sorts of Beasts."[66] Finally, he stressed the physicotheological aspects of these activities, praising those "who dissect all Animals, little as well as great; who think no part of God's Workmanship below their strictest Examination, and nicest Search."[67]

At first blush, it is difficult to see in such justifications any elevation in the status of animals. Boyle, for example, speaks of beasts being in the world for the human race to "enjoy, use, and relish." Yet inasmuch as the structures of animals pointed to the designs of the Deity, the creatures themselves were sanctified. This was particularly so for the previously despised "insects." Glanvill, for example, had pointed out that it was "the most despicable pieces of decayed nature" that betrayed stunning evidence of design. His description provides an important insight into the traditional view of insects. The category "insect" was somewhat more general than that of today and was applied to a range of invertebrate species traditionally thought not to reproduce themselves but to be generated spontaneously. In one widely accepted view, these creatures had not been part of the original creation—they receive no specific mention in the days of creation in Genesis—but had arisen out the corruption that ensued upon the Fall and had continued to do so. Insects were thus informally classified as "Creatures born of dung and corruption." In the popular taxonomy, this list could extend to "frogs, flies, wormes, mouldes, mise, crickets, bats, barnacles."[68] For successive generations of naturalists who made insects their speciality, such as Thomas Moffett (1553–1604), Jan Swammerdam, and René Réaumur (1683–1757), the argument for God's existence based on the design of small creatures was a primary justification for their study. Dutch naturalist Swammerdam thus lauded the virtues of the louse in a somewhat overstated account of the hidden virtues of this usually unwelcome creature: "Herewith I offer you the Omnipotent Finger of god in the anatomy of a louse: wherein you will find miracles heaped upon miracles and will see the wisdom of God clearly manifested in a minute point."[69] Nicolas Malebranche (1638–1715) also argued that new discoveries concerning insects had led him to "esteem what everyone despises." "The principal design of God in the formation of these small insects," he insisted, was "to adorn the universe with works worthy of His wisdom and other attributes." Thus, whereas "ordinary people despise insects . . . apparently even angels admire them."[70]

All of this meant that insects were to be admired rather than despised. Robert Hooke argued that the smallest creatures could be favorably compared with the largest, for God had expended as much "care and providence" in the production of the most lowly creature, as he had in the largest.[71] The great natural historians of the past, wrote Henry Power (1623–68), "have regardlessly pass'd by the Insectile Automata, (those living-exiguities) with only a bare mention of their names, whereas in these prety Engines (by an incomparable Stenography of Providence) are lodged all the perfections of the largest Animals."[72] If God had thought it worth the trouble to make insects, argued Abbe Pluche (1688–1761), author of a popular multivolume work on evidence of God in the natural world, we ought not think it beneath our dignity to study them: "The minutest Things in Nature were appointed to some End and Purpose; and . . . the Deity is as conspicuous in the structure of a Fly's paw, as he is in the bright Globe of the Sun himself."[73] In this manner, the structure of insect bodies came to take precedence over the classical tradition according which whatever dignity insects enjoyed was on account of their status as moral exemplars.[74]

It was not merely the intricate structures of insects that led to an elevation of their status, however. Experimentation combined with microscopic studies had led to the development of various theories of embryonic "preformation," according to which the generation of insects was effected not spontaneously but by the augmentation of a tiny creature that existed in miniature within its parent.[75] This not only dispelled the myth of spontaneous generation, but for Malebranche and others it suggested that all reproduction was to be explained mechanically, and all the generations of creatures that had ever lived and ever would live had been present in the first parent. Malebranche thus surmised that "all the bodies of Men and of Beasts, which should be born or produced till the *End* of the World, were possibly created from the *Beginning* of it."[76] Insect metamorphosis was seized upon by many naturalists as a mechanism that provided insights into the nature of human resurrection. "Worms" were thus emblems of the resurrection. As Malebranche explained, "Worms crawl on the ground. They lead there a sad and humiliating life. They make a tomb for themselves from which they depart in glory. I imagined to myself that God willed to represent the life, death, and resurrection of His Son, and even of all Christians." Not only could insects "express the divine perfections, but they are also as much as possible emblems of His beloved Son."[77] Because of its remarkable life cycle, the insect was, for Malebranche, "a natural representation of Jesus Christ, who died in order to be gloriously resurrected."[78] Malebranche's compatriot Pluche also subscribed to this view, stating that insects change their form "by a new kind of Resurrection, or Metamorphosis" that converts them "into another set of living animals." One "real animal" dies to make way for a second, which is present within the body of the first. This "appearance of Death . . . is no more than its Passage to a more amiable State."[79] These important lessons of comparative embryology, interpreted through the lens of religion, thus made possible the survival of emblematic views of animals, but on a new "scientific" basis.

All of this suggests that although early modern experimental philosophy was premised on a fundamentally different conception of nature from the medieval worldview that preceded it, important elements of the traditional moral and emblematic uses of animals still played a major role in motivating and legitimating the new scientific inquiry.

CONCLUSION

The rise of experimental philosophy during the Renaissance can be understood as an attempt to develop a set of hermeneutical procedures for rereading the book of nature. The growing conviction that nature's operations were no longer obvious to the unassisted senses led to the development of various experimental procedures and to an impressive range of laboratory instruments that could assist in the reading of nature's book of secrets. The signatures that had once immediately conveyed to our first father the uses of the creatures were now thought to have become illegible, and these lost uses could be rediscovered only after the most arduous experimental effort. The surface anatomy of animals thus was subjected to the most minute scrutiny, vivisection enabled penetration beyond the superficial level to a living, hidden, visceral world, and microscopic investigations revealed the hidden properties of natural objects that lay beneath the threshold of visibility. Trials and tests of living creatures were also called for so that nature could be observed when forced out of its normal course. In all of this, whatever reservations experimentalists might have entertained about their activities were held in check by the development of formal and public procedures that clothed acts that in themselves were at best undesirable and at worst morally reprehensible with a certain respectability. Animals themselves were recast as beautifully designed artifacts, created by the hand of the Deity. Thus, somewhat paradoxically, it was in their new and more significant role as sources of arguments for the wisdom and power of God that animals great and small came to attract the unwelcome attention of anatomists, microscopists, and vivisectors.

NOTES

1. See, for example, Gary Steiner, "Descartes on the Moral Status of Animals," *Archiv für Geschichte der Philosophie* 80 (1998): 268–91; Anita Guerrini, "The Ethics of Animal Experimentation in Seventeenth-Century England," *Journal of the History of Ideas* 50:3 (1989): 391–407; Andreas-Holger Maehle, "The Ethical Discourse on Animal Experimentation, 1650–1900," in *Doctors and Ethics: The Earlier Historical Setting of Professional Ethics,* ed. Andrew Wear, Johanna Geyer Kordesch, and Roger French (Amsterdam: Rodopi, 1993), 203–51.

2. Nathaniel Wolloch thus speaks of "theriophiles (lovers of animals) and antitheriophiles." "Christiaan Huygens' Attitude towards Animals," *Journal of the History of Ideas* 61:3 (2000): 415–32. Compare Walter Shugg, "Humanitarian Attitudes in the Early Animal Experimentation of the Royal Society," *Annals of Science* 24 (1968): 227–38.

3. William Harvey, *Movement of the Heart and Blood in Animals: An Anatomical Essay,* in *The Circulation of the Blood and Other Writings,* trans. K. Franklin (London: Dent, 1963), 7.

4. Edward Topsell, *The Historie of Foure-footed Beastes* (London, 1607), title page.

5. Conrad Gesner, *Historiae animalium,* 5 vols. (Zürich, 1551–87), I, Epistle.

6. Ibid., 23.

7. The term *vivisection* seems to have come into use in the eighteenth century; the practice predates the term.

8. Stephen Pumphrey, "The History of Science and the Renaissance Science of History," in *Science, Culture and Popular Belief in Renaissance Europe,* ed. Stephen Pumphrey, Paolo L. Rossi, and Maurice Slawinski (Manchester: Manchester Uni-

versity Press, 1991), 56; A. Rupert Hall, *The Revolution in Science* (London: Longman, 1983), chapter 2.

9. Quoted in Walter Pagel and P. Rattansi, "Vesalius and Paracelsus," *Medical History* 8 (1964): 313.

10. William Harvey, *A Second Disquisition to John Riolan* (Chicago: Encyclopaedia Britannica, 1951), 313.

11. Nehemiah Grew, *Musaeum Regalis Societatis* (London, 1681), preface.

12. Thomas Sprat, *History of the Royal Society* (London, 1667), 438.

13. See John Ray and Francis Willughby, *The Ornithology of Francis Willughby* (London, 1678), preface; William Wotton, *Reflections upon Ancient and Modern Learning,* 2d ed. (London, 1697), 258.

14. Wolfgang Franz, *The History of Brutes* (London 1670), 1–2.

15. Bacon, *De Augmentis,* in *The Works of Francis Bacon,* 14 vols., ed. James Spedding, Robert Ellis, and Douglas Heath (London: Longman, 1857–74), IV, 292–95. Compare *Works* III, 361.

16. Bacon, *Novum Organum,* in *Works* IV, 169.

17. Bacon, *Cogitationes de natura rerum,* in *Works* III, 29.

18. For the Baconian rhetoric of interrogation see Caroline Merchant, *The Death of Nature: Women, Ecology, and the Scientific Revolution* (San Francisco: Harper and Row, 1980), chapter 7; Evelyn Fox Keller, *Reflections on Gender and Science* (New Haven, Conn.: Yale University Press, 1985), chapters 2 and 3. But compare Iddo Landau, "Feminist Criticisms of Metaphors in Bacon's Philosophy of Science," *Philosophy* 73 (1998): 47–61.

19. Robert Hooke, *Micrographia* (London, 1665), preface.

20. John Wallis, *Opera mathematica* (Oxford, 1699), I, 491.

21. Galileo, *The Assayer,* in *Discoveries and Opinions of Galileo,* trans. Stillman Drake (New York: Anchor, 1957), 237f.

22. Robert Boyle, *Some Considerations Touching the Usefulness of Experimental Natural Philosophy,* in *The Works of the Honourable Robert Boyle,* ed. Thomas Birch, 6 vols. (London, 1772), II, 63.

23. On Boyle and the hermeneutics of the nature see Karen L. Edwards, *Milton and the Natural World* (Cambridge: Cambridge University Press, 1999), 59f.

24. Jean Gailhard, *A Treatise Concerning the Education of Youth* (London, 1678), 24f.

25. Juan Luis Vives, *Opera omnia,* ed. Gregorio Mayans y Síscar, 8 vols. (London: Gregg Press, 1964), IV, 422.

26. Gideon Harvey, *Archelogia Philosophica Nova, or New Principles of Philosophy* (London, 1663), 89.

27. Paracelsus, *Die 9 Bücher der Natura Rerum,* in *Sämliche Werke,* ed. Karl Sudhoff and Wilhelm Matthiessen, 15 vols. (Munich: R. Oldenburg, 1922–33), XI, 393, 397.

28. John Edwards, *A Demonstration of the Existence and Providence of God* (London, 1696), 133.

29. Richard Saunders, *Saunders Physiognomie and Chiromancie, Metoscopie,* 2d ed. (London, 1671), preface.

30. John Webster, *Academiarum Examen* (London, 1654), 76. On physiognomy and signatures see Peter Harrison, "Reading the Passions: The Fall, the Passions, and Dominion over Nature," in *The Soft Underbelly of Reason: The Passions in the Seventeenth Century,* ed. Stephen Gaukroger (London: Routledge, 1998), 49–78.

31. For occult and astrological associations see Nicholas Culpeper, *Complete Herbal* (Ware, U.K.: Wordsworth, 1995), vi; Oswald Croll, *Of Signatures* (London, 1669); Jacob Boehme, *Signatura Rerum* (London, 1651), 4; Matthew Barker, *Natural Theology* (London, 1674), 25; Saunders, *Physiognomie,* preface. For examples of advocates of the recovery of signatures see Paracelsus, *Die 9 Bücher,* XI, 393, 397; Webster, *Academiarum Examen,* 76.

32. Bacon, *New Organon,* xxiii, in *The English Philosophers from Bacon to Mill,* ed. E. A. Burtt (New York: Random House, 1967), 31; Compare Noah Biggs, *Mataetechnia Medicinae Praxeos* (London, 1651), 33.

33. Boyle, *Usefulness of Experimental Natural Philosophy,* in *Works* II, 20.

34. Guerrini, "Ethics of Animal Experimentation," 391–407; Robert Frank Jr., *Harvey and the Oxford Physiologists* (Berkeley: University of California Press, 1980), 25–30; F. J. Cole, "Harvey's Animals," *Journal of the History of Medicine* 12 (1957): 106–7.

35. Theodore Brown, *The Mechanical Philosophy and the "Animal Oeconomy,"* Ph.D. dissertation, Princeton University, 1968; Frank, *Harvey and the Oxford Physiologists.*

36. Otto van Guericke, *The New (So Called) Magdeburg Experiments of Otto von Guericke,* trans. Margaret Ames (Dordrecht: Kluwer, 1994).

37. Robert Boyle, *New Experiments Physico-Mechanical, Touching the Spring of the Air, and its Effects* (1663), in *Works* I.

38. Thomas Birch, *The History of the Royal Society of London,* 4 vols. (New York: Johnson Reprint, 1968), I, 485.

39. Guerrini, "Ethics of Animal Experimentation," 403f.

40. Leonora Cohen-Rosenfield, *From Beast-Machine to Man-Machine: Animal Soul in French Letters from Descartes to La Mettrie* (New York: Octagon, 1968), 53. See also Joseph Lavalée, *Letters of a Marmeluke* (London, 1804), 106; N. Trublet, *Mémoirs pour servir á l'histoire de la vie et des ouvrages de M. de Fontenelle* (Amsterdam, 1761).

41. Wolloch, "Christiaan Huygens' Attitude"; Alice Stroup, "Christiaan Huygens and the Development of the Air Pump," *Janus* 68 (1981): 129–58.

42. A. D. Farr, "The First Human Blood Transfusion," *Medical History* 24 (1980): 143–62. The feat was replicated in England in November of the same year, under the auspices of the Royal Society. See Birch, *History,* II, 214.

43. Wolloch, "Christiaan Huygens' Attitude," 424f.

44. For early modern discussions of animal souls, see Peter Harrison, "Animal Souls, Metempsychosis, and Theodicy in Seventeenth-Century English Thought," *Journal of the History of Philosophy* 31:4 (1993): 519–44. For Descartes's much-discussed position, see John Cottingham, "'A Brute to the Brutes?': Descartes' Treatment of Animals," *Philosophy* 53 (1978): 551–61; Peter Harrison, "Descartes on Animals," *Philosophical Quarterly* 42 (1992): 219–27; Steiner, "Descartes on the Moral Status of Ani-

mals;" Katherine Morris, "Bêtes-machines," in *Descartes' Natural Philosophy*, ed. S. Gaukroger, J. Schuster, and J. Sutton (London: Routledge, 2000), 401–19.

45. Hooke to Boyle, 10 November, 1664, Boyle, *Works*, VI, 498.

46. "An Account of an Experiment Made by Mr Hooke, of Preserving Animals Alive by Blowing through their Lungs with Bellows," *Philosophical Transactions* II (1667), 539–40; Guerrini, "Ethics of Animal Experimentation," 402.

47. John Evelyn, *The Diary of John Evelyn*, ed. E. de Beer, 6 vols. (Oxford: Clarendon, 1955), III, 549; Walter Shugg, "The Cartesian Beast Machine in English Literature, 1663–1750," *Journal of the History of Ideas* 29 (1968): 279–92, quotation on p. 231.

48. Frederik Ruysch, *Dilucidatio valvularum in vasis lymphaticis et lacteis* (1665), quoted in Guerrini, "Ethics of Animal Experimentation," 406.

49. Guerrini, "Ethics of Animal Experimentation," 398. On Boyle's attitude toward animals see J. J. Macintosh, "Animals, Morality, and Robert Boyle," *Dialogue* 35:3 (1996): 435–72; Malcolm Oster, "'The Beame of Divinity': Animal Suffering in the Early Thought of Robert Boyle," *British Journal for the History of Science* 22:2 (1989): 151–79; Yves Conry, "Robert Boyle et la doctrine cartesienne des animaux-machines," *Revue d'Histoire des Sciences* 33 (1980): 69–74.

50. Hooke, *Micrographia*, 186.

51. Nikolaus Mani, "Jean Riolan II (1580–1657) and Medical Research," *Bulletin of the History of Medicine* 42 (1974): 121–44. The one moral concern Riolan did voice was that the dissection of live animals might eventually be extended to humans, a concern that turned out to be justified in light of subsequent experiments in blood transfusion.

52. William Harvey, *Anatomical Exercises on the Generation of Animals*, trans. Robert Willis, in *Great Books of the Western World* XXVIII (Chicago: Encyclopaedia Britannica, 1951), 329.

53. Harvey, *A Second Disquisition*, 313.

54. Samuel Hartlib, *Ephemerides, The Hartlib Papers*, 30/3/54A, cited in Edwards, *Milton and the Natural World*, 61.

55. On such criticisms of natural philosophy, see Peter Harrison, "Curiosity, Forbidden Knowledge, and the Reformation of Natural Philosophy in Seventeenth-Century England," *Isis* 92 (2001): 265–90.

56. Samuel Butler, "Paedants," in *Satires and Miscellaneous Poetry and Prose*, ed. R. Lamar (Cambridge: Cambridge University Press, 1928), 166.

57. Jonathan Swift, *Gulliver's Travels* (London, 1726), Part III, chapter 5.

58. Similar requirements existed for the practice of human dissections. See Andrea Carlino, *Books of the Body: Anatomical Ritual and Renaissance Learning*, trans. John Tedeschi and Anne C. Tedeschi (Chicago: University of Chicago Press, 1999).

59. Simon Schaffer and Steven Shapin, *Leviathan and the Air-Pump: Hobbes, Boyle and the Experimental Life* (Princeton, N.J.: Princeton University Press, 1985). Compare Guerrini, "Ethics and Animal Experimentation," 394–96.

60. See Stanley Milgram, *Obedience to Authority: An Experimental View* (New York: Harper Collins, 1983).

61. Harvey, *Anatomical Exercises*, 329.

62. Boyle, *Some Considerations,* in *Works* II, 17, 84.

63. Boyle, *Usefulness,* in *Works,* II, 7.

64. Joseph Glanvill, *The Vanity of Dogmatizing* (London, 1661), 3.

65. Wotton, *Ancient and Modern Learning,* 254f.

66. Ibid., 314.

67. Ibid., 319.

68. William Gearing, *A Prospect of Heaven* (London, 1673), 98f; Thomas Draxe, *The Earnest of Our Inheritance* (London, 1613), 5f.

69. *The Letters of Jan Swammerdam to Melchisidec Thévenot,* trans. G. A. Lindeboom (Amsterdam: Smuts and Zeitlinger, 1975), Letter 19a, April 1678, 105. Compare René Reaumur, *Memoirs pour servir a l'histoire des Insectes,* 6 vols. (Paris, 1734–42), I, 4; Edwards, *A Demonstration,* part 1, 204f., 220; John Ray, *The Wisdom of God Manifested in the Works of Creation* (London, 1691), 41.

70. Nicolas Malebranche, *Dialogues on Metaphysics and Religion,* ed. Nicholas Jolley, trans. David Scott (Cambridge: Cambridge University Press, 1997), 200 and 211. Compare Malebranche, *Eloge du P. Malebranche, Oeuvres complètes,* ed. G. Rodis-Lewis, 22 vols. (Paris: Vrin, 1958–70), V, 461. Compare Edwards, *A Demonstration,* 204f.

71. Hooke, *Micrographia,* 195. Cf. Boyle, *Usefulness,* in *Works* II, 12. Also see Edward Davis, "'Parcere nominibus': Boyle, Hooke and the Rhetorical Interpretation of Descartes," in *Robert Boyle Reconsidered,* ed. Michael Hunter (Cambridge: Cambridge University Press, 1994), 157–75.

72. Henry Power, *Experimental Philosophy* (London, 1664), preface.

73. Noël Antoine Pluche, *Spectacle de la Nature: or Nature Display'd,* 7 vols. (London, 1770), I, 1, 34.

74. On moral reasons for studying animals, and insects in particular, see Peter Harrison, "The Virtues of Animals in Seventeenth-Century Thought," *Journal of the History of Ideas* 59:3 (1998): 463–85.

75. See Nicolas Malebranche, *The Search after Truth,* trans. and ed. Thomas Lennon and Paul Olscamp (Cambridge: Cambridge University Press, 1997), I.vi.3, II.vii.3; Jan Swammerdam, *Historia insectorum generalis* (Utrecht, 1669), part II, 29f; On theories of embryological preexistence see Jacques Roger, *Les Sciences de la vie dans la pensee francaise du XVIIIᵉ siecle,* 2d ed. (Paris, 1971), chapter 3.

76. Malebranche, *Search after Truth,* I.vi.3.

77. Malebranche, *Dialogues,* XI.xiii.

78. Ibid.

79. Pluche, *Spectacle de la Nature,* I, 21.

11

The Ménagerie and the Labyrinthe: Animals at Versailles, 1662–1792

Matthew Senior

The Ménagerie of Versailles, built by Louis Le Vau between 1662 and 1664, was one of the first structures to be completed as part of Louis XIV's vast domain of parks, fountains, buildings, and monuments. An extravagant display of magnificence that only a monarch could afford, the Ménagerie was an architectural innovation that served as a model for the collection and control of animals for nearly a century and a half throughout Europe.

The animal park at Versailles was, in some sense, a scale model, in design and ideology, of the entire royal project. As Pierre Lablaud observes, the Ménagerie was "a sort of miniature palace, a reduced-scale production of the much more ambitious complex being developed simultaneously around Louis XIII's palace."[1] The zoo at Versailles was the first to separate animals into groups and provide a simultaneous view of all of the animals. From the balcony of his garden pavilion, the king and his guests looked down on an octagonal courtyard joined to cages containing different kinds of animals (figure 11.1).

Like the king's apartments, the pavilion faced east, toward the rising sun; hence, the view in Aveline's engraving is from the west, toward St. Cyr. Moving counterclockwise in Aveline's drawing, from left to right, the first enclosure one sees is the Quartier des Cigognes, containing storks. The second pen, the Quartier des Demoiselles, named after its *demoiselles de numidie* (demoiselle cranes), also contained an aviary with more than forty species of exotic birds. The third yard, the Cour des Pélicans, was home to pelicans, cranes, flamingos, and wild ducks, as was the fourth enclosure, the Rond-d'eau, a habitat for storks, herons, and wading birds. The fifth compound, the Quartier des Autruches, contained ostriches, Egyptian herons, eagles, and porcupines, living in a decor of sand and rocks meant to evoke the African desert. The sixth pen, the Cour des Oiseaux, was home to civets, foxes, crows, rare pigeons, spoonbilled cranes, and exotic birds; for a time it also housed an elephant and a camel before these large mammals were moved to their own Cour de la Ferme. The seventh yard, the Basse-Cour, contained domestic

Veüe et perspective du Salon de la Menagerie de Versailles que l'on voit icy par derriere au milieu de sept Cours
remplies D'oyseaux rares et D'autres Animaux de divers pays eloignés.   fait par Aveline Avec Privilege du Roy   1689

Figure 11.1. Pierre-Alexandre Aveline, *Versailles Ménagerie* (1689).
Reproduced by permission of the Bibliotèque Nationale de France, Cabinet des estampes.

farm animals destined for the royal kitchens and tables. Lions, leopards, elephants, gazelles, and other rare animals were housed in cages constructed behind the seven main compounds. At the end of the century, Louis XIV consolidated his collection of *bêtes sauvages* by moving lions, tigers, and panthers from Vincennes to Versailles. In the years leading up to the Revolution, the Sun King and his successors managed to collect a huge number and variety of animals. Gustave Loisel's census of the animals that lived in the Ménagerie tallies up as follows: one hundred twenty-three species of mammals, two hundred thirty-nine varieties of birds, and ten species of amphibians.[2] All of these animals were on display in a fanlike structure that ensured maximum visibility and symbolized the king's dominion over the natural world.

The architectural sources for this strikingly original design cannot be directly established since Le Vau left behind no written texts on the Ménagerie.[3] By examining the architect's career against the backdrop of absolutist politics and prevailing ideas about architecture and garden design at Versailles, one can advance with varying degrees of certainty and speculation as to the purpose and meaning of the Ménagerie. Two fundamental intentions seem apparent in the design of the first modern zoo: the desire to encompass nature and make it visible from a single vantage point and the desire to confine animals and separate them according to species. Thus put on display, the animals fulfilled several purposes: they were emblems of royal prestige and amusing spectacles for the king's guests. They were studied and painted by an emerging school of *peintres animaliers* (Desportes, Nicasius, Boël, and Oudry), who were able to observe many of these exotic species for the first time.[4] And, finally, they were dissected and vivisected by members of the newly formed Académie des Sciences, who recorded their observations in collective proceedings and precise anatomical drawings.[5]

The desire to encompass and discriminate, to divide and conquer, is a theme repeated elsewhere in the park. In the Grand Canal, for example, Louis kept a small mock fleet of Dutch, French, English, and Spanish vessels, complete with crews in native attire to express his dominion over all the oceans and navies of the world.[6] The Bourbon king's personal myth was that of the god Apollo who carries the sun across the sky in a chariot, giving life and visibility to the whole world. The Ménagerie itself was designed to confer maximum visibility from a single vantage point and imply that natural life was improved, harmonized, and pacified by a rational plan.

The radiocentric design was derived from the writings of Vitruvius, which were revived by Leon Battista Alberti, the Renaissance architect.[7] The technique was used to create perspective in gardens and to integrate architecture and landscape by extending the lines and angles of buildings into the surrounding space. The plan was first used in Italy and became a commonplace in the gardens of André Le Nôtre and other classical French land-scape architects. The most original aspect of Le Vau's structure is the divi-sion of animals according to species. The animals are not to be understood as they occur in nature, mixed with other animals, but as members of a group. For the first time in history, the zoo is meant to divide and classify animals. This reflects the work of biology during the Classical Age, which focused largely on classifying plants and animals according to externally visible, minimal differences.[8]

Louis was not the first French king to surround himself with exotic ani-mals. Clovis (465–511), the first king of the Franks and spiritual ancestor of all French kings, staged animal combats in imitation of the Romans. Charle-magne (768–814) and Louis IX (1226–70) kept elephants; Francis I (1494–1547) owned lions and tigers and was known to have a leopard sleep at the foot of his bed.[9] These are heraldic uses of the animal to signify the power and prestige of the monarch and his conquest of distant lands. Animal com-bat continued to interest kings and their courts from the Middle Ages through the Renaissance. Galleries were erected to watch bears fight dogs, lions and tigers fight rhinos, and, in one instance, a cow challenge a lioness. Such encounters were interpreted as allegories of aristocratic superiority. The *fauves* triumphed over more lowly animals, or, in the case of the cow that actually vanquished the lioness, culture gained the upper hand over savage nature.

Alongside the medieval tradition of animal combat, the Renaissance saw the rise of curiosity, wonder, and the ideal of the collection. With the ex-pansion of the known world and the revival of the pantheistic idea of a cre-ative nature endowed with a soul, living animals were added to collections of stuffed animals, shells, engravings, and mechanical marvels. The aim of such collections was to show the strange diversity of nature, her freakish powers and penchant for distant analogies between sea and land creatures, stars and plant life, bodily humors and cosmic cycles.[10]

The Versailles Ménagerie is part of this line of development, but it is also radically different on certain key points. It was never the scene of animal combat; these had taken place in a small arena near the château de Vincennes, where animals were housed in what was called the Sérail des Bêtes Sauvages. The animals kept in the Sérail were exotic imported animals. The word *sérail* linked them to a feared and mysterious, non-Western political and sexual model. To seventeenth-century French men and women, the *sérail* was the space where the Sultan indulged his passions and murdered his rivals.

Versailles was meant for the purely visual pleasure of seeing a wide va-riety of animals, not the destruction of such animals in blood sports. As the French aristocracy grew in refinement, it abandoned violence in its personal conduct and aesthetic tastes as part of what Norbert Elias calls the civilizing process.[11] This different way of confining and viewing animals left its mark on the French language: the word *ménagerie,* which had previously meant a building for raising domestic animals, came to mean a royal collection of exotic animals kept for display.[12] Le Vau's Ménagerie, and its specific radial design, was identified with the French absolute monarchy and imitated at zoos in Vienna, Karlsruhe, Madrid, and Amsterdam.

SEEING ANIMALS

By studying plans and drawings of the Ménagerie and reading accounts by contemporaries, it is possible to recreate the visual experience of a seventeenth-century visitor to the site. Animals were displayed here according to a carefully choreographed sequence. Guests approached the Ménagerie by passing through a gate and crossing a gravel courtyard. Upon entering the building, visitors climbed a stairway, passed through another door, and entered a rectangular gallery decorated with portraits of animals. At this point, no animals were yet visible; they would be seen only when one entered the octagonal Salon de la Ménagerie, whose large windows and external balcony provided an expansive view of the animals on display.[13]

In *Les Amours de Psyché et de Cupidon* (1669), the poet Jean de La Fontaine gives an account of a visit he made to the Ménagerie and describes the visual effect of seeing so many animals at once: "So many species of bird are multiplied from a single species . . . the artifice and diverse imaginings of Nature [are] revealed in animals as they are in flowers."[14] Mademoiselle de Scudéry, another writer who recorded her impressions of the Ménagerie, makes similar remarks and draws attention to the role of art in the overall experience of seeing the animals. "From the Salon one can see seven different enclosures, filled with all sorts of birds and rare animals; their portraits are in the gallery, in order to prepare one for what one is about to see, or to serve as a memento after the visit."[15] Looking at animals at Versailles was always a simultaneous looking at pictures of animals. Throughout the château and the gardens, art and nature were deliberately juxtaposed and confused according to a Renaissance aesthetic that saw art as an embellishment of nature and nature as a kind of art whose principles could be understood and illustrated on a large scale.[16]

The presence of an artistic representation alongside the animals is also a reminder of the unreliability of the senses and the mediatedness of human knowledge. The eye needed to be educated. The proper human apprehension of the animal is an act of judgment, not merely the physiological process of seeing. Descartes makes this distinction in the *Méditations* in his discussion of the piece of wax, which exists in a solid, liquid, or gaseous state. We commonly say that we "see" the wax, but "we only know objects by the faculty of reason which is in us, not by the imagination or the senses."[17] In the same discussion, Descartes speculates that animals merely "see" things and are incapable of synthetic judgments: "What is there in this first perception that was distinct and evident and which would not be apprehended by the senses of the least animal? But when I distinguish the wax from its external forms, as if I had stripped away its clothes and considered it entirely naked—I can only conceive the wax in this fashion with a human spirit."[18] Just what it was, exactly, that animals saw and thought was a hotly contested issue during the Classical Age. If Descartes was sure that the beast-machines were incapable of judgment, others, following a long theriophilic tradition, were willing to ascribe passions, memory, and complicated reasoning to animals.[19]

The Flemish painter Pieter Boël (1622–74), who made in vivo sketches of animals at Versailles, focuses on the gaze of a group of exotic birds he has surprised in one of the compounds of the Ménagerie (figure 11.2). The painting ponders the depths of animal consciousness and seems to ask of its viewer, What do we look like in the minds of animals? What do animals look like in the minds of humans? The specificity of animal vision, the fact that the birds look at the painter with only one eye, for example, poses the question of the distinction between human and animal vision and, by inference, between human *jugement* and animal *sens.*

The gaze of the birds indicates the place of the *peintre animalier,* the masterful locus of the king and the painter in the classical system of representation. According to Michel Foucault, *Las Meninas,* Velásquez's masterpiece depicting the Spanish Infanta and her attendants (completed in 1656 and thus roughly contemporary with the construction of the Ménagerie) can be read as "the representation of classical representation itself and the definition of the space it opens."[20] Although the painting is characterized by both a high degree of realism and self-reference (we see the painter, with brush in hand, looking out from behind his canvas, standing alongside his models), it is also marked by "profound invisibility." The objects of the painter's gaze—King Philip IV of Spain and his queen—lie outside the painting, and the actual process of painting also remains invisible because we can't see the actual painting the artist is working on, nor can we see him in the act of painting. *Las Meninas* thus reveals the "essential void" at the heart of classical representation, "the necessary disappearance of that which founds it—the person it resembles and the person for whom it is made." The agency of man as the creator of the order of representations is invisible (and unthinkable) in this painting and in classical representation in general. The distinction established

Figure 11.2. Pieter Boël, engraving by G. Scotin, *Versailles Ménagerie, Quartier des Demoiselles* (c. 1670). (1) Muscovy ducks, (2) demoiselle cranes, (3) black-crowned cranes, (4) Canada geese, (5) Guinea fowl, and (6) great bustards. Reproduced by permission of Bibliotèque Nationale de France, Cabinet des Estampes.

within the painting between seeing reality and seeing art also destroys any direct link of resemblance between the work of art and "the person it resembles." Delivered from this obligation, the work of art thus stands as a "pure representation."

The role of animals in this newly created space of representation is to serve as pure objects. "The dog, stretched out on the floor, is the only element in the painting that neither sees nor moves because its only purpose, with its rough outline and the light playing on its satin coat, is to be seen as an object."[21] *Las Meninas* represents a kind of anthropology in which humans see and make representations, whereas dogs and other animals are simply objects, displaying a blank, unreflective gaze, just as their minds are incapable of self-awareness. Human vision, in all its intensity, gazes out of the painting and ponders the distinction between representation and reality. In the painting, the dog looks tiredly at the floor, uninterested in the drama of representation going on around it. It does not exchange glances with human subjects, nor does it encounter its own gaze and its own subjectivity, as the painter Velásquez does.[22]

One of the West's favorite myths about the difference between human and animal vision is the story of Zeuxis, an early Greek painter who sought to win a competition for the best artist in Athens by painting a mural of grapes so convincing that birds flew up and tried to peck at the fruit. Zeuxis was defeated in the contest by Parrhasius, a rival painter who sketched in a curtain around the picture of the grapes and succeeded in fooling Zeuxis, who asked that the curtain be drawn back to fully reveal his painting. The Greeks considered deceiving a human to be a greater feat than tricking animals.[23]

With these references in mind, the effect of the animal *regard* in Boël's painting is multiple. It adds a naturalistic aspect to the painting, as the naïve, natural seeing of the birds confirms the existence of the spectator and the painter. According to the beliefs of the period, the animal gaze would be an uncritical, confused look, wedded to appearances, capable of confusing painted grapes with real ones. Here, unlike in *Las Meninas,* the position of the painter and the spectator is engaged by animal glances. Does this confirm the same order of representation that Foucault sees in the Velásquez masterpiece?

In this painting, the artist seems interested in taking several steps toward animal consciousness. He has abandoned the panoptical position afforded by the Ménagerie and joined the animals in their own world, inside one of their compounds. Cut off from the global view of all of the animals in their quarters, we see the central pavilion from a different kind of "bird's-eye view." However, in addition to registering a moment of pure animal vision, the painting also powerfully inscribes a position of human authority and rationality on the scene. The birds seem to be captured by the artist in a totally natural, unrehearsed pose. The moments frozen in time by the drawing are the few seconds during which the birds stare warily at a human intruder before returning to their feeding and foraging. The animals do not exchange glances among themselves but look in unison outside of their world toward the place of representation. We see the birds as *observed,* interrupted in their natural movements and artificially arranged in a series of oppositions that confirm the scientific and social paradigms that governed Versailles. The birds are drawn in profile so the viewer can compare their extravagant plumage and sinuous forms. They are assigned numbers and names, continuing the process of separation of the animals in the Ménagerie down to the level of individual species with unique names.

The most striking species, the *demoiselles* (demoiselle cranes) and *oyseaux royals* (black-crowned cranes) are in the foreground, with the *oyseau royal's* head and plumage clearly elevated above the heads of the other birds. The lower domestic birds, the ducks, geese, and guinea fowl, are smaller and closer to the ground, about to return to their feeding. The order of nature depicted in this painting is thus a political order. The more noble, royal birds are the most worthy of representation and dominate all of the birds by their external grandeur and magnificence. The exotic animals gathered by the king from the four corners of the world thus confirm that there is a monarchical order in nature that is faithfully revealed at Versailles. The position of the painter is thus a position of reason and royal insight. In a certain sense, Boël's *Quartier des Demoiselles* turns out to be a *Las Meninas,* a carefully composed tableau of royal *suivantes* who evoke a human presence and a human ordering that is all the more powerful for its being invisible.

Jean-Baptiste Oudry (1686–1755) was similarly interested in the gaze of his animal subjects, whose eyes seem to confirm the opinion of his contemporary, Jacques-Henri Bernardin de Saint-Pierre: "Each species of animal has certain traits that express its character. The fiery and disquieting eyes of the tiger announce its ferocity and perfidiousness."[24] By the mid-eighteenth century, scientific and philosophical views of animal consciousness had shifted: animals were accorded sentiments such as anger, fear, and love that they shared with humans.[25] But however much animals shared certain sentiments with humans, there was still an absolute difference between animals and humans, especially violent ones, such as Oudry's panther (figure 11.3). The prominent bars of the cage in this painting suggest a limit between human culture and wild animal nature, reminding the viewer that one of the prime functions of the Ménagerie was to contain nature and subject it to the monarchical order of peace and rationality.

Figure 11.3. Jean Baptiste Oudry, engraving by Pierre-François Basan, *Panther Cage* (1739). Reproduced by permission of the Bibliothèque Nationale de France, Cabinet des Estampes.

DISSECTION AND DIFFERENCE

The Cartesian metaphor of stripping objects and seeing them naked is evident in the work of the Academy of Sciences, founded by Louis XIV in 1666. Claude Perrault, its chief anatomist, conducted dissections of animals from the Ménagerie and recorded them in his *Mémoires pour servir à l'histoire des animaux* (1671). In contrast to earlier Renaissance natural histories, which sought the prodigious and the strange, Perrault and his associates were looking for consistency and order in nature. In the preface to the *Mémoires,* the author states that nature does not vary in its laws. Perrault also took great care in illustrating the *Mémoires.* He was a very capable draftsman and worked closely with Sebastien Leclerc to produce precise drawings of the animals as both living creatures and dissected specimens. The *Mémoires* specify that the artist who records the dissections must also be a scientist: "It is important not so much to represent well what is seen, as to see well what should be represented." In this view of representation, judgment and scientific knowledge take precedence over naive vision.[26]

One of Leclerc's engravings and the accompanying commentary by the Académie show the different kinds of vision and knowledge that surrounded animals at Versailles. The animals in question are two species of monkey that Perrault and his colleagues dissected: the *sapajou* and the *guenon.* The chained monkeys can be seen playing, with the château and the Labyrinthe clearly visible in the background. The Labyrinthe, designed by Charles Perrault, the brother of Claude Perrault the anatomist, contained statues and placards illustrating scenes from Aesop's fables. Thus Leclerc's engraving shows animals to be the objects of scientific knowledge but also of play and literary allegory (figure 11.4).

In general, the ape had a checkered reputation in the Western tradition. In the Middle Ages, the animal was considered to be an incarnation of the devil.[27] Because of its similarity to humans, it was often accused of being a deceitful imitator and a fraudulent usurper. One of La Fontaine's fables, "The Dolphin and the Monkey," is typical of this stereotype. During a shipwreck, a monkey jumps onto the back of a dolphin to save himself. The Dolphin thinks the Monkey is a man and so asks him, in the course of their conversation, "Have you ever visited Pirée?" The Monkey replies, "Yes, I know him well." The Dolphin, knowing that Pirée is the name of a city on the Greek coast, understands that he has a monkey on his back, not a man, so he hurls the Monkey off his back into the sea.[28] Another La Fontaine fable, illustrated with a statue in the Labyrinthe, concerns a monkey who puts on the clothes of a boy and is captured as a result. According to an absurd and supposedly historical account of a simulating monkey from the sev-

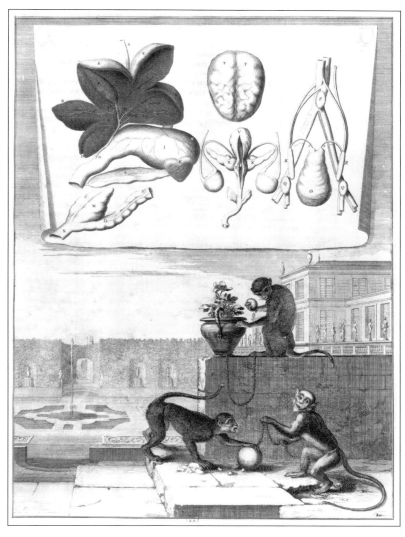

Figure 11.4. Sebastien Leclerc, *Sapajous et Guenon,*
from Claude Perrault, *Mémoires pour servir à l'histoire des animaux* (1676).
Reproduced by permission of the Bibliotèque Nationale de France.

enteenth century, the philosopher and writer Cyrano de Bergerac killed a monkey in a duel because the animal was dressed in gentleman's clothing, including a sword hanging by its side. This particular monkey was a well-known fair and carnival performer named Fagotin, mentioned in one of Molière's plays.[29]

In the *Mémoires,* Perrault takes up the question of the resemblance between monkeys and humans. Dissection reveals that monkeys have many similarities to humans as well as differences. Leclerc's drawing carefully records the similarities and differences between the monkey's hands and those of humans. However, the ultimate distinction, as in La Fontaine's fables and Descartes's philosophy, turns out to be speech. According to Perrault, apes have the same muscles and vocal equipment as humans, but, lacking reason, they cannot talk. "Speech is an action much more particular to man than the hand. Monkeys do not have reason. They have the necessary organs but not reason itself."[30]

Leclerc's engravings of the monkeys juxtapose the living, playful animals and their dissected organs. The château and the Labyrinthe suggest the other dimensions of the monkeys' lives: they are pets of the courtiers and living links to the literary, moralized world of Aesop, Perrault, and La Fontaine. The organs are separated and drawn against a white background for the purpose of scientific illustration; this part of the engraving is Cartesian analysis, not naturalistic painting. The curled edges of the dissection sheet underscore the fact that the viewer is looking through several layers of illusion and representation to arrive at an abstract, artificial tableau. The presentation of the organs actually looks like a botanical drawing. (Botany eclipsed anatomy during the Classical Age, according to Foucault, because the forms and differences of plants are external and visible.)[31] The aim of this kind of representation is to see minimal differences, to see things clearly and distinctly, according to the Cartesian criteria of clear and distinct ideas.

Claude Perrault's anatomical illustrations and observations accomplish the same work of unmasking the dissimulating monkey as the fables of his brother and La Fontaine. The monkey's physiological nature hangs over his head, preventing him from usurping a higher place in the natural order. The animal's internal organs are like a ball and chain, weighing it down, making it part of the spectacle of Versailles and preventing it, like many ambitious social climbers, from rising above its assigned place.

By studying the hidden structures of animals, Perrault hoped to understand major functions, such as digestion, reproduction, and muscle contraction, according to simple mechanical principles, as William Harvey had done for the circulation of blood. Perrault subscribed to Harvey's theories concerning circulation and became involved in debates about transfusion.

In 1667 he succeeded in transfusing blood between two dogs. The next year, Perrault's colleague Jean-Baptiste Denis attempted a transfusion between a man and a dog; the man died, and his survivors sued Denis.[32] To advance science along these pathways, it was necessary to vivisect, as Perrault states: "The living animals on which experiments will be made shall be dogs, pigs, sheep, calves donkeys, cows, and horses."[33]

ANIMAL ACTS

Science was not the only purpose of keeping animals at Versailles; their most important function was to entertain guests of high rank. Louis received the Papal Nuncio and the Doge of Venice and held receptions for his mistresses. Exotic gifts from other monarchs were displayed (an elephant given by the King of Portugal and three crocodiles from the King of Siam) as well as animals from France's commercial and colonial empire (gazelles and ostriches from Egypt, a cassowary bird from Madagascar, and parrots and leopards transported by the fleet of the Compagnie des Indes).[34]

Animals were used extensively in elaborate royal pageants staged at Versailles. One of the fundamental reasons for the construction of the entire palace and garden complex was to hold rituals of the monarchy in large outdoor theaters that incorporated sculpted trees and alleys from the gardens into the perspectival settings of the stage. An early example of such *fêtes*, and one that set the tone for the entire reign, was the Plaisirs de l'Isle Enchantée, held between May 7 and 13, 1664. Louis appeared in the pageant as Roger, the hero of Tasso's *Orlando Furioso*, who is held captive on an enchanted isle. In the opening phases of the pageant, different elements of the cosmos came to pay homage to the king. The four seasons of the year were represented by women riding on the backs of animals borrowed from the Ménagerie.[35]

As opposed to the scientific use of animals, here they express enchantment and wonder. Louis is the master of France and the world. He commands time and space. Orange trees grow in winter, and animals from around the world are assembled to demonstrate the king's mastery over the seasons and the continents of the world. Versailles was an enchanted palace, and Louis XIV was its magician. It was described as such by André Felibien, a contemporary. "Everyone immediately saw this Palace as a magical place, for it was begun at the end of winter and finished in the spring, as if it had sprung from the earth along with the garden flowers that surrounded it."[36] The art of the king rivaled and superseded nature, as Felibien claimed: "One can say of Versailles that it is a place where Art works on its own, and that Nature seems to have abandoned in order to allow the king, by performing, if I may say so, an act of creation to bring forth numerous magnificent works and an infinite number of extraordinary things."[37]

These wonders included mechanical birds in the Grotto of Thetis whose songs were produced by a water-driven organ. In a curious mixture of the old and new, animals from Aesop's *Fables* and Ovid's *Metamorphoses* were in reality automatons, as Descartes had declared them to be. Through the mysterious mechanical power of the monarch, ancient myths were brought back to life; using modern science and engineering, Louis revived the golden age of myths and fables.

DISCIPLINARY SPACE

In addition to being a complex interface of art and nature, the Ménagerie was, according to Michel Foucault, the original model for a new political use of space. *Discipline and Punish* contains a brief passage speculating that the inventor of the Panopticon, Jeremy Bentham, might have been inspired by the Versailles Ménagerie: "The Panopticon is a royal menagerie; the animal is replaced by man, groups of species by single individuals, and the king by the machinery of a furtive power."[38] According to Foucault, Enlightenment disciplinary institutions such as the prison, the school, the hospital, and the army barracks were derived from the zoo. Looking at Aveline's engraving (figure 11.1), the humans in the drawing appear to be the same size and are situated on the same grid as the animals they observe. Foucault speculates that Bentham may have seen the Ménagerie, but, in fact, the historical connection between confining humans and animals had already been made in the seventeenth century. The same architect who designed the Ménagerie, Louis Le Vau, was also the chief architect for Louis XIV's grand project for confining the sick, the criminal, and the insane at the Hôpital Général. The Eglise de La Sapêtrière, whose final plan was submitted by Le Vau in 1669, used the same octagonal design as the Ménagerie and was similarly innovative in its day for separating the Hôpital's inmates and personnel into distinct groups so that all could assist simultaneously at religious ceremonies without infecting or coming into contact with one another.[39]

Another historian, Henri Ellenberger, drawing parallels between the treatment of animals and the mentally ill, emphasizes the common point of entertainment and public spectacle that marks the history of zoos and mental hospitals. Bedlam Hospital in London, like a public zoo, depended in large part for its financial support on admission fees. Animals and psychiatric patients were expected to be amusing; they were subjected to the same cruel treatment by crowds and developed the same disorders of confinement.[40]

CHARLES PERRAULT'S VISIONS
OF THE MÉNAGERIE

Charles Perrault (1628–1703), author of the Mother Goose fairy tales and brother of the anatomist and architect Claude Perrault, makes several references to the Ménagerie in his writings that reveal the symbolic importance of this site and the role it played in the larger ideological and artistic schemes of Versailles. In "La Peinture" (1668), a long panegyric to Louis XIV and Charles Le Brun, Perrault invokes Apollo to describe the past and predict the future of painting. Not surprisingly, France has a glorious role to play. After Greece and Rome, the arts will attain their "supreme degree of perfection" in France because "the greatest King on earth" will offer brilliant subjects for artists to paint. History, portraiture, architecture, landscape, and garden painting will all reach their zenith during Louis's reign. The Ménagerie is mentioned as a worthy subject in this program: "A thousand wandering herds / Of all of the different species of animals / Once scattered across the Universe / Will be gathered together in this charming enclosure."[41] Another purpose of animal painting in Louis's age will be to illustrate military victories: bears, lions, tigers, and panthers will be the "fearsome trophies" of conquered lands.[42]

Further references to the Ménagerie occur in Perrault's fairy tale *Peau d'Ane* ("Donkey Skin"). A beautiful princess flees her father's court and incestuous embraces, wearing an ugly donkey skin to disguise her natural beauty. The father is described in terms that could refer only to Louis: "There was once a King, the greatest on earth, gentle in peace, terrible in war, comparable only to Himself." The princess escapes far away to another kingdom where, like the Prodigal Son, she accepts the lowliest employment of all—feeding pigs—surrounded by uncouth peasants who name her according to the skin she wears, Peau d'Ane. However, the farm where she works is adjacent to a magnificent Ménagerie built by a "powerful and magnificent King"—another Louis. It contains the same species of exotic birds kept at the Ménagerie: "Poules de Barbarie, Râles, Pintades, Cormorans, Oisons musqués, Canes Petières, et mille autres oiseaux de bizarres manières" ("African Guinea fowl, rails, common Guinea fowl, cormorants, Muscovy ducks, little bustards, and a thousand other strange birds"). The birds are enclosed in ten separate cages, similar to the seven compounds of the Ménagerie.

HYDRAULIC SWAN SONGS

A third set of references to the Ménagerie in Perrault's work occur in *Le Labyrinthe de Versailles,* published in 1777.[43] The Labyrinthe was first created by André Le Nôtre between 1664 and 1667, almost contemporary with the construction of the Ménagerie. Compared with that of earlier medieval and Renaissance mazes, its layout was fairly simple. What made it a marvel and ensured its place as one of the chief attractions of the gardens were its thirty-nine fountains based on scenes from Aesop's fables. According to contemporary accounts, the animals were considered extremely lifelike. Created by the renowned sculptors Tuby, Le Gros, and Houzeau, the lead statues owed their naturalness to the fact that the sculptors and painters who made the statues had observed real animals in the Ménagerie. Unfortunately, only a few of the statues have survived, with faint traces of the original paint. The polychrome richness of the original animals and fountains can be appreciated in paintings from the period by Cotelle.[44] Perrault published a souvenir book of the Labyrinthe, containing engravings by Leclerc and texts from Aesop in French verse. Noting that the animals were convincingly real ("si bien faits au naturel"), Perrault explained that they seemed to be alive because water gushed from their mouths, giving them not only "life and action" but also "voices that express their passions and thoughts."[45]

There are several paradoxes inherent in the animal statues of the Labyrinthe. They were sculpted and painted to be as natural as possible, illustrating a common idea that art should imitate nature. The fact that the animals were hydraulic machines also reinforced and illustrated Descartes's hypothesis of the *bête machine*. The animals' language was, materially, nothing more than the sound of rushing water, and their passions and thoughts were purely mechanical responses to external stimuli. But the animals were also deliberately illusory and scientifically heretical on several levels. The language they spoke in fable and verse was subtle and rational, something Descartes deemed animals to be incapable of. They behaved in ways that were utterly unrealistic according to even the most naive natural history of the day. Monkeys ride on the backs of dolphins, rats discuss putting bells around the necks of cats, and so on. These are literary animals, and the Labyrinthe was a deliberate, achieved illusion, a bringing back to life of a mythical golden age.

The combination of exacting details, based on the observation of real animals, with fanciful stories brings science and myth together and makes them collaborate in creating a renaissance of the mythical past, adding glory and enchantment to Louis's reign. Animals were studied as scientific objects at Versailles; they were also displayed as signs of the submission of nature to royal control, and they were admired simply for their beauty and diversity. Live animals were used in pageants to show the magnificence and wonder of the court and to suggest that Versailles was an Eden, an Arcadia, a golden age of myth and fable. In the Labyrinthe, a very modern and distinctly Cartesian form of animal entertainment and poetry makes its appearance: the combination of engineering and fantasy to produce mechanical fables. The animal fountains illustrate themes that resonate with contemporary court society (as had La Fontaine's *Fables,* published immediately before the completion of the Labyrinthe), but the mechanical rendition of these stories gives them a new, mechanistic inflection.

The entry to the Labyrinthe was guarded by two statues, one representing Aesop, depicted as an aged, physically unattractive man carrying a book, and the other Cupid, a winged androgynous figure holding a ball of thread. The thread alludes to Ariadne's help in guiding Theseus through the Cretan labyrinth. According to Perrault, Cupid wanted to build a labyrinth at Versailles because love itself is a maze. "I am a labyrinth," Cupid tells Apollo. The statue of Aesop represents the wisdom necessary to guiding oneself through the twists and turns of love. The Aesopean animals, "full of ruse and address," can teach humans many valuable lessons about love. The narrative thread of Aesop's fables allows one to experience the pleasures of love without losing one's way.

In the first fable, "Le Duc et les Oiseaux" ("The Owl and the Birds"), a group of smaller birds surround an owl and angrily direct their voices— streams of water—down upon his head. The moral of the story, according to Perrault: the owl is a violent and rough bird with a raucous voice. "Any wise man who enters the Labyrinthe of Love must be gentle in his language, gallant and proper in his attire, not at all a *loup-garou* (werewolf)."[46]

In the Labyrinthe, as at Versailles, the language of love and political intrigue must be gentle, gallant, and restrained. Brute force will always fail. Rivalry, intrigue, and seduction are played out in a field of language, as figured by the water issuing from each animal's mouth. The animals in the Labyrinthe have become courtiers, after the fashion of Norbert Elias; they have ceased playing the role of violent, warring aristocrats, as in the Sérail des Bêtes Sauvages at Vincennes. The general political lesson, as Chandra Mukerji has observed, is a conservative one: do not try to rise above your place in the natural hierarchy.[47] Some advancement, by dint of hard work, intrigue, and ingenuity, is permitted, but those who lack self-awareness and knowledge of their essential nature are doomed to failure. Monkeys who become kings or pretend to be humans are captured, deposed, or drowned. Jays who try to become peacocks by adding false feathers to their own soon lose their borrowed attire—meaning that those not blessed with good looks and suave discourse should stay away from gallantry. There is one fable, however, whose message is decidedly subversive. A group of frogs beg Jupiter to give them a king. The god consents and sends them a stork, who promptly proceeds to devour them all, one after the other.

Animals that cross or confuse natural distinctions between species are ostracized. A bat, difficult to classify because it exhibits both mammalian and avian characteristics, is excluded from both classes of animals and condemned to fly alone at night because it betrayed the birds and joined the mammals in a war between the two groups. A monkey who has become king by wearing a crown and making a spectacle of himself falls into a trap set by a fox, who tells him to look for a treasure in the exact spot where the trap is hidden.

Love is almost uniformly represented as a cruel, predatory instinct. A hawk offers a birthday party to a group of baby birds, only to devour them all once they arrive at her house. The moral here is that when a beautiful woman has several suitors, they will all be gobbled up. In another fable, an attractive woman is again represented as a hawk swooping down on a group of defenseless chicks. The baby birds are saved *in extremis* by a mother hen who pushes them into a cage. The lesson offered here: one must hide from the gaze of a cruel woman and seek the affection of one who "treats you better."

Another theme is the need to distinguish between appearance and reality, the need to recognize the specific nature of one's adversary and to answer one lie with another. A fox tries to persuade a rooster to fly down from his perch and join him on the ground because a truce has been declared among all animals. The rooster agrees to do so only when two greyhounds he sees approaching from a distance, bearing the good news, have joined them. The fox understands he has been outwitted and flees.

What is notable about these stories is that not a single one is really about erotic love. Except for two stories of maternal instinct, the fables treat consistently of political rivalry and ruse. The stories are certainly polysemous. They could be read as allegories of almost any human situation in which competing interests are expressed through various rhetorical strategies. According to Michel Conan, the decision to read the fables according to a courtly love coda is characteristic of the social games being played at the time, especially in the salons.[48] However they were interpreted, the fables suggest that, in politics as in love, human behavior is based on bestial strivings expressed in bestial rhetoric, aptly represented as pure hydraulic force.

As is always the case with fables and fairy tales, the Labyrinthe stories appeal to regressive, childish fears and gratifications.[49] Animals are constantly threatened with being eaten, beaten, captured, drowned, seduced, or humiliated. Sometimes these fears or pleasures are realized, as in the case of the frogs being devoured by the Heron-King and the baby birds being eaten at the hawk's birthday party. One enigmatic fable seems emblematic of the particular spin that mechanization puts on oral gratification. "A Dragon wanted to chew on an Anvil. A File said to him: 'You'll just break your teeth instead of chewing on the Anvil. I alone, with my teeth, can eat you and any-thing else here!' "[50] Perrault strains to come up with a courtly love interpre-tation. When one's lover is mad, he says, one must not respond in anger, like the dragon. Instead, the gentle action of the "sweet File" is called for. Upon reflection, there is perhaps much wisdom in this advice, but the story also has something to say about oral pleasures in a mechanized world. The ma-terial object, the anvil, resists the oral devouring by the dragon. It cannot be eaten in the same fashion as baby birds and frogs. The mechanical object, like the mechanical fable, can be consumed only by a sweet file, a slow, ma-terial wearing away. It is hard to say exactly what sort of aesthetic pleasure this is. It is certainly a restrained, sublimated pleasure, an aesthetic and sex-ual satisfaction in exacting, calculated work, perhaps supplemented by the auditory pleasure of hearing the file do its work.

One final fable seems to be a fitting conclusion to a discussion of the po-etics of mechanical animal voices: the story of the dying swan. It is one of the last fountains, and Perrault accords the swan the highest marks for its lover's discourse. According to the well-known legend, the swan sings a final beautiful song when it senses its death approaching. Unlike most of the speech in the Labyrinthe, the words of the swan seem gratuitous, disinter-ested, poetic. Upon hearing a swan sing, a stork asks him, "Why do you sing?" "Because," the swan replies, "I am going to die." Perrault interprets the fable to mean that when the lover is dying of love, his or her language becomes most eloquent and convincing. The swan song is the rarest of na-ture's auditory performances, a one-time event that translates this beauti-ful bird's essence into sound. This seems to be the ambition of Perrault, to translate into sound the artificial animals of the Labyrinthe. That sound would most fittingly be the voice of the perpetually dying hydraulic swan.

ANIMAL LIBERATION

Because the Ménagerie was so thoroughly identified with royal power, it is not surprising that it came under attack during the Revolution. The *philo-sophes* considered it a scandal that beasts should be well fed while people starved. The article "Ménagerie" in the *Encyclopédie* (1765) declared, "Me-nageries must be destroyed when people are lacking bread; for it is shame-ful to feed animals at great expense while people are starving to death."[51] In addition to being seen as a superfluous luxury, the Ménagerie was crit-icized in the second half of the eighteenth century because of a growing sentiment that animals were denatured by captivity. Buffon, in an entry to the *Histoire naturelle des oiseaux* devoted to the *outarde* (great bustard)— the same bird that appears in Boël's *Quartier des Demoiselles*—argued that animals confined in menageries behave in an "altered and constrained manner, unworthy of the scrutiny of a philosopher, for whom the only beautiful nature is, if you will, nature that is free, independent, and wild."[52]

When the Revolution came, attempts were made to liberate or destroy animals in the Ménagerie and other princely collections, just as other victims of royal incarcerations, such as inmates in the Bastille and the Hôpital Général, were similarly freed. On August 10, 1792, a committee of Jacobins arrived at Versailles, demanding "in the name of the People and of Nature [that] liberty be restored to creatures that leave the hands of their Creator free and are unjustly detained by tyrants."[53] Some of the animals were set free in the woods around the château; others were transported to the Jardin du Roi, which had been renamed the Jardin des Plantes. Inevitably, there were conflicts between the *philosophes'* desire to study free animals and the practical and symbolic advantages to be gained by transferring the Versailles animals to the Jardin des Plantes.

Bernardin de Saint-Pierre, in his "Mémoire sur la nécessité de joindre une ménagerie au Jardin des Plantes de Paris," written to the Committee of Public Safety in 1792, argued for a new kind of zoo, one that would overcome the cruelty of confinement by gentle treatment and the fostering of friendships between different animal species and between humans and animals. The newly appointed director of the Jardin des Plantes believed that by use of patient taming techniques in captivity, humans could actually "perfect" wild animals and return them to an Edenic state in which they no longer fought among themselves or feared cruel treatment at the hands of humans. In a story that reverses the interspecies violence of Oudry's *Panther Cage,* Bernardin de Saint-Pierre describes how a dog and a lion—tellingly, the lion is described as *le roi des animaux* and *un terrible despote*—became steadfast friends behind the bars of the Ménagerie. "Their friendship is one of the most touching spectacles that nature can offer to the speculations of a philosopher."[54] No longer the mirror of royal power, nature, as displayed in the new menagerie, would become a school of virtue for the entire population of Paris. "This school, necessary for the study of nature's laws, can . . . influence the behavior of people whose ferocity toward each other starts with the mistreatment of animals."[55]

Despite a grand gesture of rupture and discontinuity, the Versailles animals and their cages were moved to the seat of republican sovereignty in Paris. Although animals and humans were supposedly returning to a state of Arcadian bliss and virtue, it cannot be forgotten that an absolute difference still prevailed between humans and animals, all the more dangerous because it was veiled in effusions of sentimentality. Writing about domestic animals, Buffon declared, "It is because of his natural superiority that man reigns and commands. He thinks, and, as a consequence, he is master of those beings that do not think."[56] The same Buffon, with the help of the architect Verniquet, drew up plans for a vast modern menagerie containing animals from Europe, Africa, America, and Asia, as well as human inhabitants, on display, living in the same compounds as the animals from their native lands. "A Laplander or Greenlander, even an Eskimo, would believe, in some way, that he was in his native land, just like the animals."[57] The Versailles Ménagerie, a form of royal power and knowledge synonymous with the *ancien régime* since the late Renaissance, had ceased to exist. A more humane form of taming had taken its place as a model for displaying and improving animals and humans.

NOTES

1. Pierre-André Lablaude, *The Gardens of Versailles,* trans. Fiona Biddulph (London: Zwemmer, 1985), 72. The best source on the Ménagerie remains Gustave Loisel, *Histoire des ménageries de l'antiquité à nos jours,* 3 vols. (Paris: Octave Doin, 1912); see also Alfred Franklin, *La Vie Privée d'autrefois,* vols. 21, 22 (Paris: Plon, 1897); Alfred Marie, *Naissance de Versailles* (Paris: Vincent, Fréal, 1968); Gérard Mabille, "La Ménagerie de Versailles," *Gazette des Beaux-Arts* 116 (1974): 5–36; Alfred and Jeanne Marie, *Versailles au temps de Louis XIV* (Paris: Imprimerie Nationale, 1976); Robert Berger, *In the Garden of the Sun King: Studies on the Park of Versailles under Louis XIV* (Washington, D.C.: Dumbarton Oaks, 1985); Bob Mullen and Garry Marvin, *Zoo Culture* (Urbana: University of Illinois Press, 1987); Masumi Ireye, "Le Vau's Ménagerie and the Rise of the Animalier: Enclosing, Dissecting, and Representing the Animal in Early Modern France," Ph.D. dissertation, University of Michigan, 1994; R. J. Hoage and William Deiss, *New Worlds, New Animals: From Ménagerie to Zoological Park in the Nineteenth Century* (Baltimore: Johns Hopkins University Press, 1996); Louise Robbins, *Elephant Slaves and Pampered Parrots: Exotic Animals in Eighteenth-Century France* (Baltimore: Johns Hopkins University Press, 2002); Eric Baratay and Elisabeth Hardouin-Fugier, *Zoos: Histoire des jardins zoologiques en occident, XVIe–XXe siècle* (Paris: La Découverte, 1998).

2. Loisel, *Histoire,* 2:170–83.

3. Baratay and Hardouin-Fugier, *Zoos,* 64.

4. On the *animaliers,* see Hal Opperman, *Jean-Baptiste Oudry (1686–1755) with a Sketch for a Catalogue Raisonné of His Paintings, Drawings, and Prints,* 2 vols. (Chicago: Garland, 1977), and *J.-B. Oudry, 1686–1755* (Fort Worth, Tex.: Kimbell Art Museum, 1983); Madeleine Pinault, *The Painter as Naturalist from Dürer to Redouté* (Paris: Flammarion, 1991).

5. On Perrault and the Académie, see Antoine Picon, *Claude Perrault, 1613–1688, ou la curiosité d'un classique* (Paris: Picard, 1988).

6. Edouard Pommier, "Versailles: The Image of the Sovereign," in *Realms of Memory: Rethinking the French Past,* 3 vols, ed. Pierre Nora, trans. Arthur Goldhammer (New York: Columbia University Press), 3:293–322, 300.

7. Baratay and Hardouin-Fugier, *Zoos*, 65. The authors also argue that the recently codified rules of classical theatre (unity of time, space, and plot) were a key influence on the Ménagerie, which, like other theatricalized settings at Versailles, was meant to provide "un spectacle de rêve," based on the marvels of nature and human art.

8. The design of the Ménagerie could be seen as an instance of the "exhaustive ordering of the world" that Michel Foucault describes as the organizing principle of science during the Classical Age. *Les Mots et les choses: Une Archéologie des sciences humaines* (Paris: Gallimard, 1966), 89. Le Vau's fanlike structure was surely an attempt organize animals, plants, flowers, water, trees—all of nature—into a tableau.

9. Franklin, *La Vie Privée*, 21:12.

10. Krzysztof Pomian, *Collectors and Curiosities: Paris and Venice, 1500–1800*, trans. Elizabeth Portier (Cambridge: Cambridge University Press, 1990); Antoine Schnapper, *Le Géant, la licorne, et la tulipe: Collections et collectionneurs dans la France du XVIIe siècle* (Paris: Flammarion, 1988).

11. Norbert Elias, *The Civilizing Process*, trans. Edmund Jephcott (Oxford: Basil Blackwell, 1978).

12. The *Dictionnaire de L'Académie française* gives both meanings: (1) "A place built near a farm for fattening and raising animals, birds, etc" and (2) "In the houses of Princes, a Ménagerie is the place where foreign and rare animals are kept."

13. Mabille, "La Ménagerie," 32–33.

14. Jean de La Fontaine, *Œuvres Complètes*, 2 vols., ed. Pierre Clarac (Paris: Gallimard, 1958), 2:128.

15. Mademoiselle de Scudéry, *La Promenade de Versailles*, ed. Allen Weiss (Paris: Mercure, 1999), 56.

16. According to Edouard Pommier, the Galérie des Glaces illustrates one of the underlying themes of Versailles, the desire to deliberately confuse art and nature: "With its fascinating mirrors, the galérie des Glaces brought nature inside the palace: art and nature mingled in a single ambiguous space that was at once real and imaginary." Pommier, "Versailles," 315.

17. René Descartes, *Méditations métaphysiques*, ed. Florence Khodoss (Paris: PUF, 1974), 51.

18. Ibid., 49.

19. For debates on the nature of the animal soul in the seventeenth century, see Henri Busson and Ferdinand Gohin, *Jean de La Fontaine, Discours à Mme de la Sablière* (Geneva: Droz, 1967); Lenora Rosenfield, *From Beast-Machine to Man-Machine: The Animal Soul in French Letters from Descartes to La Mettrie* (New York: Oxford University Press, 1941).

20. Foucault, *Les Mots*, 31.

21. Ibid., 29.

22. According to the latest evidence, most animals lack the ability to recognize themselves in mirrors, and this is proof of their general inability to attain human

mental states. Gordon Gallup and Daniel Povinelli, "Can Animals Empathize?," *Scientific American* 94 (1998): 66–75.

23. See W. J. T. Mitchell's discussion of this story in *Picture Theory: Essays on Verbal and Visual Representation* (Chicago: University of Chicago Press, 1994), 329–44.

24. Jacques-Henri Bernardin de Saint-Pierre, *Oeuvres Complètes,* 12 vols. (Paris: Méquignon-Marvis, 1818), 5:105.

25. Bernardin de Saint-Pierre revised Descartes's famous axiom: "I thus substitute this argument for Descartes' which seems more simple and general: *I sense, therefore I am (Je sens donc j'existe)*. It can be applied to all of our physical sensations, which alert us much more frequently as to our existence than thought does." According to Bernardin de Saint-Pierre, the human being feels two kinds of sentiments: an "animal" sentiment, which confers a sense of the body and its "misery," and "le sentiment de la Divinité," which only humans possess. The sentiment of Divinity is aroused by contemplation of Nature and is at the root of generosity and many other human virtues. Ibid.

26. Claude Perrault, *Mémoires pour servir à l'histoire des animaux* (The Hague: P. Gosse, 1731), 3.

27. Franklin, *La Vie Privée,* 21:12.

28. Charles Perrault, *Le Labyrinthe de Versailles* (Paris: L'Imprimerie Royale, 1677), 30.

29. Emile Campardon, *Les Spectacles de la foire* (Paris: Berger-Levrault, 1877), xiv.

30. Perrault, *Le Labyrinthe,* 229.

31. Foucault, *Les Mots,* 149.

32. Picon, *Claude Perrault,* 38.

33. Perrault, *Le Labyrinthe,* 33.

34. Jean-Bernard Lacroix, "L'approvisionnement des ménageries et les transports d'animaux sauvages par la Compagnie des Indes au XVIIIe siècle," *Revue Française d'Histoire d'Outre Mer* 65 (1978): 153–79.

35. Marie, *Naissance,* 44–53.

36. Quoted in Pommier, "Versailles," 301.

37. Ibid., 299.

38. Michel Foucault, *Discipline and Punish: The Birth of the Prison* (New York: Vintage, 1979), 203.

39. Robert Poujoul, "La Salpêtrière hier et aujourd'hui," *L'Hôpital à Paris* (August 1982): 24–25.

40. Henri Ellenberger, "The Mental Hospital and the Zoological Garden," in *Animals and Man in Historical Perspective,* ed. Joseph Klaits (New York: Harper and Row, 1974): 59–92.

41. Ibid., 227.

42. Ibid., 233.

43. On the Labyrinthe, see Marie, *Naissance;* Michel Conan, "Métamorphoses des labyrinthes de jardin de la moitié du XVIème à la moitié du XIXème siècle," *Coloquio Artes* 63 (1984): 22–54; Alain Marie Bassy, "Les fables de La Fontaine et le

labyrinthe de Versailles," *Revue Française d'Histoire du Livre,* 3ème trimestre (1976): 126–42.

44. Marie, *Naissance,* 123.

45. Charles Perrault, *Contes,* ed. Jean-Pierre Collinet (Paris: Gallimard, 1981), 239.

46. Ibid., 242.

47. Chandra Mukerji, *Territorial Ambitions and the Gardens of Versailles* (Cambridge: Cambridge University Press, 1997), 285.

48. Conan, "Métamorphoses," 46.

49. For a discussion of oral pleasure in fairy tales, see Louis Marin, *Food for Thought,* trans. Mette Hjort (Baltimore: Johns Hopkins University Press, 1989), 29–38.

50. Perrault, *Contes,* 245.

51. Quoted in Loisel, *Histoire,* 2:159.

52. Quoted in Richard W. Burkhardt Jr., "Le comportement animal et l'idéologie de domestication chez Buffon et chez les ethologues modernes," in *Buffon 88: Actes du Colloque international pour le bicentenaire de la mort de Buffon,* ed. Jean Gayon (Paris: Vrin, 1992), 573.

53. Loisel, *Histoire,* 2:163. This story might be apocryphal because its originator, Paul Huot, was a royalist sympathizer and may have been trying to ridicule the Jacobins. See Robbins, *Elephant Slaves,* 214, for a discussion of this incident.

54. Bernardin de Saint-Pierre, "Mémoire sur la nécessité de joindre une ménagerie au Jardin des Plantes de Paris," in *Oeuvres Complètes,* 12:639. Visitors to the Jardin des Plantes today can see a statue commemorating the lion-dog friendship.

55. Ibid., 661.

56. Georges-Louis Leclerc, Comte de Buffon, "Les animaux domestiques," *Histoire Naturelle, Générale et Particulière,* 15 vols. (Paris: Imprimerie Royale, 1749–67), 4:170.

57. Quoted in Loisel, *Histoire,* 2:320.

❦ CONTRIBUTORS

BRIAN CUMMINGS is a reader in English in the School of European Studies at the University of Sussex. He is the author of *The Literary Culture of the Reformation: Grammar and Grace* (Oxford University Press, 2002).

ERICA FUDGE is a senior lecturer in English literary studies at Middlesex University. She is the author of *Perceiving Animals: Humans and Beasts in Early Modern English Culture* (Macmillan, 2000. Reprint. University of Illinois Press, 2002) and *Animal* (Reaktion Books, 2002) and coeditor, with Ruth Gilbert and Susan Wiseman, of *At the Borders of the Human: Beasts, Bodies, and Natural Philosophy in the Early Modern Period* (Macmillan, 1999). She is also an associate editor of the journal *Society and Animals*.

ELSPETH GRAHAM is a reader in early modern studies and the head of literature and cultural history at Liverpool John Moores University. She is coeditor, with Hilary Hinds, Elaine Hobby, and Helen Wilcox, of *Her Own Life: Autobiographical Writings by Seventeenth-Century Englishwomen* (Routledge, 1989) and has published on the writings of seventeenth-century religious radicals, Milton, and autobiography. She is finishing a book-length manuscript on twentieth-century fiction and life writing and is also working on a project involving seventeenth-century land and animals.

PETER HARRISON is a professor of philosophy at Bond University, Gold Coast, Australia. He is author of *"Religion" and Religions in the English Enlightenment* (Cambridge University Press, 1990) and *The Bible, Protestantism, and the Rise of Natural Science* (Cambridge University Press, 1998). He has also published extensively on attitudes toward animals and nature in the early modern period in such journals as *The Journal of the History of Ideas, Philosophical Quarterly, The Journal of Religion,* and *The Journal of the History of Philosophy.*

JAMES KNOWLES is a reader in English at the University of Stirling. He is coeditor, with Jennifer Richards, of *Shakespeare's Late Plays: New Essays* (Edinburgh University Press, 1999) and, with Gene Giddens, of *The Roaring Girl and Other Plays* (Oxford University Press, 2001). He has written extensively on the masque, including Jonson's *Entertainment at Britain's Burse,* in *Representing Ben Jonson* (Macmillan, 1999) and is editing Jonson's masques and entertainments for the New Cambridge *Works of Ben Jonson* (to appear in 2003–5).

KATHRYN PERRY teaches part-time in the School of English, University of Reading. Her Ph.D. thesis is titled "Political Animals: Spenserian Beast Satire, 1591–1628" (University of Reading, 2002). She has also published an article on the early modern book trade.

JULIANA SCHIESARI is a professor of comparative literature at the University of California at Davis. She is the author of *The Gendering of Melancholia: Feminism, Psychoanalysis, and the Symbolics of Loss in Renaissance Literature* (Cornell University Press, 1992) and coeditor, with M. Migiel, of *Refiguring Woman: Perspectives on Gender and the Italian Renaissance* (Cornell University Press, 1992). Her book *Dogs and Domesticity: Pets, Bodies, and Desire from the Renaissance to the Present* is forthcoming from Duke University Press.

MATTHEW SENIOR is an associate professor of French at the University of Minnesota at Morris. He is author of *In the Grip of Minos: Confessional Discourse in Dante, Corneille, and Racine* (Ohio State University Press, 1994) and coeditor, with Jennifer Ham, of *Animal Acts: Configuring the Human in Western Culture* (Routledge, 1997).

ERICA SHEEN is a lecturer and director of film in the School of English at the University of Sheffield. She is coeditor, with Annette Davison, of *American Dreams, Nightmare Vision: The Cinema of David Lynch* (Wallflower Press, 2003) and coeditor, with Lorna Hutson, of *Literature, Politics and Law in Renaissance England* (Palgrave, 2004) and is completing studies of Shakespearean theater and of film as intellectual property.

ALAN STEWART is a professor of English and comparative literature at Columbia University and associate director of the Arts and Humanities Research Board Centre for Editing Lives and Letters in London. He is the author of *Close Readers: Humanism and Sodomy in Early Modern England* (Princeton University Press, 1997) and *Philip Sidney: A Double Life* (Chatto and Windus, 2000) and coauthor, with Lisa Jardine, of *Hostage to Fortune: The Troubled Life of Francis Bacon* (Victor Gollanez, 1998). His most recent book is *The Cradle King: A Life of James VI and I* (Chatto and Windus, 2003), and he is editing Francis Bacon's correspondence for publication by Oxford University Press.

S. J. Wiseman is a reader in early modern literature and culture at Birkbeck, University of London. She is the author of *Aphra Behn* (British Council, 1996) and *Drama and Politics in the English Civil War* (Cambridge University Press, 1998) and coeditor, with Erica Fudge and Ruth Gilbert, of *At the Borders of the Human: Beasts, Bodies, and Natural Philosophy in the Early Modern Period* (Macmillan, 1999).

❧ INDEX

The University of Illinois Press
is a founding member of the
Association of American University Presses.

Composed in 10.5/13 Adobe Minion
with Minion & Woodtype Ornaments display
by Type One, LLC
for the University of Illinois Press
Designed by Dennis Roberts
Manufactured by Thomson-Shore, Inc.

University of Illinois Press
1325 South Oak Street
Champaign, IL 61820-6903
www.press.uillinois.edu